TERRORISM AS CRIME

MARK S. HAMM

TERRORISM AS CRIME

From Oklahoma City to Al-Qaeda and Beyond

New York University Press   •   *New York and London*

NEW YORK UNIVERSITY PRESS
New York and London
www.nyupress.org

© 2007 by New York University
All rights reserved

Library of Congress Cataloging-in-Publication Data
Hamm, Mark S.
Terrorism as crime : from Oklahoma City to Al-Qaeda and beyond / Mark S. Hamm.
p. cm.
Includes bibliographical references and index.
ISBN-13: 978-0-8147-3695-1 (cloth : alk. paper)
ISBN-10: 0-8147-3695-5 (cloth : alk. paper)
ISBN-13: 978-0-8147-3696-8 (pbk. : alk. paper)
ISBN-10: 0-8147-3696-3 (pbk. : alk. paper)
1. Terrorism. 2. Radicalism. 3. Terrorism—United States.
4. Radicalism—United States. 5. Criminology. I. Title.
HV6431.H364   2006
364.1—dc22   2006029835

New York University Press books are printed on acid-free paper,
and their binding materials are chosen for strength and durability.

Manufactured in the United States of America
c 10 9 8 7 6 5 4 3 2 1
p 10 9 8 7 6 5 4 3 2 1

For New Orleans

Let history be a witness that I am a criminal.

—Osama bin Laden

Quoted in The 9/11 Commission Report.

Contents

Acknowledgments

Buddhists say that the secret of Zen lies in just two words: not always so. Much the same can be said of terrorism, and I have many to thank for helping me search for answers.

For their patience with things I have no patience for, thanks to Jennifer Brown, Peggy Strobel, David Skelton, and Charles Norman at Indiana State University.

For bringing this research the light of print, I thank Ilene Kalish at New York University Press.

The ideas flowing through this work were shaped by an outstanding group of scholars. Thanks to Pat Lauderdale, Henry Brownstein, Marcus Felson, Ronald Akers, Gregg Barak, Bob Bohm, Victoria Bedford, and Lynn Chancer. Thanks also to veteran terrorism researchers Brent Smith, Kelly Damphousse, Christopher Hewitt, Jeff Ross, Josh Frelich, Adam Silverman, Mark Potok, and Brian Levin.

I owe a special thanks to Jeff Ferrell and Mike Presdee for their humor when the clouds gathered; and to Ken Tunnell, Fran Hoffmann, Cecile Van de Voorde, and Terry Cox for their kindness when the rains came.

To Lou Hamm and Marla Sandys, I owe something more than thanks.

Proceeds from this book go to the New Orleans Musicians' Relief Fund, a non-profit support group founded in response to the devastation of Hurricane Katrina.

Introduction

The Criminology of Terrorism

Our world is flooded with images of terror. Each day, it seems, we are hammered by a televised rain of suicide bombings, mass murders, and assassinations. Historically this represents a seismic shift in the nature of terrorism, a shift from the symbolic to the concrete. Nowhere is this change more evident than in the media reporting of violence committed in the name of Islamic extremism.

Live terrorist TV was born at the 1972 Summer Olympics in Munich when the Palestinian group Black September broke into the dormitory rooms of the Israeli team and took eleven athletes and coaches hostage. As some 900 million television viewers followed attempts made by German authorities to negotiate with the guerrillas, cameras captured extraordinary footage of a lone Palestinian gunman, his head covered by a dark hood, standing on a balcony of the dormitory. In the end, though, things went terribly wrong, and the terrorists killed all of their hostages. Yet these murders were carried out in secret, far from the camera's eye, and Munich was framed as a political crisis of the Middle East.

In contemporary America, terrorism garners a disproportionately large share of news coverage where it is typically presented through the frame of private stories—stories of fallen firefighters, soldiers, airline pilots, subway riders, and others. As such, television reporting highlights the personal (and the extremely emotional) aspects of terrorism's global criminal threat at the expense of its broader political content. For American viewers, this human focus has resulted in a nightly ritual of random death, which exposes the public to images symbolizing the nation's vulnerabilities. Through international satellite television networks and the video capabilities of the World Wide Web, millions of people are now able to watch hijackings, torture, missile firings, and suicide bombings. Today, not only can we watch terrorists trample and hack their victims to death; we can even watch beheadings over the Internet.

The hard rain of awful imagery demonstrates that the whole point of terrorism is fear. And fear, as it turns out, has unleashed a long-standing American fascination with Christian doomsday prophecy. This has led to a spectacular rise in sales for books, movies, and music with apocalyptic themes—some of which has been remarkably prescient. "Some things are just too terrible to be true," growled Bob Dylan on *"Love and Theft,"* his nightmarish album of dread and uncertainty, eerily released on September 11, 2001—the same day, of course, that al-Qaeda perpetrated the single greatest act of terrorism in human history. Shortly thereafter, *Time*/CNN conducted a poll showing that four out of every ten Americans thought about the implications of the daily news for the end of the world, and six out of ten believed the future would unfold in accordance with the Book of Revelation.[1] Yet beyond the grisly headlines and doomsday prophesies a far more important change is now taking place in the world of terrorism itself.

Throughout the post–World War II era, terrorism was strategic warfare on the cheap. Terrorism was state-sponsored, low-level military activity which used the threat of violence to influence international relations. Terrorism, as the saying goes, was diplomacy by other means. Since the collapse of communism, however, there has been a marked decline in state-sponsored terrorism. Instead, terrorists are increasingly turning to criminal activity as an alternative means of support.

This development represents a *privatization* of terrorism that parallels the movement by many nations in the past decade to convert their state-supported industries to privately owned companies. Although the criminal methods used by terrorist groups range from the highly sophisticated to the most basic, they all serve a common purpose: the crimes provide *logistical* support for terrorism. That is, crimes are committed to supply terrorists with money, material, personnel, training, communication systems, safe havens, and travel. Far from being mere accouterments strapped onto the terrorist's agenda, these crimes are the lifeblood of terrorist groups.

In the past these crimes included counterfeiting, bank robbery, theft, and fraud. But this is only a partial listing of crimes committed by terrorists today. To the list we can add kidnapping and espionage; smuggling of drugs, guns, military arms, biological weapons, exotic jewelry, cigarettes, and even baby formula; tax evasion, money laundering, cell phone and credit card theft; immigration violations, passport forgery; extortion, arson, human trafficking, and prostitution. The goal of this book is to examine terrorists' involvement in these crimes and describe law enforcement's opportunities to detect and prevent them.

WHY ANOTHER BOOK ON TERRORISM?

More than one hundred books on terrorism have been published since the attacks of September 11, 2001.[2] Some offer invaluable perspectives on the human dimension of terrorism and its relationship to social, cultural, and political processes: Daniel Benjamin and Steven Simon's *The Age of Sacred Terror,* Richard Clarke's *Against All Enemies,* Steve Coll's *Ghost Wars,* Rohan Gunaratna's *Inside Al Qaeda,* and *The 9/11 Commission Report* are but a few outstanding examples. What sets this book apart is that it focuses explicitly on the terrorism-crime connection. This connection has not gone unnoticed in Washington. Today FBI agents are collaborating with CIA agents to hunt down criminal gangs with suspected ties to terrorist cells. Informants for the Drug Enforcement Administration are being used to provide intelligence on drug traffickers who are financing anti-American insurgency movements. And the military, traditionally accustomed to preparing for battles against conventional armies, is retraining itself to fight asymmetrical conflicts against borderless criminal syndicates that also finance acts of terrorism.

This book explores these developments, along with an often overlooked assumption about terrorism. That assumption is simply this: because terrorism involves criminal activity, its perpetrators will display varying degrees of competency. Like all criminals, some terrorists will be extremely competent in carrying out their transgressions; some will be minimally competent; and some will be utterly inept.

I concentrate on the ways in which terrorists have engaged in crimes for logistical purposes by analyzing their actions via two leading criminological approaches: the routine activity perspective and social learning theory. The purpose is to determine the extent to which terrorist-oriented criminality has distinguishing features. This is, after all, the ordinance of sociology: to find general principles, along with situation-specific and history-specific qualifications of deviance. In this case, of course, we're talking about phenomenal acts of deviance capable of affecting the stability of nation states.

The routine activity approach used by criminologists "shows how crime feeds off the larger system of daily activities . . . It focuses on crime events and situations, that is, specific acts rather than general offender propensities."[3] By examining thoroughly these crime events and situations and by placing them in a wider system of daily activity, the routine activity perspective concentrates on how offenders create opportunities for crimes to occur.

Yet a founding father of criminology, Edwin Sutherland, would argue that opportunity alone is not enough to pull off a successful crime. Sutherland would contend that something else is needed. Something that precedes and even trumps the opportunity to commit crime: namely—criminal skill or trade craft.[4] According to what criminologists would deem as social learning theory—the central emphasis of which is that criminal activity involves techniques of committing the crime—such skills are acquired through "deliberate tutelage, training, and socialization" of offenders.[5]

Consider, for example, the exploits of an American terrorist cell known as the Aryan Republican Army (ARA). The ARA was a gang of white supremacists who zigzagged across the Midwest, hitting bank after bank for a period of two years (1994–95). In all, the ARA robbed twenty-two banks, netting some $500,000. This money was used to support a series of terrorist attacks that included armored truck heists, sabotaging public utilities, derailing trains, attempted assassinations, and bombings. Their goal, as incredible as it may sound, was to overthrow the federal government.[6]

From a criminological perspective, what may be most instructive about this crime spree is not the ARA's successful bank robberies, but those instances in which robberies were thwarted, averted, and otherwise prevented through the routine activities of public safeguards—bank security measures, police surveillance, and citizen involvement. While the ARA got away with twenty-two bank robberies, at least that many were prevented through routine activities. My goal is to identify these sorts of routine activities and show how they benefit public safety and serve as effective counter-terrorism measures. At the same time, I also ask questions informed by my social learning theory: What specific skills are needed to accomplish terrorist-oriented crimes? How are skills learned or transmitted from one person to the next? What can be done to influence these variations in association?

Criminologists who use routine activity theory also employ the concept of situational crime prevention. This consists of identifying a series of methods, which ultimately become routine activities, for removing crime opportunities from immediate situations. As criminologists, we ask: How can specific types of crime be made more difficult for terrorist groups? How can technology and transportation systems be used to accomplish this aim? How can surveillance techniques be used to track terrorist activity?

These are the types of questions that are addressed in the following pages. The book explores an array of crimes committed by terrorist groups and then applies the two theories, social learning and routine activity, in order to determine criminal "successes" and "failures." In terms of the latter, then, the research represents a best-practices approach to the control of terrorism. While social learning and routine activity theory have never been applied to terrorism research before, several well-publicized cases do, indeed, speak to the practical significance of integrating these perspectives as a means to understanding our best practices in these dangerous times.

Consider the alert Pakistani immigration officials who, upon a routine security inspection at Karachi Airport in 1998, detained a suspicious-looking Jordanian citizen named Mohamed Odeh. Upon being questioned, Odeh not only admitted to his participation in the recent U.S. embassy bombing in Nairobi, Kenya, but also admitted to being a member of al-Qaeda. This gave the FBI its first solid lead connecting Osama bin Laden to the East African embassy attacks. A routine border inspection also led to the arrest of Algerian Ahmed Ressam, the bin Laden soldier who was later convicted for plotting to bomb the Los Angeles International Airport during the 2000 millennium celebration. Both Ressam and Odeh were unskilled in international travel and crossing borders without gaining notice. (Ressam, in fact, suffered from tuberculosis at the time and was so disoriented from fever that he got lost trying to cross from Canada to Washington state.) In effect, the routine activities of public guardians removed from these men the opportunity to kill more innocents.

Finally, consider the Minneapolis FBI agents who routinely responded to a call concerning the suspicious activities of Zacarias Moussaoui at a local flight training school. (The terrorists who piloted the planes on 9/11 all learned to fly in U.S. flight schools.) The decision to arrest Moussaoui on August 15, 2001, on an immigration violation prevented him from receiving any more flight training. It is even within the realm of possibility that Moussaoui's arrest also kept him from becoming the twentieth hijacker of September 11—thus allowing the heroic passengers of Flight 93 to overcome their terrorist hijackers and to spare lives on the ground and more, since the hijackers' target was reportedly the U.S. Capitol.

TERRORISM AND CRIME

Each terrorist group is unique and must be explained in the context of its own natural culture and history.[7] For example, with the erosion of state support, some terrorist groups such as the Irish Republican Army turned to organized crime. During the early 1970s, U.S. law enforcement cracked down on IRA fund-raising efforts in America, thus forcing the IRA to find new sources of revenue. Rather than turn to the Irish gangs, the IRA began to commit crimes normally associated with ethnic organized crime groups.[8] These crimes included smuggling livestock, cars, and weapons; running protection and extortion rackets; managing underground brothels; orchestrating prison breaks; bank robbery, tax evasion, and construction fraud.[9] The IRA ran saloons and even bought its own fleet of taxi cabs, eventually forcing out its competitors and cornering the Belfast transportation market.[10]

Terrorist groups have historically been reluctant to participate in the international drug trade, fearing that their involvement would lead to a decline in support from state sponsors.[11] But the attrition of state support has lifted this prohibition.[12] The most instructive example is perhaps the Colombian leftist group, M-19. While the Colombian drug cartels had no vested interest in the group's politics, in the mid-1980s drug lord Pablo Escobar found his alliance with M-19 to be a profitable one. Escobar's syndicate produced cocaine in Colombia and prepared shipments for international distribution. M-19 supplied transportation out of the country and protection against government raids. M-19 was paid well for its services, and its ranks swelled along with its capacity for violence, thereby establishing a connection between terrorism and the drug trade that would be emulated worldwide.[13]

There are many ways to participate in drug trafficking, though, and some terrorist groups have done so by producing, smuggling, and selling their own narcotics. The Burmese insurgents, who go by the name of the United Wa State Army, operate one of the world's most formidable drug-smuggling rings. The organization, which cultivates and traffics opium and heroin out of the Golden Triangle, has recently moved into the burgeoning methamphetamine market.[14] Other terrorist groups limit their involvement to the "upstream" phase of drug trafficking—the cultivation stage, where risks and profits are low.[15] Other groups tax opium and coca producers, provide safe havens for cultivators, and refine drugs. And still other terrorist organizations, particularly in North Africa, have become racketeering syndicates, smuggling drugs and humans, as well as selling pirated CDs, DVDs, and sportswear.[16]

No matter the method, in each case there is a clear transition into organized crime because drug smuggling is *by definition* an organized crime. During the Kosovo conflict, the Kosovo Liberation Front sold heroin in Europe to raise money for their cause. The Revolutionary Armed Forces of Colombia (FARC) continues to draw revenues from the narcotics trade, as do terrorist groups in Spain, Sri Lanka, Turkey, and Lebanon.[17] One author argues that Yasser Arafat was involved in the drug trade for nearly twenty years.[18] Another study suggests that Hezbollah has generated revenues by protecting Middle Eastern heroin labs.[19] There is also substantial evidence that the drug trade was a source of revenue for the Taliban prior to 9/11. By taxing growers, the Taliban received money from Afghanistan's position as supplier of nearly 80 percent of the world's opium.[20]

It would be a mistake to assume, however, that all terrorist groups make the transition to organized crime. Organized crime—and especially transnational organized crime—requires a clandestine network of collaborators. Because small terrorist cells lack these resources, they are more likely to engage in such brazen acts of banditry as bank and jewelry store robbery. Not only do these robberies fill the terrorist's war chest, they have the potential to create "force multipliers"—or the illusion of increased strength.[21] The six-member ARA carried out its bank robberies with hand-held radios, pipe bombs, grenades, and assault rifles. Once they even used a rocket launcher, when in reality, a pistol would have done. These force multipliers increased the striking potential of the gang without increasing its personnel.

The force-multiplier strategy has been used to great effect by such disparate groups as West Germany's Baader-Meinhof gang, the Chilean Movement of the Revolutionary Left (MIR), Egypt's al-Jihad, Jemaah Islamiyah (al-Qaeda's affiliate in Southeast Asia), and the Order, a neo-Nazi gang active here in the United States. Baader-Meinhof supported its operations through a series of small-cell bank robberies that were executed with military precision.[22] The MIR collaborated with French criminals in the biggest-ever bank robbery in France at St. Nazaire during the early 1980s.[23] In 1981, citing the Koran on the right to take spoils won in a war with infidels, al-Jihad conducted a spree of armed robberies against Christian-owned jewelry stores in Cairo; the funds went toward supporting a plan to assassinate President Anwar Sadat.[24] Jemaah Islamiyah financed the 2002 Bali bombings through jewelry store robberies that netted over five pounds of gold.[25] The Order raised money through counterfeiting, bank robbery, and a spectacular 1984 armored truck heist that netted the gang $3.6 million.[26]

Small cells are often capable of great crimes. Illich Ramirez Sanchez—better known as Carlos the Jackal—once single-handedly so terrorized the French government that it not only released a Japanese terrorist from a prison cell in Paris, but also paid Carlos a $300,000 ransom. On another occasion, aided by six accomplices, he took the OPEC conference hostage at gunpoint inside its Vienna headquarters. In exchange for releasing his hostages, the governments of Saudi Arabia and Iran paid Carlos an astounding $50 million ransom.[27]

One of the most complex aspects of terrorism is weapons procurement. The greatest opportunities for buying weapons of mass destruction are no doubt in the former Soviet Union. After the collapse of communism, the Soviet military left weapons and equipment behind in the newly emerging states on the periphery of the Soviet Union. The Soviet military also left weapons and equipment behind in Afghanistan following its 1989 retreat.[28] These materials have been used to equip new nationalistic forces in Armenia, Azerbaijan, and Tajikistan, but more importantly they have found their way into the hands of al-Qaeda.[29] Such a threat came into full relief in 2002 when al-Qaeda used a Russian anti-aircraft missile in a failed attempt to shoot down an Israeli commercial airliner over Kenya. Some such materials are sold on the black market, others are sold through independent weapons merchants; either way, al-Qaeda's leadership has also attempted to acquire nuclear arms through these channels.[30]

In other cases of arms procurement, the criminological implications are complicated. In 1993—the year his name cropped up in CIA reports as a financier of terror—Osama bin Laden arranged to buy a used aircraft in the United States through a former Afghan jihadist then living in Arizona. At the sprawling bone-yard of the Davis-Monthan Air Force base outside Tucson, bin Laden's associate paid cash for a T-39 jet.[31] Was a crime committed here? If so, who was the perpetrator?

Such questions do not arise when terrorists steal weapons from military installations and commercial establishments. In 1985, two members of the Red Army Faction (RAF, formerly the Baader-Meinhof gang), murdered a U.S. soldier near the American Air Force base at Frankfurt, shooting him in the nape of the neck in order to steal his ID card and gain access to the base.[32] The RAF was also involved in a series of raids on Switzerland's loosely guarded military armories. In one attack, gunmen made off with more than two hundred rifles, five hundred revolvers, and four hundred grenades.[33] The RAF also once broke into a Belgian stone quarry and stole a cache of explosives.[34] Similar tactics have been used by American terrorists. Timothy McVeigh and Terry Nichols broke into a Kansas limestone quarry and stole dynamite, Tovex sausages, detonator cord, and blasting caps—explosives that were later used in the Oklahoma City bombing.[35]

Money laundering may be the most sophisticated crime engaged in by terrorist groups, especially when it is committed in the Arab world. Since 1998, entire operational divisions of the U.S. Departments of Defense and Justice have devoted massive resources to understanding bin Laden's financial affairs. Analysts generally agree that these attempts have been frustrated by one impenetrable reality: bin Laden's assets (estimates put the figure between $35 million and $300 million) are privately held in Muslim nations of the Middle East and Africa. These are closed societies, infused with a culture of secrecy and deeply suspicious of U.S. intentions in those parts of the world. It will be years, then, before researchers have the information necessary to make informed decisions about money laundering in the bin Laden case.

That said, research suggests that the most important link between money laundering and terrorism is to be found in the operations of Hamas. The organization has tens of thousands of supporters and sympathizers throughout the world. Many supporters in America already hold U.S. passports, allowing them to travel to Israel where they are able to enter the Palestinian territories, sometimes bringing with them hundreds of thousands of dollars for Hamas military authorities. Such crimes—which involve no banking record, no instance of passport fraud or immigration violation, and no connection to terrorist watch lists—leave nothing behind connecting launderers to their organization.[36]

Finally, research indicates that the skills needed to accomplish terrorist-oriented crimes have often been learned in paramilitary training camps. Many of these camps were once endowed, equipped, and staffed by state sponsors. Foremost among them were those established in Libya. During the 1970s, Muammar al-Gaddafi poured millions of dollars into training camps situated in the Libyan desert. Carlos the Jackal trained there, along with the Japanese Red Army, the Baader-Meinhoff gang, and the IRA, all of whom learned how to use explosives and automatic weapons there, as well as how to create false documentation and encryption techniques.[37] As of 1999, Iran, Syria, and Sudan continued to offer terrorist training to Hezbollah and al-Jihad.[38]

Most of this training has now been privatized. Prior to the 1994 ceasefire, the IRA regularly trained its members in weaponry, explosives, and information technology. Former soldiers and security and intelligence specialists lent their assistance. The IRA also exchanged training in explosives with other terrorist groups, in return for those groups' providing the IRA's members with safe housing and transportation.[39]

Privately owned paramilitary camps have offered logistical support to terrorists in the United States since the late 1970s. The Order trained at camps in Arkansas and Idaho, while the ARA did their training at Elohim City, a remote Christian Identity enclave located near the Arkansas-Oklahoma border. Members of both gangs learned trade crafts in automatic weaponry, grenades, and explosives, drawing on such works as *The Blaster's Handbook* and the *Homemade C-4* manual.[40] Terrorist training in the United States has not been limited to American right-wing groups: the Islamic extremists who carried out the 1993 World Trade Center bombing took part in commando-style training at gun ranges in New York and Connecticut.[41]

Al-Qaeda's training camps have been the subject of global attention. Interviews with defectors indicate that these camps provided the most elaborate terrorism training the world has ever known.[42] Al-Qaeda recruits were required to undergo a three-part basic training. First, recruits were instructed in the use of light weapons, ranging from pistols to automatic weapons. Then, they moved on to explosives, including C-4, dynamite, grenades, detonators, and anti-personnel mines. In the final phase, recruits were instructed in the use of heavy weaponry, such as anti-aircraft missiles. The training was augmented with rigorous physical conditioning, religious indoctrination, and class-room instruction. The standard reference work was a multi-volume, 7,000-page manual called *Encyclopedia of the Afghan Jihad.* Most of the material in the *Encyclopedia* was adapted from stolen U.S. and British military manuals; its purpose was to teach guerrilla tactics in a wide range of environments—urban, non-urban, mountain, desert, or jungle. Subjects included security and intelligence; manufacturing arms; to-pography and land surveys; booby-trapping; bombing buildings, stat-ues, and bridges; and shooting down aircraft.

From basic training, men were sent to a second camp designed to fit their assigned mission. There were three areas: guerrilla warfare and *sharia* (Islamic law); advanced training in techniques of assassination and bombing; and specialized training. In specialized training, the ji-hadists were taught techniques of surveillance and counter-surveil-lance along with methods for encrypting Internet communications and perpetrating identity, credit card, and cell phone theft, as well as pass-port fraud; they also prepared for suicide bombings. Graduates of this program were known as "the travelers." Among them was the Egypt-ian Mohammed Atta. The greatest acts of terrorism in the post–com-munist era, including the attacks of 9/11, would not have been possible without the support of privately owned terrorist training camps.

RESEARCH THAT MATTERS

In a landmark work entitled "Academic Research and Government Pol-icy on Terrorism," Israeli terrorism scholar Ariel Merari sets forth a standard for policy-oriented research on terrorism. Merari begins by ac-knowledging what every terrorism researcher knows, but seldom ad-mits—that government officials have failed to utilize academic re-search. There are a number of reasons for this, Merari argues, but they all boil down to one thing: the existing body of scientific knowledge about terrorism does not justify a more serious attitude on the part of policy makers because it fails to offer useful information. So, Merari ad-vises, "Before we complain that the client does not appreciate our mer-chandise, we must be sure that the goods are good, that the client really needs them and that he does not already have a better product that he makes on his own."[43] How, then, do we assure that the "goods are good"?

We do so by first recognizing what is *not* good—that is, by identifying types of research which are unlikely to capture policy makers' attention. Topping this list are discussions of terrorist personalities based on examinations of political manifestos and communiqués. Next are studies based solely on other writers' conclusions or impressions. Terrorism studies that lack empirical grounding are next, followed by studies that are either too theoretical or too statistical to have practical value. The more researchers rely on these methods, the farther they stray from accepted norms of social science research. The farther researchers stray from those norms, the more they distance themselves from reality. The result is research that resembles solipsism rather than twenty-first-century social science.

But the alternative—employing methods that *are* likely to produce research that will matter—is no cake walk. The frustrations are well known to researchers: compared to data on common criminality, data on terrorism are hardly accessible for the academic researcher. This is because intelligence and law enforcement agencies are reluctant to share their information with outsiders; because the clandestine nature of terrorist organizations and the ways by which intelligence is obtained rarely enable data collection that meets accepted academic standards; and because the conditions prevailing in those parts of the world where terrorism is often gestated (e.g., Pakistan) lack anything approaching a domestic scientific infrastructure to accommodate terrorism research. In addition to such limitations, terrorism itself is an inherently difficult subject for research because its heterogeneity makes generalizations questionable. "Moreover," Merari concludes, "the customary tools of psychological and sociological research are almost always inapplicable for studying terrorist groups and their individual members."[44]

Given these obstacles, Merari identifies three criteria for determining what types of research should be promoted:
(1) Research that has relevance for policy decisions. To achieve a threshold of relevancy, studies should deal specifically with the problem of terrorism on the basis of solid factual knowledge (e.g., official records and reports, as well as interviews with investigators, intelligence analysts, and law enforcement personnel).
(2) Studies that capitalize on the relative advantage of academia over government in the particular type and area of research. Because they usually have more time on their hands, academic researchers are typi-

cally able to conduct more thorough research than government workers. In terms of theory and specialized methods, academics' knowledge frequently exceeds that of public servants charged with formulating responses to terrorism. These advantages should be exploited.

(3) In-depth studies of specific terrorist groups, describing ideology, motivations, structure, decision-making, demographic characteristics, etc. Sociological and political science studies are not necessarily dependent on direct access to terrorists (in the way that psychological studies are) and may therefore be conducted utilizing mostly publicly available information.

Terrorism as Crime

Terrorism as Crime follows in this policy-oriented tradition. It features six in-depth case studies, comparing crimes committed by domestic right-wing and international jihad groups. By putting the meat on the bone of criminality, I hope to vividly describe the opportunities and skills that made terrorist-oriented crimes possible (criminal "successes"); and to clearly identify the events and lack of skills that prevented other crimes from occurring ("failures").

The six cases were not randomly selected, nor were they selected for the sake of convenience. Rather, they were selected through a statistical analysis of the American Terrorism Study (ATS) database. The ATS, compiled over a twenty-year period by criminologists Brent Smith and Kelly Damphousse, is the most comprehensive database ever assembled on crimes committed by terrorist groups.[45] The ATS is comprised of indictments and court records gathered from the case files at the federal district courts where the cases were adjudicated. The database contains information on 447 terrorists, and their organizational affiliations, tried in federal courts between 1978 and 2002. The sample represents roughly 80 percent of the population of persons indicted in federal courts for "terrorism-related" offenses during these years.[46]

I conducted a secondary analysis of the ATS by first dividing terrorist groups into two categories consisting of domestic-right wing groups (24 different groups), on the one hand, and international jihad groups (5 groups), on the other. Among the twenty-four domestic right-wing groups, a total of 846 criminal counts were handed down in support of terrorist objectives. Among the five international jihad groups, a

Table 1

Distinguishing Features of Terrorist-Oriented Criminality

Crimes	Counts Against Terrorist Groups	
	Right-Wing	International
Aircraft & motor vehicle	1	48
Explosive materials	75	197
Firearms	102	3,057
Mail fraud	77	19
RICO violations	57	21
Robbery & burglary	18	0
Machine guns, destructive devices	224	33

$x^2 = 2, 167, df = 6, p < .001$

total of 704 counts were issued in support of terrorist objectives. The "terrorism-related" counts covered a wide range of crimes: from racketeering, robbery, and conspiracy to drug smuggling, arms trafficking, and mail fraud.

Statistics were then applied to these data in order to create a baseline of knowledge that can be used to shed light on the central research question: To what extent does terrorist-oriented criminality have distinguishing features? That question is answered empirically in Table 1. The table shows that international groups are more likely than domestic groups to commit aircraft- and motor vehicle–related crimes; crimes using explosive materials; and firearms violations. Conversely, right-wing groups are more likely to commit mail fraud; RICO violations (racketeering); robbery/burglary; and violations related to machine guns and destructive devices.[47]

Further analysis revealed that, among international groups, the majority of aircraft and motor vehicle crimes (54.2 percent) were committed by the terrorists responsible for the 1993 World Trade Center bombing in New York City. Therefore, the 1993 World Trade Center bombers were selected for the first case study. They are the subject of Chapter 1.

The analysis also showed that the majority of criminal counts against international groups for violations of explosive materials (32.5 percent) were attributed to al-Qaeda. All of these counts involved al-Qaeda's simultaneous 1998 bombings of the United States embassies in Kenya and Tanzania. Al-Qaeda was also responsible for the overwhelming majority (97.4 percent) of firearms violations among international groups. These counts involved the embassy bombing in Nairobi,

Kenya. Accordingly, both cases (the attacks in Kenya and Tanzania) are examined in Chapter 2.

The research then turns to the domestic groups.[48] Over the years, a total of seventeen different domestic groups have been indicted on crimes related to machine guns and destructive devices. The greatest percentage of these indictments (26.3 percent) was brought against the Covenant, the Sword, and the Arm of the Lord, a survivalist group active in Arkansas, Missouri, and Oklahoma during the early to mid-1980s. They are the subject of Chapter 3.

Most of the RICO violations for domestic groups (78.9 percent) were committed by the Order, a legendary gang of neo-Nazis active in the Pacific Northwest in the mid-1980s. Their case is presented in Chapter 4. And the greatest percentage of robbery/burglary crimes among domestic groups (38.9 percent) was committed by the aforementioned Aryan Republican Army—the subject of Chapter 5.

To summarize, then, purposive sampling was used to focus on the greatest number of criminal counts set forth in indictments against domestic right-wing and international jihad groups between 1978 and 2002. During this period, nearly six thousand terrorism-related criminal counts were brought against fifty-nine different groups. From this pool, I selected six cases based on the most significant statistical differences between international and domestic right-wing organizations. Simply put, of the fifty-nine terrorist groups tried in the United States over the past twenty-five years, the six cases examined here represent the most criminally severe.

The primary source material for the case studies is trial transcripts and related court documents. This material is then enriched by interviews both with FBI agents who worked the cases and with several convicted terrorists, as well as by government intelligence, investigative reports, previous research, and related scholarship. Because crime does not occur in a social vacuum, the narratives also include biographies of the terrorists along with descriptions of their organizations, strategies, and plots. It is crucial to note that the terrorist groups studied committed numerous crimes, *not just the ones referenced in the ATS database;* thus, these other crimes are examined as well. I also consider the actualities of daily criminality inside terrorist groups by paying attention to such factors as technology, religion, charismatic leadership, intra-group conflict, terrorism's cultural codes and mythologies, as well as the role of women and government informants inside the groups.

Then, in the final chapter, I offer a new way of thinking about security challenges by applying the findings to the threat of terrorism facing the United States in the aftermath of terrorist bombings in Casablanca, Madrid, London, the invasion of Iraq, and other recent developments.

What Can Be Learned from This Book?

Again, the primary source materials for this book are the transcripts of the major terrorism trials of our times, including cases both foreign and domestic. In their masterful work on Islamic terrorism, *The Age of Sacred Terror,* former National Security Council directors Daniel Benjamin and Steven Simon describe these transcripts as "a treasure trove. Reading through nearly fifty thousand pages of testimony, we learned more about the rise of the new terrorism than we ever could have expected. In many instance, we discovered information so crucial that we were amazed that the relevant agencies did not inform us of it while we were at the NSC."[49] The same can be said for crimes committed by other terrorist groups. The transcripts provide a gold mine of information that has largely been ignored in previous research.

The main finding of this work is that the most successful method of both detecting and prosecuting cases of terrorism is through the pursuit of conventional criminal investigations. By focusing on crimes committed by terrorist groups, investigators may well preempt larger operations designed to kill thousands of innocent people. This represents a significant departure from other recent terrorism studies which tend to emphasize broader factors such as global politics, religious movements, and a host of grievances associated with ethnic and nationalistic conflicts. The focus of this book is explicitly criminological. By focusing on past cases of terrorism, and the evidence accumulated from prosecuting and studying them, the research indicates that the best practices of investigators should be directed to crimes that facilitate the operation of complex organizations. When this strategy is employed, a clear pattern of precursor activity across diverse organizations becomes clear. All terrorist groups require money, material, transportation, identity documents, communications systems, and safe havens to accomplish their aims. Crimes that finance these operations should be the top priority for investigators because terrorist groups cannot operate without engaging in them.

Included among those crimes are bank robberies, credit card theft, document counterfeiting, motor vehicle–related offenses, money laundering, and smuggling weapons of mass destruction. These are the specific types of crimes that those charged with combating terrorism should focus on. The same holds true for criminologists and others interested in the lived reality of contemporary political violence. By tightening our focus on the criminality of terrorist groups, we are able to reduce the problem of terrorism to its common denominators, thereby removing some of the mystery that shrouds these organizations. Once the hype and political hysteria surrounding terrorism is removed, we are able to understand the vulnerabilities of different kinds of terrorist groups.

Those vulnerabilities can be identified only through a careful analysis of criminal failures. The case studies will show that terrorists are rarely the "criminal masterminds" we have been led to believe they are. The greatest failures of jihad groups involve cultural conflicts that manifest themselves in such seemingly innocuous transgressions as passport fraud, immigration infractions, and traffic violations. In addition, as pointed out earlier, their Achilles heel is an inability to cross international borders without attracting attention. True, jihadists rarely have criminal records. Rather, they are inexperienced criminals—sometimes staggeringly so—who often fail to conceal incriminating evidence. Likewise, they often do not possess the criminal skills necessary to transform opportunity into terrorism, nor do they set up contingencies in the event that their terrorist plots go awry.

Domestic terrorists fail in different ways. There are failures when it comes to counterfeiting, insurance scams, constructing weapons of mass destruction, and maintaining internal security. But their greatest failure comes from living a pipedream—or, what we might call the showcasing of imagery and style. Jihadists would never dream of using appearances or panache to make ironic statements about their violence. Domestic terrorists are just the opposite: they present themselves to the world as entertainers, thereby turning terrorism into a theatrical performance. One needs only to make a cursory reading of Timothy McVeigh's apocryphal ghostwritten autobiography, *American Terrorist: Timothy McVeigh & the Oklahoma City Bombing*, to appreciate this insatiable need to be famous. Such a constant craving for attention has attracted the likes of such infamous right-wing American terrorists as Jesse James, John Wilkes Booth, and Eric Rudolph. The pursuit of celebrity has trumped their ideology, their purpose, and their mission. And this is their Achilles heel.

Criminal successes also turn on cultural forces. Jihad groups tend to rely on low-level operatives to perform menial criminal acts necessary for a terrorist strike. These operatives are recruited less for their criminal skills than for their connections to local communities and attendant opportunities to exploit routine activities. In contrast, it is the jihad leaders with specialized training who are responsible for successes in surveillance, financing, communications, breaching airline security, smuggling explosives, and bomb building.

The situation in domestic groups is quite different. They tend to recruit individuals specifically for their criminal competencies. Often headed by charismatic leaders, domestic groups are most successful at acquiring false identity documents, manufacturing illegal firearms, and armored truck and bank robbery. They are surveillance experts, skilled in the craft of deception, who often spend weeks taking into account the taken-for-granted order of daily routines in and around their targets.

There are also some important similarities between these groups. Perhaps most interesting are the attempts made by domestic terrorists to forge alliances with international jihadists, uncovered in this book. But both domestic and jihad groups have also financed their operations through counterfeiting. Both have stolen arms, explosives, and equipment from military installations. Both have exploited military training for terrorist purposes. And both have proven exceptionally vulnerable to infiltration by informants.

How can all of this information benefit policy makers and increase public safety? For starters, because the book systematically evaluates the entire content of terrorism trials, the results summarize concisely the relative role of criminal activity within various terrorist groups. From a legal perspective, this is important because U.S. prosecutors have historically indicted terrorists, not on terrorism charges, but on criminal charges. This research pinpoints the *distinct* ways that terrorists' goals are compromised by poor criminal skills and an inability to fully exploit routine activities associated with counter-terrorism measures. If criminal activity is the lifeblood of terrorist groups, then choking off the blood supply begins with identifying these differences.

Another set of implications involves specific legal strategies for controlling terrorism that may produce meaningful intelligence. For example, because terrorism involves complex criminal conspiracies, prosecutors are always interested in knowing if a defendant has information on these conspiracies. This volume explains how previous conspiracies were created. It also explains how they ultimately broke down under the weight of their own obsessions. Appreciating the ways in which terrorists have created the opportunities to marshal their conspiracies, and the organizational factors that led to their downfall, may prove beneficial to intelligence analysts.

Finally, different crimes require different skills and opportunities, and identifying these differences may take law enforcement a step closer to prevention. Recent events certainly suggest as much: increased airline security along with heightened awareness of passport fraud, identity theft, and immigration violations have all made criminal opportunities tougher for terrorists to create. There is no doubt that closing down training camps in Afghanistan and Arkansas has reduced criminal skill development among potential terrorists. This work complements those security advances. Through its study of government documents, original interviews, and investigative reports, as well as its incorporation of previous research—all of which shed further light on the information contained in nearly three hundred thousand pages of court records—the book offers detailed accounts of the specific techniques involved in terrorism-related criminality.

To be sure, applying these findings to the current terrorist threat is like shooting at a moving target. Not only do terrorists groups change over time, but so does their criminality. Thus, for example, after years of idleness, and before agreeing to lay down their arms for good in 2005, the IRA renewed its criminal activity through a series of Belfast bank robberies and warehouse heists. IRA operatives were also involved in training FARC militias (Revolutionary Armed Forces of Colombia) in the use of explosives. Prior to that training, FARC bombings were unheard of in Colombia; since the training, FARC has committed some two dozen bombings, including a rocket-propelled attack on the nation's capitol building.[50] Here in the United States, the radical right's terrorism continues, only now their plots involve the procurement of biological and chemical weapons.[51] The Moroccan immigrants responsible for the 2004 Madrid train bombings raised money by peddling hashish and Ecstasy. Islamic terrorists in France are turning to the lucrative trade in counterfeiting goods, forgery, and credit card fraud. Italian mobsters and Islamic terrorists have formed links in arms and drug trafficking. And al-Qaeda's criminal portfolio now includes insurance fraud and antiquities smuggling assisted by criminal gangs in the central and south Asian heartlands. In fact, U.S. investigators have found that some of the most useful intelligence on al-Qaeda has been collected from informers or infiltrators of these criminal gangs, leading a group of analysts to conclude that al-Qaeda's "criminal connections may prove to be the Achilles' heel of the organization."[52] I would argue that that is most certainly the case and that because it is, we can gain crucial insights into the processes and forces of terrorism by understanding the origin and meaning of crime inside terrorist groups.

PART I

GLOBAL CRIME AND TERRORISM

I

Criminal Stupidity and the Age of Sacred Terrorism

The First World Trade Center Bombing

Scholars have traditionally explained terrorism by placing it within an historical context. Efforts have also been made to describe terrorism through the contexts of changing global politics, ethnic and nationalistic conflicts, and religious movements. Other writers have concentrated on the personal pathologies of terrorists as well as on the social pulls and pressures that influence the dynamics of terrorist groups. And still others have focused on the conceptualization of terrorism as a form of communication. Once we appreciate the enormous variety of social, political, cultural, and individual features of terrorism, we can understand why it is such an overwhelming subject of study.

This work takes an entirely different approach by assuming that terrorism is first and foremost a criminal matter. This strategy was well-known to terrorism investigators long before the attacks of 9/11. "Terrorists are criminals," said a veteran FBI counter-terrorism official in 1998, "and we use criminal investigations to go after them."[1] These investigations focused on such highly sophisticated affairs as building bombs and coordinating terrorist cells to such mundane activities as breaching airport security and motor vehicle violations. Some terrorists will show signs of criminal brilliance in carrying out these activities. Richard Clarke, the former counter-terrorism czar for both Presidents Bill Clinton and George W. Bush, comments on this trait in his analysis of Islamic terrorists. "These people are smart," Clarke writes, "many trained in our colleges, and they have a very long view."[2] But this is not true for all terrorists, Islamic or otherwise, no more than it is accurate to say that all car thieves are superlative criminals. Some terrorists will be only marginally competent in carrying out their activities. And some will be completely incompetent.

The terrorists who perpetrated the attacks of September 11 were no exception to this basic principle of criminology. In a speech delivered at the University of California, Los Angeles, in February of 2004, Presidential candidate John Kerry pointed out that the 9/11 attacks could have been prevented had U.S. law enforcement and intelligence communities coordinated information on the hijackers' driving records. "In the months leading up to September 11," said Kerry, "two of the hijackers were arrested for drunk driving—and another was stopped for speeding and then let go, although he was already the subject of an arrest warrant in a neighboring county and was on a federal terrorist watch list."[3] Although drunk driving and speeding may seem like extremely careless actions for terrorists to engage in, such infractions are not uncommon.

For example, less than ninety minutes after detonating a massive truck bomb in front of the Alfred P. Murrah Federal Building in Oklahoma City on April 19, 1995, Timothy McVeigh was arrested for driving without a license plate. What kind of criminal bombs a federal building, killing 169 and injuring hundreds more, and then drives off in a car that does not have a license plate, an act that led directly to his capture?

As incredible as they are, these cases pale in comparison to the criminal ineptitude displayed in the 1993 World Trade Center bombing, the focus of this chapter.[4]

BACKGROUND

Around noon on Friday, February 26, 1993, a group of Islamic extremists drove a bomb-laden van into the underground parking lot of New York's World Trade Center complex and, using a timer, set the bomb to detonate. At 12:18 p.m., the bomb exploded, killing six and wounding over a thousand others, thus presaging the September 11, 2001 attacks on the same building. Six days later, the FBI made its first arrest in the case. This arrest was based on what prosecutors would later call a "ludicrous mistake" made by one of the conspirators. As we shall see, this mistake was not an isolated incident. Rather, throughout the conspiracy, criminal patterns were overlooked by law enforcement. Time and again authorities could have taken the terrorists off the streets if only police and immigration officials had enforced the letter of the law.

The Poor Immigrant

Mohammad Salameh was born in the town of Biddya, on what was then the Jordanian-controlled West Bank, on September 1, 1967—shortly after the "Six-Day War" between Israel and her Arab neighbors. Extremism was a family trait, due mainly to the influence of relatives on his mother's side. Salameh's maternal grandfather was a member of the PLO, as was his maternal uncle, who served eighteen years in an Israeli prison for terrorism.[5] In 1968, the Salameh family relocated to Zarqa, Jordan, where Mohammad's father, a Jordanian soldier and Palestinian, was stationed. Mohammad grew up there in a bleak lower-class neighborhood, along with his parents and ten brothers and sisters. From an early age, humiliation became part of his emotional landscape. There were a number of reasons for this.

First was the Black September massacre of 1970—an event initiated by Jordan's King Hussein after he ordered a campaign to relocate Palestinians to refugee camps. During the relocation, three-year-old Mohammad Salameh was shot by a Jordanian soldier and hospitalized under inadequate medical conditions. Several years later, Mohammad's father retired from the military and took on odd jobs; yet he was unable to make ends meet, and the family slipped into abject poverty. Then another problem arose. Mohammad was the oldest of the eleven Salameh children, and he would prove to be the least accomplished. He functioned at a below-average level of intelligence, had few interests, and little ambition. Even within his own family, Mohammad Salameh was an outcast.

After graduating from high school, Salameh took entry exams to become a student at the University of Jordan, where he planned to study law or medicine. Failing those exams, he ended up majoring in Islamic studies. There is no evidence of his participation in fundamentalist movements, though, and upon graduating, he entered Jordan's austere job market. Unable to find work, Salameh was reduced to selling candy on the streets.[6] Sensing that employment opportunities would be better in America, and seeking to avoid Jordan's mandatory military service, he applied for, and was granted, a five-year visa to the United States. Borrowing money from his family, Salameh bought a one-way ticket to New York City.

He arrived in early 1988. Barely able to speak English and with no job skills, Salameh found that employment opportunities were no better than those he had left behind. Often destitute, he bounced from one menial job to the next until he ended up in a refugee center in Jersey City, New Jersey. There he began attending the Masjid al-Salaam mosque.

The Assassin

The Jersey City mosque was led by a radical Palestinian immigrant named Sultan el-Gawli, who by 1988 had attracted a following of struggling young Middle Eastern émigrés.[7] Among them was a round-faced, thirty-two-year-old Egyptian refugee who was a walking testament to the theory that terrorism is caused by individual pathology.

El Sayyid Nosair was born in 1955 near Port Said, Egypt, to a family that was also displaced following the Six-Day War in 1967. Nosair was raised in Cairo and went on to study industrial design and engineering at Helwan University. He graduated in 1978 and apparently spent some time in the training camps of the Arab terrorist Abu Nidal. Nosair immigrated to America in the early 1980s and settled with family friends in Pittsburgh. Nosair found work as a diamond cutter in a jewelry store and married a despondent, overweight Irish-American woman who had recently converted to Islam.

Nosair's life began to unravel shortly after that. He was fired from his diamond cutting job in 1983, in part because he had begun proselytizing co-workers in the name of Islam. In 1985, a woman from the Pittsburgh mosque filed battery charges against Nosair, and later another person accused him of assault. Eventually cleared of both charges, Nosair was nevertheless ostracized from the local Muslim community. Unemployed, with three children and a wife to support, Nosair relocated to Jersey City where he found work in a power plant. But in 1986, Nosair was electrocuted on the job. The accident left him impotent, disabled, depressed, and unemployed. He began taking the anti-depressant medication Prozac. In mid-1987, Nosair went to work as a heating and air conditioning repairman in the Criminal Courts Building in Manhattan.

By this time, Nosair had become a fixture at the Jersey City mosque where his rabid hatred of the United States for its pro-Israel policies went into overdrive. Nosair's fanaticism eventually so alienated his brethren at the mosque that he began praying at home with a small circle of other disenfranchised worshipers, including Mohammad Salameh. And soon the impressionable Salameh became Nosair's disciple.

In 1989, Nosair and Salameh became involved with the al-Kifah Refugee Service Center located in the al-Farooq mosque on Atlantic Avenue in Brooklyn. The Service Center was founded by a charismatic Islamic scholar named Abdullah Azzam, whose influence among volunteer mujahideen soldiers fighting the Soviet army in Afghanistan was legendary. Among his devotees was the young Saudi millionaire Osama bin Laden. Under Azzam's leadership, the al-Kifah Service Center functioned as a recruiting and propaganda arm for the Afghan mujahideen. Clandestinely, the Service Center also engaged in counterfeiting and producing phony passports to enable Muslim volunteers to travel to America.

Through their involvement with the Service Center, Nosair and Salameh met three other refugees who would become part of an unfolding criminal conspiracy. But unlike Nosair and Salameh, all three would enter the conspiracy with considerable talent. The first was a giant thirty-year-old Egyptian-born New York City cab driver named Mahmud Abouhalima—known as "Mahmud the Red" because of his hair. The Red was a hardened combat veteran who had survived two tours of duty in Afghanistan; there he had developed a reputation for fearlessness, often volunteering for mine-sweeping missions. Emblematic of his jihadist background, Abouhalima continued to wear his military fatigues and combat books as he walked the streets of Brooklyn. The second was a twenty-seven-year-old Palestinian named Bilal Alkaisi, also a veteran of the Soviet-Afghan war. And the third was twenty-five-year-old Nidal Ayyad, a naturalized American citizen, born in Kuwait to Palestinian parents, who had recently graduated with a degree in chemical engineering from Rutgers University. These five men (Nosair, Salameh, Abouhalima, Alkaisi, and Ayyad) formed the nucleus of the first Islamic terrorist cell in the United States.

In the spring of 1989, Nosair's cell began conducting paramilitary training exercises at the Calverton Gun Range on eastern Long Island. There, they participated in basic firearms training taught by a Black Muslim from Brooklyn named Richard Smith. Smith also sold Nosair's crew an assortment of rifles, shotguns, assault weapons, and grenades.[8] That summer, the training was expanded to include survival and surveillance courses taught by a U.S. Army Special Forces instructor, Ali

Mohamed, at Nosair's apartment in Jersey City. Alkaisi,who had been an explosives trainer in bin Laden's camps, also added a course on rudimentary bomb building.

As the training progressed, Nosair sought the approval of Azzam and other spiritual leaders, including the blind Egyptian cleric Omar Abdel-Rahman, considered one of the most accomplished religious scholars in all of Islam. By the summer of 1989, Nosair was in regular contact with Abdel-Rahman, who was then being held under house arrest by the Egyptian government. At length, Nosair and Abouhalima launched a campaign to bring the blind sheik to New York. In one audio cassette to Abdel-Rahman, Nosair boasted, "We have organized an encampment. We are concentrating here." Indeed they were, and this led to the cell's first of many motor vehicle violations.

By now, Nosair had moved the firearms training to the High Rock Shooting Range in Naugatuck, Connecticut. On August 29, 1989, a state trooper stopped a suspicious-looking car carrying six Middle Eastern men near the range. Upon searching the vehicle, the officer found a small arsenal of semi-automatic weapons and several out-of-state license plates. The guns were legally purchased and licensed to the driver, a local gun dealer of Albanian descent. A computer search showed that the extra license plates were registered to one El Sayyid Nosair. This brought Nosair to the attention of the FBI, yet his name meant little to them at the time.[9]

Soon thereafter, Nosair planned his first terrorist strike in the United States. This involved a plot to set off bombs in the Atlantic City casinos, yet the scheme never came to fruition. Nosair took a step closer to implementing another plan later that year. On December 8, Soviet premier Mikhail Gorbachev was on a state visit to New York. As Gorbachev's motorcade passed through Manhattan, Nosair threw a homemade grenade at the premier's limousine, but the device failed to detonate, and Nosair's assassination attempt went unnoticed by law enforcement.[10] Yet Nosair was relentless. In April 1990, he set off a crude pipe bomb at a gay bar in Greenwich Village, causing three minor injuries. Again Nosair got away unnoticed.[11]

A month later, Nosair's spiritual mentor, Sheik Abdel-Rahman, arrived in New York after absconding from house arrest in Egypt. Abdel-Rahman began preaching at the al-Farooq mosque in Brooklyn and then at the Jersey City mosque. Sometime that summer, the blind sheik issued a fatwah, calling on his Muslim brothers to rob American banks and kill Jews anywhere they were found. Ten years earlier, Abdel-Rah-man's fiery oratory had inspired the creation of the Egyptian Islamic Jihad—the organization responsible for the assassination of Egyptian president Anwar Sadat. Now Abdel-Rahman would inspire Nosair and his confederates to carry out another assassination, this time on American soil.

In the fall of 1990, Mahmud Abouhalima struck up a relationship with a Lebanese Muslim, then living in Texas, named Wadih el-Hage. From el-Hage (who would later become a personal emissary for bin Laden and a key figure in the 1998 bombing of the American embassies in East Africa), Abouhalima attempted to buy weapons to use against the Jewish Defense League—classified as a terrorist organization by both the U.S. State Department and the Israeli Knesset—and its outspoken fifty-eight-year-old founder, Rabbi Meir Kahane. Simultaneously, Nosair began stalking Kahane.

On the evening of November 5, Kahane gave a speech on the expulsion of Palestinians from Israel at the Marriott Hotel in Manhattan. In the crowd stood Nosair, wearing a yarmulke to disguise himself as a dark-skinned Sephardic Jew, along with Bilal Alkaisi. Mahmud the Red was in his cab outside the hotel, and Mohammad Salameh sat behind the wheel of a green sedan a block away. As Kahane left the crowded ballroom, Nosair approached him with a coat draped over his arm.

Suddenly, Nosair pulled a .357 revolver and fired two shots into Kahane's jugular vein, killing him. As the crowd erupted in chaos, Nosair ran from the room, shouting, "It's Allah's will!" At the door, an elderly man grabbed Nosair around the neck; Nosair shot him in the leg and fled.

Once he and Alkaisi reached the street, Alkaisi ran toward the green sedan as Nosair jumped into a cab. Three blocks away, Nosair realized that he was in the wrong cab (security had shooed the Red away from the hotel) and told the driver to stop. As Nosair sprinted toward the sedan, he was confronted by a U.S. postal police officer who told him to halt. Nosair fired one shot at the officer, hitting him in his bullet-proof vest. The officer fired back, hitting Nosair in the chin and bringing him to his knees.

When Alkaisi reached the sedan, he shouldered Salameh over to the passenger's seat and took the wheel. Alkaisi hit the accelerator and fled the scene, leaving Nosair bleeding on the sidewalk. A police report later stated that witnesses saw "two bug-eyed Middle Eastern men in the front seat of a green sedan careening the wrong way down Park Avenue."[12]

THE PLOT

When police searched Nosair's apartment they discovered forty-seven boxes of documents, including training manuals from the Army Special Warfare School at Fort Bragg, North Carolina, and copies of teletypes related to the war in Afghanistan that had been routed to the Secretary of the Army and the Joint Chiefs of Staff. There were bomb-making manuals in the boxes, as well as maps of landmark New York locations, including the Statue of Liberty, Times Square, the Holland Tunnel . . . and the World Trade Center. Detectives also found a notebook in which Nosair had written (in Arabic) about the destruction of the enemies of Allah "by means of exploding the structure of their civilized pillars." It would be years, however, before investigators would understand the significance of these documents.

Abouhalima and Salameh were found staying at Nosair's former residence after the assassination and were taken into custody by New York City police. A background check showed that in 1990 Salameh had lied on an immigration document, falsely claiming that he had been in the United States since 1982, and that he had left briefly in 1987. Both men denied their involvement in the Kahane murder, and, lacking evidence to the contrary and ignoring Salameh's immigration violation, police released them without filing charges.

Nosair was locked up in the Manhattan house of detention and charged with first-degree murder. Yet he received numerous visitors, including the Red and representatives of the blind sheik. To cover his legal costs, supporters created the El Sayyid Nosair Defense Fund, to which Osama bin Laden made a $20,000 contribution.

Nosair's trail began in late 1991. His defense—which was led by famed civil rights attorney William Kunstler—claimed that Nosair had not fired the gun that killed Meir Kahane, and that Kahane had actually been shot by one of his own followers. Each day, a small group of Muslim men paced the sidewalks in front of the courthouse, fulminating against Israel, the United States, and the alleged political persecution of Nosair. Taking advantage of this situation, the New York office of the FBI placed among these supporters an informant named Emad Salem, a forty-three-year-old former Egyptian military officer. People have various motivations for becoming an FBI informant; Salem was motivated by money. Over the next year and a half, Salem would receive $500 a week, plus expenses, for information he provided to his FBI handlers. With that income in mind, Salem ingratiated himself with the blink sheik and ultimately became his private bodyguard.

In a surprise decision, on December 21 the jury acquitted Nosair of Kahane's murder. Outside the Manhattan courthouse, Nosair's supporters cheered the verdict as the Red hoisted Kunstler onto his shoulders. News photographers captured the moment, and the next morning's *New York Times* featured a front-page photograph of the impoverished Palestinian immigrant Mohammad Salameh.[13]

Acquitted of murder, Nosair was nevertheless convicted of shooting the postal police officer and the other man who tried to prevent his escape from the Marriott, and he received a seven to twenty-five-year sentence in the state prison at Attica. The Muslim fundamentalists continued to support Nosair, arranging bus trips to Attica from the New York and Jersey City mosques. Emad Salem, the FBI informant, was among them. In the summer of 1991, Nosair began talking to his supporters about "underground people" who were planning to construct twelve pipe bombs to be used in the assassination of the judge who sentenced Nosair, along with a Brooklyn assemblyman, and ten "Jewish locations" in New York.

Nosair's plot was also taking shape on another front.

The Decoy

With Nosair in stir, the rest of the cell began to quarrel over who would become their new emir (leader). To settle the matter, they drew straws. Salameh won, causing Alkaisi to eventually leave the group. But this created another problem because Alkaisi was the cell's only bomb builder.

The story of how Ramzi Yousef came to fill this void is shrouded in mystery. One theory is that Abdel-Rahman recruited him into the cell. Another holds that Mahmud the Red recruited him—the two having met in Afghanistan around 1991. And other theories have been proposed. One is that Osama bin Laden enlisted Yousef into the plot though Yousef's older cousin, Khalid Sheikh Mohammad (who would go on to become the principle architect of the 9/11 attacks). Another is that Yousef was an Iraqi intelligence agent sent to New York by Saddam Hussein to avenge Iraq's defeat in the Persian Gulf War. And still another is that no one recruited him at all. Yousef would later say that his initial plan was to visit New York, acquire a U.S. passport, identify potential targets, and then return to Pakistan to raise funds for his operation. But once in New York, he decided to raise money there and proceed with a terrorist attack. While the impetus for Yousef's joining the cell remains unclear, what *is* known is that he entered the conspiracy by dint of a complex scheme to breach U.S. airline security. For our purposes, *who* sent him is incidental to this exploitation of a routine activity within the transportation industry.

The ploy centered on a young pizza deliveryman from Houston, Texas, named Ahmad Ajaj. Like Mohammad Salameh, Ajaj was a Palestinian refugee who had been brutalized as a child by soldiers in the conflict over occupied territories. On April 24, 1992, Ajaj flew from New York to Peshwar, Pakistan, using the alias "Ibraham Salameh," and from there he made his way to a terrorist training camp along the Afghanistan-Pakistan border known as Camp Khaldan. Apparently lacking necessary credentials, Ajaj was sent to Saudi Arabia to obtain a letter of recommendation. On May 16, Ajaj flew to Saudi Arabia, via the United Arab Emirates (UAE), where he procured a letter of introduction requesting that the leader of Camp Khaldan provide the bearer with training in the use of weapons and explosives. Ajaj returned to Pakistan, again via the UAE, arriving on June 14. Shortly thereafter, he began taking a course on bomb building at Camp Khaldan taught by Ramzi Yousef. Yousef specialized in building bombs to destroy large buildings, such as American embassies. With this instruction, the plot to bomb the World Trade Center was set in motion.

On September 1, Yousef and Ajaj left Karachi for New York on Pakistani International Airlines, flying first class. Details of their passage through U.S. Customs speaks volumes about how institutionally ill-prepared American law enforcement was to combat terrorism prior to 9/11.

On the evening of September 1, Yousef and Ajaj exited the plane separately and approached the arrival lanes at JKF International Airport. Yousef had only one small carry-on bag, and he was an amazing sight to behold. The twenty-five-year-old Yousef was a slender 6' 2" with a brown beard and a pock-marked face. He was dressed in what has been called a "harem suit"—Ali-Baba type pants, a shirt with balloon sleeves, and a brightly-colored silk jacket and vest. His startling appearance was only the beginning of some highly unusual events.

Yousef presented himself to Immigration and Naturalization Service (INS) officer Martha Morales by handing over his boarding pass, issued in the name of "Mohammad Azan." Then Yousef handed over an ID card from an organization called the Al-Bunyan Islamic Center. Another name appeared on that card—"Khurram Khan"—but on the back was a signature for Ramzi Ahmed Yousef. After showing Morales his Iraqi passport, which appeared to be authentic but lacked a U.S. visa, Yousef claimed that he was fleeing the oppressive regime of Saddam Hussein and needed asylum.

Ajaj stood nearby at a second desk. Traveling under the alias "Khurram Khan" (the same name that appeared on Yousef's ID card), Ajaj handed his International Student Identification card and Swedish passport to INS inspector Robert Malafronte. Noticing that the laminate covering the passport photo was too thick, Malafronte peeled back the photo's corner from the edge of the page, revealing the picture of another man. In addition to these problems, Ajaj's passport did not contain a visa. Realizing that he was in trouble, Ajaj shouted to the inspector: "My mother was Swedish! If you don't believe me check your computer." Malafronte then took Ajaj into an office for questioning.

As this was going on, Morales escorted Yousef to an interview room for questioning as well. Speaking excellent English with a British accent, the immigrant stated that he was traveling alone and admitted that his real name was Ramzi Yousef. Yousef said that he was born in the UAE in 1967, though he was now a citizen of Pakistan. He explained the discrepancies in his identification documents by claiming that he had obtained the "Mohammad Azan" boarding pass from a Pakistani government official by paying him a $2,700 bribe. As for the asylum request, Yousef charged that he had recently been beaten by Iraqi soldiers when he was in Kuwait because they thought he was a member of a Kuwaiti guerrilla organization.

Morales then searched Yousef's belongings. Among his possessions was an identity card from an Islamic organization in Arizona, along with checks from Lloyd's Bank of London and an address book listing what Morales would later call "unusual places [in America] for someone to visit who had just come from halfway around the world."

All of this raised Morales's suspicions, and she informed Yousef that he had broken the law by attempting to make in illegal entry into the

United States. Morales fingerprinted and photographed Yousef and confiscated his passport. She then recommended to her supervisor, Mark
Cozine, that Yousef be detained. "I felt he might pose a danger to the
United States," said Morales. Yet Morales was overruled by Cozine on
the grounds that the INS Detention Center was full. So Yousef was released on his own recognizance and told to appear before an immigration judge at a later date to determine his asylum claim—despite the facts
that Yousef had not only committed several acts of immigration fraud
(traveling under three different identities and lying to an INS official); he
had also given inspectors evidence linking him to Ahmad Ajaj.

And the questioning of Ajaj had led to an amazing discovery. Upon
searching his possessions, Malafronte and Cozine found what prosecutors would later call a "terrorist kit." In his briefcase, Ajaj carried fake
passports from Jordan, Saudi Arabia, and Britain, all issued in different
names. In one of Ajaj's bags, the inspectors found several handwritten
journals, a couple of magazines—one of which featured a picture of
Saddam Hussein on the cover—along with some manuals containing
detailed instruction on the assembly of pipe bombs and large improvised bombs. There were also military guides on carrying out successful terrorist operations, complete with aerial photographs, assembly instructions for rocket launchers, and ingredients for bomb building.
Four videos were discovered—one featured a suicide bombing of an
American embassy, another gave a chemistry lesson on manufacturing
explosives—along with a document entitled "Facing the Enemies of
God Terrorism Is a Religious Duty and Force is Necessary." Finally, a
manual entitled "Rapid Destruction and Demolition" gave instruction
on complicated chemical formulas needed for making bombs capable
of destroying large buildings. Those chemicals included urea nitrate,
aluminum powder, nitroglycerine, and lead azide. Printed beneath the
manual's title were Arabic words initially mistranslated as "The Basic
Rule." Later, these words were retranslated as "Al-Qaeda, The Base."

A closer look at Ajaj's passport revealed that his June 14, 1992, Pakistani entry stamp was counterfeit. Adding to what was now a litany of
immigration infractions, Malafronte and Cozine also discovered evidence connecting Ajaj to Ramzi Yousef. In Ajaj's bag they found an airline ticket issued to "Mohammad Azan"—the name that Yousef had just
admitted to his INS inspector was an alias.

Some commentators have argued that Ajaj was a "mule" for
Yousef's bomb-building manuals. A more likely scenario is that Ajaj

had previously agreed with Yousef that he would carry the terrorist kit in his own bags to distract inspectors, thereby maximizing Yousef's chances of getting through customs. In this scenario, the terrorist kit, the counterfeit entry stamp, and Ajaj's outburst were all decoys intended to deflect the INS's attention away from Yousef and facilitate his processing. This was a premeditated plan intended to exploit the routine activities of busy INS inspectors.

Shortly after 5:00 a.m. on September 2, after more than eight hours of questioning, INS charged Ajaj with passport fraud and handed him over to the Wackenhut Correctional Corporation, a private contractor, for incarceration in a converted warehouse in Queens. The evidence linking Yousef to Ajaj would be ignored.

Organization

Yousef told officer Morales that he would be traveling on to Houston, Texas, but that turned out to be another lie. Wasting no time, he took a cab from JFK to the al-Farooq mosque where he met up with Abouhalima. The next day, Abouhalima arranged a meeting between Yousef and Abdel-Rahman; then the Red helped Yousef obtain a truck driver's license so that he would have a legitimate identification card. The following day, Yousef moved into an apartment with Mohammad Salameh at 34 Kensington Avenue in Jersey City—a residence that Salameh shared with five other Middle Eastern men. Among these men, Yousef was known as "Rashid, the Iraqi." By this time, Salameh's immigration jacket had become riddled with problems. In addition to his 1990 violation and his being questioned as a suspect in the Kahane assassination, Salameh was called into INS offices in August of 1992 to fill out an affidavit to reactivate a lapsed immigration application.

In early October, seeking more privacy, Salameh and Yousef relocated to a two-room apartment at 251 Virginia Avenue, less than a mile from Kensington Avenue. This apartment they shared with a quiet young Egyptian student named Ashref Moneeb. Yousef then began making dozens of overseas phone calls, often talking loudly for hours with contacts in Pakistan, Jordan, Iraq, Israel, Saudi Arabia, Turkey, and even Yugoslavia. Among them were numerous calls to his cousin, Khalid Sheikh Mohammad. Yousef and Salameh also began holding meetings with other conspirators, including Abouhalima, Nidal Ayyad, an enigmatic Iraqi named Abdul Yasin—who also began living at 251

Virginia Avenue after his arrival in the United States in late June, 1992—and the informant Emad Salem, who around this time warned his FBI handler that the Muslim group was planning to carry off a catastrophic bombing in New York. That would require money for rent, phone calls, vehicles, storage fees, and eventually bomb-building components.

After settling in to the apartment, Salameh and Ayyad opened several bank accounts using the Jersey City Islamic Center as their mailing address. These accounts have become the subject of extensive speculation. According to interviews with law enforcement and State Department officials published in the *New York Times* (April 25, 1993), over the next four months more than $100,000 was allegedly funneled to the conspirators through the accounts. Possible sources for this revenue were the Muslim Brotherhood of Egypt, along with unknown parties in Iran, Saudi Arabia, and Kuwait.[14] The sum, considerable enough, was allegedly only a drop in the bucket. Research conducted by the Federal Library of Congress concludes that, at the time, Mahmud Abouhalima was involved in a fraudulent coupon-redemption scam in New York that generated as much as $200 million for Middle Eastern terrorist activities.[15] There is no mention of these finances in court documents. In fact, years later, the post–9/11 investigative committees would conclude that the cell had meager resources at its disposal. Specifically, those investigations show that on November 3, 1992, Salameh received a $660 wire transfer from Yousef's uncle, Khalid Sheikh Mohammad, in Qatar.[16]

In any event, one of the first things Salameh did with the money he shared with Ayyad was to call Jordan and ask his father to buy a Palestinian woman who would be willing to marry him. (This never happened.) Then he moved on to more practical matters. On November 18, Salameh payed $533 for a dark green 1978 Chevy Nova to be used in transporting equipment and materials needed to make a bomb. (This casts doubt on the claim that the conspirators had significant sums at their disposal. If so, why would Salameh settle for a cheap used car?) Then he began searching for a place to stockpile explosives. He found it at the Space Station, a Jersey City rental facility on Mallory Avenue. On November 30, Salameh (using the alias "Kamal Ibraham") withdrew $3,400 from an account he shared with Ayyad and used a portion of that money to rent a 10′x10′ storage shed for $90 a month.

The same day, Yousef (also using the alias "Kamal Ibraham") placed an order for chemicals at a local firm called City Chemicals.

These chemicals included one thousand pounds of urea nitrate, more than a hundred pounds of nitric acid, and sixty gallons of sulphuric acid.[17] Yousef paid $3,615 in cash and arranged for the chemicals to be delivered to Salameh at the Space Station. At the same time, Yousef also began calling surgical supply companies for the gloves, masks, and rubber tubing he needed to build the bomb. Ayyad attempted to supplement the bomb-building ingredients by using his job as a chemical engineer at Allied Signal, a large New Jersey chemical business, to locate a firm willing to sell him tanks of compressed hydrogen. And finally, through Mahmud the Red, Salameh obtained a quantity of smokeless powder (an explosive component) that he stored at the Space Station as well.

By this time, however, the FBI had lost track of the Nosair-Salameh conspiracy. Emad Salem's handler, special agent John Antivec, had come to doubt the veracity of the informant's intelligence. And so the bureau had severed relations with Salem back in July when he refused to follow protocol regarding criminal investigations.[18]

In mid-December, the quiet Egyptian student, Ashraf Moneeb, told Salameh that he and Yousef had to leave the apartment because they were making too much noise with their incessant overseas telephone calls. On New Year's Day, 1993, Yousef moved to an apartment at 40 Pamrapo Avenue in Jersey City. Though Salameh would never live at the apartment himself, he was the occupant of record. Using the alias "Alaa Mahrous," Salameh paid $1,100 in cash for one month's rent and deposit and told the landlord that he would need the apartment for one year. This apartment would become known as the bomb factory.

Strategy

By now the plot to bomb twelve "Jewish locations" had been abandoned. That plan was based on a classic terrorist strategy: a series of small bombings whose primary objective was to terrify local populations, but not kill or maim on a mass scale. Ramzi Yousef had in mind something more awesome. As Mahmud the Red confirmed to a cellmate, who later turned state's evidence: "Yousef showed up on the scene and escalated the plot."

Yousef subsequently told interrogators that his desire was to kill 250,000 Americans. That figure was not selected at random: it was the number of victims Yousef thought were killed by the American atomic bombs dropped on Nagasaki and Hiroshima. It is commonly reported that Yousef targeted the World Trade Center for its symbolic value. According to his confession, though, Yousef believed that if he could build a bomb powerful enough to topple the Twin Towers, one into the other, he could murder on a scale that would teach the United States that its "terrorism" in Japan, Vietnam, and the Israeli-occupied territories of Palestine justified an equal response—a sentiment that was shared by Abouhalima.[19] "Terror for terror," as Yousef once said. The same logic would, of course, be employed to devastating effects by bin Laden in 2001.

Yousef's biography reveals that he possessed the skill and ideology necessary to carry out his mission. Born in Kuwait on April 27, 1968, Yousef (whose real name is Abdul Karim) was the son of a Pakistani engineer who worked for Kuwaiti Airlines. Yousef was raised in a rural Palestinian community in Kuwait where he excelled at school, especially in math and science. Yet within Kuwaiti society, Palestinians were treated as second-class citizens—a factor that formed the central grievance underlying Yousef's later commitment to terrorism. Yousef was highly intelligent, spoke four languages (Arabic, Baluch, Urdu, and English), and graduated with a degree in engineering from the West Glamorgan Institute in Swansea, Wales, in 1989. Here, investigators believe, Yousef began to hone his skills in electronics and explosives.

Following graduation, Yousef returned to Kuwait and found work as a communications engineer in the National Computer Center of the Ministry of Planning. Although he had joined a chapter of the Egyptian Muslim Brotherhood in college, there is little to suggest that Yousef was a devout Islamic warrior. During these years Yousef fashioned himself as something of an international playboy. He was also known to beat his young wives, and he refused to fast during the Muslim holy month of Ramadan. More than anything, Yousef was a self-proclaimed freedom fighter for the liberation of Palestinians.

Following the Gulf War, sometime in late 1990, Yousef went to Afghanistan for training at Camp Khalden, where he learned basic bomb building. But Yousef's political beliefs, combined with his broad knowledge of electronics and explosives, destined him for greater things. In the summer of 1991, Yousef traveled to the Philippines where he conducted explosives training for the terrorist group Abu Sayyaf. In 1992, he returned to Camp Khaldan and began teaching a course in explosives. And it was here that he met Ahmed Ajaj and planned his daring entrance into the United States.

That entrance had all the earmarks of an operation designed by Palestinian terrorists. Twenty years earlier, for example, an advance team for the Black September terrorists—responsible for the 1972 Munich Olympics massacre—also used a decoy to breach airport customs. Nearly two weeks before the attack, three Black September operatives, two men and a woman, landed in Frankfurt carrying suitcases containing firearms. A customs officer singled out one of the suitcases and demanded that it be inspected. Upon opening the suitcase, though, a male inspector found that it was bursting with lingerie and women's clothing. When the frilly underwear was laid out on a table, the female terrorist, posing as the wife of one of the men, looked on indignantly. Embarrassed by the display of women's undergarments, the German customs inspector waved the Palestinians through, free to transport their weapons on to Munich.[20]

The Bomb Factory

The Pamrapo Avenue apartment fit the specifications in Ajaj's manuals as an ideal base for waging an urban terrorist attack. It was actually an old garage that had been converted to an apartment with two bedrooms, a kitchen, a bath, and a living room. The apartment was in a quiet residential neighborhood, hidden from the street on the ground floor, thus permitting a quick escape in the event of a police raid or emergency. The only thing missing was a refrigerator, but this was resolved by Abouhalima who purchased one from a local appliance store.

The bomb building began in early January. Twice a week, the Red and Abdul Yasin brought sealed buckets of chemicals from the Space Station to the bomb factory. In the living room, Yousef and Salameh worked late into the night transforming the urea nitrate and nitric acid into an explosive by soaking the chemicals in water inside a blue trash can. "The preparation took commitment," writes journalist Simon Reeve. "The chemical fumes from the mixture were horrendous, choking Yousef's lungs when he removed his respirator, staining the walls with a bluish tint and rusting the inside doorknob and the hinges of the back bedroom door."[21] (The government would later contend, however, that most of the chemicals were mixed at another unidentified location.)

Each day, when the newest batch of explosives had dried into a mash on spread-out newspapers, the terrorists loaded it into five-gallon buckets and drove them to the storage shed. Meanwhile, Nidal Ayyad assumed responsibility for constructing a remote control timing device at his home in Maplewood, New Jersey.

The explosives would serve as the main charge for the bomb. Placed beneath it would be three large metal tanks of compressed hydrogen gas. Nitroglycerine, mixed with lead azide and then frozen in the refrigerator, would act as the initiator. Yousef added sodium cyanide to the mix, thinking that the vapors could go through ventilation shafts and elevators of the Twin Towers. Once attached to a fusing system consisting of two twenty-minute lengths of non-electrical smokeless powder fuses, the initiator would explode, triggering the main charge. The bomb would weigh roughly two thousand pounds.[22] The plan was to load the device into a rental van and drive it to the World Trade Center parking basement, where it would be detonated by the remote control timing device.

Throughout this period, Yousef continued his trans-Atlantic telephone calls. He also used the phone to stay in touch with Ahmad Ajaj, still in INS custody for passport fraud, in a successful attempt to get his hands on Ajaj's bomb building manuals. Yousef needed those manuals in order to follow the bomb-building formulae to a tee. This search for perfection was Yousef's trademark, manifested in various practice bombings that he made in the weeks preceding the World Trade Center attack. On several occasions, Yousef left the Pamrapo Avenue apartment to test small-scale versions of the bomb in the New Jersey countryside. Ironically, this search for perfection nearly got him killed. More precisely, Mohammad Salameh's poor driving skills almost derailed the entire operation.

On the night of January 23, Salameh and Yousef left a meeting at the Red's apartment in suburban New Jersey and drove toward the country in the Chevy Nova. In the trunk were Yousef's manuals and chemicals for a small bomb. Just after 1:00 a.m. on January 24, as they passed through the small town of Avenel, Salameh lost control of the Nova. The car skidded off the blacktop, hit a curb, and came to a stop in the front yard of an apartment complex. Salameh was thrown from the vehicle and ended up flat on his back on the ground. Yousef was slumped over in the passenger seat with some lacerations and a severe back injury. The Nova was a total wreck.

When the police arrived, Salameh was walking around in a daze. The officers became suspicious, and for good reason. The roads were clear. There was no ice or snow. The area was well lit, and the accident had occurred on a simple curve. So, because the Nova had hit the curb with such extreme force, the officers assumed that Salameh must have been drunk.

But he was not drunk. Salameh was simply a horrible driver; or, as his attorney would later argue, "Salameh is one of the world's worst drivers"—which is precisely why Alkaisi had shouldered him out of the driver's seat after the Kahane assassination back in 1990. Salameh had received his driver's license only five months before the accident—after failing four driver's tests since 1992. Salameh had even failed the vision test—twice. Nevertheless, he would remain the cell's driver.

Salameh's injuries were minor, but Yousef spent the next five days recuperating at the hospital in Rahway, New Jersey. Yet he continued to show a single-minded determination. Using the phone in his hospital room, he first called Abouhalima and told him to retrieve the manuals and chemicals that had been stored in the Nova's trunk (which went unchecked by police). The Red visited the police impound where he was allowed to clean out the evidence. Next, Yousef placed calls to several chemical companies and arranged for deliveries of even more exotic explosive components—aluminum, magnesium, and ferric oxide as well as more nitric acid—to the Space Station. While this was going on, Ayyad continued his efforts to locate a chemical firm willing to sell him compressed hydrogen.

With the Nova gone, Ayyad used his corporate account at Allied Signal to rent a red Oldsmobile for Salameh. (This casts more doubt on the theory that the cell had access to large sums of money. If so, why would Ayyad use his corporate account to rent a car, thereby leaving a paper trail?) While Yousef was in the hospital, Salameh and the Red loaded a small bomb into the Olds and drove deep into the Pennsylvania woods where they successfully set it off. When Yousef returned to the bomb factory on January 29, the conspiracy entered its final phase.

COUNTDOWN

On February 12, Yousef (using falsified documents in the name of "Abdul Basit Mahmud Abdul Karim") paid cash for a first-class airline ticket to Amman, Jordan, with a connecting flight to Pakistan. The flight was scheduled to leave on Friday, February 26—the day of the bombing.

On February 14, Salameh made the eight-hour drive from Jersey City to Attica prison in upstate New York where he visited his hero, El Sayid Nosair.

On February 16, Ayyad called in sick to Allied Signal and joined Salameh in a reconnaissance of the World Trade Center. With Salameh at the wheel, they drove into the underground garage. Ayyad got out and drew a rough map of the garage floor plan that would later be analyzed by Yousef. On their way back to Jersey City, another driver slammed into the rented Olds. Hampered again by Salameh's driving, the two men spent the rest of the afternoon filing an accident report at a Jersey City police precinct.

On Sunday, February 21, a twenty-one-year-old Palestinian named Eyyad Ismail arrived at JFK airport on a flight from Dallas. Ismail, it is assumed, was an associate of Ahmad Ajaj and had come to New York to aid Yousef.

Two days later—Tuesday, February 23—Ayyad rented another car, again using his corporate account, this time a red Chevy Corsica. Ayyad then drove Salameh to the DIB Leasing Agency on Kennedy Boulevard in Jersey City. The franchise was also the local Ryder truck agency. Salameh approached an agent and asked: "How do I go about renting a Ryder truck?" The agent presented Salameh with three rental options. After making a phone call (presumably to Yousef), Salameh said that he needed a panel van and that he needed it at least until Sunday. Salameh presented his New York driver's license, listed his address as the Jersey City Islamic Center, and gave a telephone number for the apartment at 34 Kensington Avenue.

After forking over a $400 cash deposit and signing a one-week rental agreement in his own name, Salameh was handed a white plastic key chain. In a move that would later have drastic repercussions for law enforcement—and would preempt the possibility for the prevention of the bombing through a simple routine activity—the leasing agent had mistakenly written down an incorrect license plate number on the key chain. Salameh then drove off in a yellow one-ton Ford Econoline van bearing an Alabama license plate and somehow made it back to the bomb factory without having an accident.

The next day—Wednesday, February 24—Salameh and Ayyad drove the Corsica to the Trade Center parking garage on a final scouting mission. They returned to Jersey City where Abdul Yasin took Salameh on a practice drive with the Ryder van. Meanwhile, Nidal Ayyad, now back at his desk at Allied Signal, finally reached a firm willing to sell him compressed hydrogen. That afternoon, AGL Welding Supply of Clifton, New Jersey, delivered three large tanks of the compressed gas to Yousef and Salameh at the Space Station. When another conspirator arrived in the Ryder van, followed by Abouhalima in a dark blue Lincoln (a car he used for his new job as a chauffeur), the manager told Salameh to remove the tanks from the premises because it was too dangerous to store them in the shed. So Salameh, the Red, Yousef, and perhaps Yasin (the manager recalled seeing four "Arab-looking" men) hoisted the tanks and the other bomb-making components into the van.

That night, the van was pulled up to the back door of the Pamrapo Avenue apartment where Yousef supervised the bomb's construction inside the cargo hold. During this time-frame, someone dropped Salameh off at the Shop-Rite grocery store on Kennedy Boulevard. Around 9:00 p.m., he entered the store and bought several bags of groceries. And then, to establish an alibi for the following day, Salameh called the Jersey City police and reported the Ryder van stolen. Two officers came to the parking lot at about 10:00 p.m. Salameh jumped in the backseat of the cruiser and was taken to the West District police station. It is unknown whether the officers checked the status of Salameh's visa. If they had, the officers would have found that Salameh was now an illegal immigrant.

On the way, Salameh gave the key chain to one of the officers who punched into his computer the license number that appeared on the chain. Because the number was incorrect, the officer drew a negative ID on the vehicle. Once at the station, Salameh filled out a report indicating that he had gone into the grocery store and that when he had come out, the van was gone. To back up his story, Salameh produced the time-stamped grocery receipt. Yet another part of his story—that he had rented the van for an *entire week* to help a friend move some furniture—was met with derision. One officer told Salameh that his story amounted to "bullshit." Nevertheless, the police report could not be filled out until the correct license plate number was known. So Salameh was told to go back to the Ryder dealer the next day, get that number, and then return to the West District station to complete the paperwork. Salameh left the station around midnight with plans to do just that.

THE ATTACK

Around 3:30 a.m. on Friday, February 26—the second anniversary of the ending of the Gulf War—Salameh pulled the Ryder van away from the bomb factory with Yousef at his side. Moments later, he turned into an all-night Shell gas station on Kennedy Boulevard, followed by Mahmud the Red in his Lincoln and Ayyad in the red Corsica.

The station attendant, a man named Willie Moosh, walked toward the customers and asked what they wanted. From the van's passenger seat, Yousef said, "Fill it up." As Moosh topped off the Ryder and then the Lincoln, Yousef slid out of his seat and began circling the van, giving Moosh a clear look at the man he would later describe as "a horse face surrounded by a beard." Once the filling was completed, the Red paid Moosh twenty-one dollars, Yousef got back into the van, and then all three drivers started their engines.

As they were leaving, Salameh noticed a white Jersey City police car coming down Kennedy Boulevard. Salameh stopped, and Yousef jumped from the van, threw open the hood, and called to Moosh to bring him a can of water. By the time Moosh got there, Salameh had exited the van as well. Then the police car passed. There stood the two Middle Eastern men in front of the Ryder van that was reported stolen the night before. Yet because the Ryder agent had written down the wrong license plate number on the key chain, the passing officers were not on the lookout for a Ryder van bearing Alabama plates.

Once the cruiser passed, Ayyad motioned to the others, pointing toward Route 440. Yousef slammed the hood down, without using the water, and got back in the cab. What happened next is almost beyond belief.

Mohammad Salameh, the accident-prone motorist, slipped back behind the van's driving wheel. His visa had expired a month earlier, marking his third immigration hassle in as many years. Since then, he had been in the clutches of local law enforcement no less than three times, the most recent being only hours before when he gave Jersey City police information that did not check out. He had also visited the nation's most notorious Islamic terrorist behind the walls of Attica. Still, the illegal immigrant with poor eyesight who had flunked his driving test four times steered the truck bomb seven miles through the Holland Tunnel, negotiated the congested traffic of lower Manhattan, and ignited a clash of civilizations.[23]

Details of the attack are incomplete. Witnesses recall seeing a tall, muscular, redheaded "Egyptian" browsing through CDs at the J&R Music store next to the World Trade Center at about noon. Some fifteen minutes later, other witnesses spotted a yellow Ryder Ford Econoline van idling next to a Dodge Ram on the ramp of the B-2 level of the Trade Center's underground garage, near the south wall of the north tower. A yellow Port Authority van was in a nearby parking space. When the Port Authority van pulled away, the Ryder took its place. Two Middle Eastern men got out of the van and entered a red car that trailed them. Then the red car pulled away.

At 12:18 p.m., an enormous wind ripped through the underground garage, tearing through cars and concrete walls and collapsing much of the B-2 level. The payload bounced off the underside of the north tower and gouged a huge crater where the van had been parked. In one imperceptible instant, nearly seven-thousand tons of concrete, steel, and other material was displaced by the blast. Sewage lines and water mains ruptured, threatening the stability of the container wall holding back the Hudson River. And, of course, there was the human toll: six people were murdered, and more than a thousand were injured.

AFTERMATH

Some three hours later, Salameh returned to the Ryder agency in Jersey City. Appearing excited and confused, he stated to an employee that the van had been stolen from a grocery store parking lot the night before, and then presented the key chain. "I want refund," said Salameh, referring to the $400 cash deposit he had left for the van. The employee told Salameh that he had to report the theft to the police and produce a copy of the police report before he could get the deposit back. That evening, after driving Yousef and Ismail to JFK airport, Salameh went back to the West District police station and spoke with a desk officer. He related his story about the stolen van and requested a copy of the police report that had been filed the previous evening. The officer, in turn, told Salameh that they couldn't complete the report without a correct license plate number—the same information Salameh had been given the previous evening.

Salameh was now back at square one. He then made three trips between the Ryder agency and the police station, trying to resolve the license plate issue. By now, Yousef had landed in Jordan, and the other conspirators were planning to flee the country as well. Salameh had a plan of his own, more or less. On Monday, March 1, he used his last sixty-nine dollars to purchase a child's plane ticket (thus nailing the coffin shut on the theory that the World Trade Center bombers had significant resources) to Amman, Jordan, via Amsterdam, scheduled for March 5. (Abdul Yasin had already purchased a ticket on the same flight.) Salameh took the ticket to customs and obtained a Dutch visa, but he needed the $400 from the van deposit to upgrade his ticket to an adult fare. Nidal Ayyad, on the other hand, was staying put. He continued working at Allied Signal as if nothing had happened. But that wouldn't last long.

Early Sunday morning, February 28, bomb technicians working near the crater found a three-hundred pound fragment from a vehicle frame which displayed inordinate explosive damage. The next day, March 1, they found a dot matrix vehicle identification number (VIN) displayed on the fragment. The VIN was traced to a 1990 Ford Econoline van owned by the Ryder agency in Jersey City. One phone call later, FBI agents determined that the van had been rented by one Mohammad Salameh who claimed that the van had been stolen the day before the bombing.

On Tuesday morning, March 2, an anonymous letter was received by the *New York Times* taking credit for the bombing on behalf of the "fifth battalion of the Liberation Army." The letter explained that the World Trade Center attack was undertaken in retaliation for America's support of Israel, adding that future attacks would be imminent unless all U.S. aid to Israel was suspended. Later that day, FBI agents arrived at the Ryder agency in Jersey City to learn more about Salameh. Following the interview, agents enlisted the manager's help in nabbing him.

Salameh finally got the police report on the morning of March 4. He phoned the Ryder agency with the news and was told to come over and settle his business. Salameh walked into the agency shortly after 10 a.m. and was greeted by a "loss prevention agent" who was actually an undercover FBI agent. Outside, dozens of agents were fanned out on rooftops, in vans, and even in the trees. The media had caught wind of the operation, so two television trucks and several reporters were in the area as well.[24] Salameh, of course, was well known to the Jersey City police because of his motor vehicle problems. He was also known to the New York office of the FBI due to the information provided by the informant Emad Salem.

The undercover agent launched into a series of questions concerning the van, often doubling back and asking the same thing several times, all in an attempt to flummox Salameh, who eventually threw up his hands and exclaimed: "I want justice! This is not justice!" Finally, at 10:28 a.m. the agent came to terms with Salameh and agreed to refund $200 of the deposit. Salameh thanked him profusely and then stepped out the door. He took several steps into the parking lot and was surrounded by a team of agents in FBI wind breakers.

CRIMINAL STUPIDITY AND THE AGE OF SACRED TERROR

Salameh said that he was living at 34 Kensington Avenue in Jersey City, and within an hour agents were combing the place for evidence; eventually, they discovered a link between Salameh and the Space Station. They also found Abdul Yasin at the apartment, and his interrogation yielded a wealth of information, including the location of the bomb factory. (Yasin was released by the FBI and left the country the next day.) Ahmad Ajaj, who had recently completed his sentence for passport fraud, was arrested on March 9. On March 10, agents arrested Nidal Ayyad at his home. Phone records showing calls to the Space Station, joint bank accounts with Salameh, and inquiries into buying explosives would have been enough to implicate him in the attack. But when agents searched his computer at Allied Signal, not only did they find a draft of the letter to the *Times* taking responsibility for the bombing, but they also found a deleted sentence to that letter which read in part: "Unfortunately, our calculations were not very accurate this time." Mahmud Abouhalima was captured in Egypt and tortured by Egyptian intelligence agents before being handed over to the FBI on March 25.[25] On the same day, Bilal Alkaisi turned himself in, even though he had nothing to do with the bombing. The interrogation of these men led to a windfall that surprised even the FBI. Several months later, agents linked Salameh to a plot involving the blind sheik and eight other Islamic extremists to blow up the United Nations, the Lincoln and Holland tunnels, and the George Washington Bridge.

Salameh's desperate attempt to retrieve his $400 cash deposit on the Ryder van was the thread that unraveled the entire conspiracy. It was also the event that created a dangerous mind-set for American law enforcement. Once they tied him to the van, the FBI did not consider Salameh to be smart enough or aggressive enough to be a key figure in the World Trade Center attack. The FBI had good reason to believe as much. Referring to Salameh, a fellow mosque member later told investigators: "He is stupid. This man doesn't have the courage to kill an animal."[26] After his arrest in Islamabad following a shootout with Pakistani authorities on February 7, 1995, Ramzi Yousef characterized Salameh's decision to retrieve the $400 deposit as "Stupid." Even *The 9/11 Commission Report* agreed with this assessment of the bombing. "[T]he public image that persisted was not of clever Yousef," says the *Report*, "but of stupid Salameh going back again and again to reclaim his $400 truck rental deposit."[27] The image of Salameh returning to collect the deposit therefore left a lasting impression on law enforcement: no group that relied on someone that stupid could possibly pose a serious threat to the United States. And so, the World Trade Center bombing was considered nothing more than the work of a loosely affiliated group of Islamic extremists with no larger agenda. Yet armed with 20/20 hindsight, a different picture emerges.

Yousef resurfaced in Bangkok, Thailand, during the winter of 1994—by then the world's most wanted terrorist. There, he went to work planning a series of terrorist strikes, including plots to assassinate the pope and President Bill Clinton when they visited the Philippines in 1995. Yousef and his associates also began gathering material for another bombing—this one a stupendous conspiracy, called the Bojinka Project, to blow up eleven U.S. passenger airliners over the Pacific Ocean. The bombs were to be made of a liquid explosive designed to pass through airport metal detectors. But first Yousef would wage a symbolic attack against Israel.

After constructing a one-ton bomb similar to the one used in the World Trade Center attack, Yousef and his gang loaded the bomb into a truck on March 11 and set out for the Israeli embassy in downtown Bangkok. Yet the Bangkok driver was even worse than Salameh; it seems that Yousef deliberately chose simple-minded men with poor driving skills as his comrades. En route to the embassy, the driver crashed the truck bomb into a taxi-motorcyclist and then careened into a car at one of the city's busiest intersections, rendering the bomb inert. The aborted attack was considered a farce, yet, even as the attack was a failure this view itself failed to recognize a defining characteristic of jihadist criminality. Mohammad Salameh, Ahmed Ajaj, the Black September woman with her frilly undergarments, and the incompetent driver in Bangkok—all were human decoys used by their leaders to circumvent counter-terrorism routines of the state. All of them were manipulated by jihadists with exceptional criminal skills. Years later, Vincent Cannistraro of the CIA's Counterterrorism Center would tell a reporter that once in the United States, Ramzi Yousef recruited a group of "useful idiots" to help him with the World Trade Center operation, and it was these "idiots" who were left holding the bag when Yousef quickly fled the country.[28]

At the time, however, many within the U.S. intelligence community considered the World Trade Center bombing a farce. In addition to Salameh's criminal ineptitude, the bomb was deemed a technical failure inasmuch as it failed to topple the 107-story north tower into its twin a few yards away. When Yousef was brought back to America, he was flown over the still intact Twin Towers. "We would have brought them down," he told FBI agents, "if we had enough money." Even so, the nature of the attack and its investigation had overshadowed a deeper problem: namely, both had the unintended consequence of obscuring the need to analyze the nature and extent of the threat of Islamic terrorism to the United States. *The 9/11 Commission Report* concludes that the investigative processes used to solve the World Trade Center case did not "allow for aggravating and analyzing facts to see if they could provide clues to terrorist tactics more generally—methods of entry and finance, and mode of operation inside the United States."[29] In a word, the U.S. law enforcement community had vastly underestimated terrorism's global criminal threat.

Following Yousef's capture in Islamabad on February 7, 1995, agents discovered an underlying plan that was anything but farcical. The urea nitrate–based bomb was actually just a backup plan for Yousef. According to U.S. intelligence, in the months preceding February 1993 Yousef tried to obtain radioactive material for a nuclear bomb big enough to wipe out the population of southern Manhattan. It was later determined that the alleged source of the radioactive material was Osama bin Laden.[30]

Eventually indications of a connection between Yousef and bin Laden were recognized. In June 1998, United States Attorney Mary Jo White filed a sealed indictment against bin Laden in a New York federal court, two months before al-Qaeda attacked the American embassies in East Africa.

2

Vulnerabilities of the Jihad— Prelude to 9/11

The U.S. Embassy Bombings in Kenya and Tanzania

In August 1998, al-Qaeda orchestrated two simultaneous bombings against the United States embassies in Nairobi, Kenya, and Dar es Salaam, Tanzania. The Nairobi bombing killed 213 people and injured some 4,500. The Dar es Salaam explosion killed 11 and wounded 85. The attacks were the most devastating terrorist assaults the United States had suffered overseas since the bombing of the Marine barracks in Beirut in 1983. The FBI investigation—which came to light in four terrorism trials held in New York between 1998 and 2001—offers not only a wealth of information on the routine activities exploited by al-Qaeda in these attacks, and the skills used to do so, but also an abundance of evidence concerning al-Qaeda's criminal activities, and, consequently, vulnerabilities. As we shall see, the embassy bombings were a direct result of the U.S. government's failure to recognize and act in response to these criminal vulnerabilities. Likewise, the government's ability to solve the case ultimately turned on these same vulnerabilities.

BACKGROUND

The East African bombing case became the FBI's largest overseas investigation up to that point in history. It involved 375 FBI agents, myriad cultural and technological obstacles, and a widespread terrorist conspiracy spanning four continents. The Bureau's major breakthrough came with the arrest and interrogation of two key conspirators.

The War Hero

The first was a twenty-two-year-old Saudi Arabian named Mohammed Rashid Daoud al-Owhali.[1] Like Osama bin Laden, al-Owhali came from a wealthy and devout Saudi family. Al-Owhali was born in Liverpool, England in 1977, while his father was pursuing graduate work there. The family returned to Saudi Arabia a year later. Al-Owhali's road to extremism began in his early teenage years when he was introduced to such unorthodox Islamic tracts as *The Love and Hour of the Martyrs* and *Jihad,* a magazine published by bin Laden's network of Afghan mujahideen. Al-Owhali was captivated by the protagonists of these works—brave Islamic warriors who died fighting in the Soviet-Afghan war and were rewarded with eternal life in paradise. For more than a decade (1979–1989), some twenty-five thousand Islamic militants, from nearly thirty countries around the world, had streamed into Afghanistan to join the anti-Soviet jihad. Among these jihadists, the Saudis were some of the most committed. For them, the war was more than a struggle to defeat the Soviets. It was a conflict waged both on earth and in heaven.[2]

After high school, Al-Owhali enrolled in the Mohamed bin Saud religious university in Riyadh, but dropped out after the second year to pursue his dream of fighting for the Muslim cause in Bosnia or Chechnya. To prepare for the battle ahead of him, al-Owhali left Saudi Arabia in 1996 and moved to Afghanistan where he underwent basic training at Camp Khaldan.

Al-Owhali was instructed in the use of light weaponry, explosives, and communications. He proved to be an excellent trainee and was granted an audience with Osama bin Laden. Bin Laden spoke softly of the jihad against America—the campaign to drive U.S. military forces from the Arabian Peninsula—and encouraged al-Owhali to pursue additional training. Al-Owhali did just that. In 1997, he received advanced military training in three different al-Qaeda camps. This included instruction in intelligence and counter-intelligence, hijacking, kidnapping, and seizing buildings, with priority given to planning attacks against U.S. military bases and embassies. Following the training, al-Owhali met with bin Laden again and pleaded with the Qaeda leader to send him on a jihad mission on behalf of al-Qaeda. Al-Owhali's goal was to join with a band of brothers in search of a new holy war in the tradition of the courageous mujahideen who had forced Soviet troops out of Afghanistan. Bin laden advised al-Owhali to be patient—his mission would come in time.

Al-Owhali then took a military assignment to fight alongside Taliban forces against the government of Afghanistan. Joining the Taliban near Kabul, he soon fell ill with tuberculosis. One of the men who treated him was an al-Qaeda fighter from Saudi Arabia known as "Azzam" (a.k.a., Jihad Mohammed Ali); he had evidently taken his name from Abdullah Azzam, the chief ideologue of non-Afghan volunteers drawn to fight with the mujahideen against the Soviets. As a result of this medical attention, al-Owhali would come to revere Azzam. And Azzam, in turn, would have a significant influence on the life of Mohammed al-Owhali. Azzam encouraged his protégé to think beyond the conflict in Afghanistan, to concentrate on a "bigger mission, a better mission that we could be doing."

Once al-Owhali recovered from his illness, he participated in a major attack that resulted in the Taliban's defeat in Kabul. While many fighters were killed in this battle, al-Owhali distinguished himself by maintaining a Taliban stronghold. Greeted as a war hero upon his return to the camps, he was granted the privilege of carrying his rifle anywhere he went as a symbol of his bravery. And in time, the young Saudi was singled out for a personal jihad mission. Each step of the way, he would be handled by Azzam. The mission would require even more skill development, so al-Owhali was sent to a camp near Kabul where he received specialized training in the operation and management of a terrorist cell, including instruction on conducting target surveys using still photographs and videos.

The Explosives Expert

The second conspirator was thirty-four-year-old Mohamed Saddiq Odeh.[3] Odeh was born in Saudi Arabia in 1965 and raised in Jordan. In 1986, he enrolled as an engineering student at the Far Eastern University in Manila, Philippines. During his studies, Odeh became active in Islamic societies and underwent a life-changing experience after being introduced to tape-recorded and video lectures by the legendary Abdullah Azzam. An early spiritual mentor of bin Laden, Abdullah Azzam is believed to have coined the term "al-Qaeda," or The Base.

During his final year at the university, Odeh decided to quit school and make his way to Afghanistan to join the mujahideen who were then engaged in a civil war against the Soviet-backed government of Mohammad Najibullah. (It took three years for the mujahideen to oust the Najibullah regime. This paved the way for the Taliban takeover in 1996.) In October 1990, Odeh arrived at the Farouq camp, where he underwent basic training in light weaponry. From there, Odeh moved to a second level of training where he was taught topography, map reading, and explosives. And from there, he moved to advanced training involving rocket launchers, mortars, and surface-to-air missiles. Along the way, Odeh also became a combat medic.

In 1991, Odeh was sent to Jalalabad, Afghanistan, where he cared for wounded mujahideen behind enemy lines. Odeh was subsequently injured in an air raid and was sent to Pakistan where he received treatment for a head wound. Upon his recovery, Odeh went back to Afghanistan where he received more advanced training—this time on tactics of seizing military bases and embassies. In March 1992, Odeh took a religious *bayat,* meaning that he pledged his allegiance to Osama bin Laden.

Odeh was then sent to the Sadeek camp where he received advanced explosives training under the direction of al-Qaeda's premier bomb technician, the Egyptian Abdel Rahman (also referred to as Abdel Rahman Yasin.) This involved sophisticated instruction on bomb building, including the computation of mathematical formulae for configuring detonator cord and blasting caps; the melting of TNT into "shape charges" that can be aimed at a target; and the mounting of bombs with electrical, mechanical, and fuse detonators.

In late 1992, with the war against the Najibullah regime now over, Odeh met a former Egyptian special forces military officer turned al-Qaeda operative, Saif al-Adel, who persuaded him to volunteer for service in Somalia. At the time, al-Qaeda's mission in Somalia was to aid Muslims engaged in widespread interclan fighting and to oppose United Nations peace-keeping forces in the country. American troops became targets of al-Qaeda after they entered Somalia in 1993. "The snake is America," said bin Laden at the time, "and we have to stop what they are doing. We have to cut the head of the snake."[4] Accordingly, in 1993 Odeh traveled to Somalia via Kenya, where he trained Islamic fighters of the Um Rehan tribe in small arms and battlefield medicine. Joining some 250 fighters sent to the country by bin Laden, Odeh remained in Somalia aiding clan leader Mohammed Farah Aideed for seven months.

In 1994, Odeh moved to Mombasa, Kenya, along with two other al-Qaeda veterans of the Somalia conflict: an Egyptian named Mustafa Mohamed Fadhil and a Kenyan named Fahid Mohammed Ally Msalar (referred to in court documents by his first name, Fahid, or sometimes as "Fahad"). At the time, both men worked for an export business based in Dar es Salaam, Tanzania. Odeh subsequently married a Kenyan woman he met through Fadhil; the wedding was attended by Fadhil, Fahid, and another al-Qaeda member known as "Harun." (Weddings are important to al-Qaeda. In 1999, Mohammed Atta and Marwan al-Shehhi attended the wedding of a fellow Muslim at a radical mosque in Hamburg, Germany—an event considered by investigators to have been an important gathering for the core members of the 9/11 plot. Moreover, the attack itself was referred to by Atta and the others as "the wedding."[5]) These four men—Fadhil and Fahid in Dar es Salaam, Odeh and Harun in Nairobi—would ultimately comprise the core membership of the Qaeda teams responsible for bombing the East African embassies.

In late 1994, Odeh was visited in Mombasa by al-Qaeda's top military commander, Mohammad Atef, who provided Odeh with the financial backing to purchase a seven-ton aluminum fishing boat. This boat would play an important role in the embassy plot. Over the next three years Odeh used the boat to sell other crews' catches at ports up and down the west coast of the Indian Ocean. Using the boat's cargo as cover, Odeh and his confederates also began to gather and transport bomb-building components commonly used in al-Qaeda training camps, including TNT and detonator cord (known by the code word "tools"). These explosives were smuggled by Fahid from a source in Tanzania, along with hand grenades ("potatoes") and fake travel documents ("goods").

In March 1997, Odeh and Mustafa Fadhil were sent back to Somalia on a special mission for bin Laden. Their objective was to provide bin Laden with a military assessment of the Islamic struggle in the war-torn country. Seven months later, after having successfully completed his mission, Odeh returned to Kenya and moved to the tiny village of Witu, near the Somalia border, where he set up a furniture business with his brother-in-law, Omar, who lived in Mombasa. In Witu, Odeh lived piously with his wife and child in a mud hut. He had no telephone, no electricity, and no running water. He read only the Koran and hated all things Western.[6]

The Fatwahs: Afghanistan, Winter 1998

On February 23, 1998, bin Laden issued a renowned fatwah proclaiming that it was the duty of all Muslims to kill Americans. "In compliance with God's order," it read, "we issue the following fatwah to all Muslims: the ruling to kill the Americans and their allies, including civilians and military, is an individual duty for every Muslim who can do it in any country in which it is possible to do it." The same month, bin Laden and Ayman al-Zawahiri, the leader of the Egyptian al-Jihad (EIJ), endorsed a joint fatwah under the heading, "International Islamic Front for Jihad on the Jews and Crusaders," which also stated that Muslims should kill Americans, including civilians, anywhere in the world. This proclamation marked the merger of al-Qaeda and the EIJ as an international terrorist threat. "Bin Laden and al-Zawahiri appear to have expanded al-Qaeda not only to protect power," writes the former senior U.S. intelligence official known as "Anonymous" in his book *Through Our Enemies' Eyes*, "but also to disperse assets, thereby making it more flexible and redundant and thus more difficult for its foes to strike a truly disabling blow."[7]

In March 1998, Mohammed Odeh attended a meeting of al-Qaeda operatives in Mombasa. Bin Laden had dispatched a personal emissary to the meeting, carrying a message: it was now time for the operatives to begin preparations for leaving Kenya and Tanzania. Odeh and the others were told to get their personal affairs in order and to gather passports and money for their departure from the region. Bin Laden's missive concluded that their departure would "come soon." This signaled the activation of al-Qaeda cells in Nairobi and Dar es Salaam.

Around the same time, Azzam sent Mohammed al-Owhali to Yemen to obtain a passport. From there, al-Owhali was ordered to Pakistan where Azzam introduced him to Khalid Sheikh Mohammed (architect of the 9/11 attacks, to whom the CIA refers by his initials, KSM). It was KSM who finally gave al-Owhali his jihad mission: he would join Azzam in an anti-American operation in East Africa.

KSM told al-Owhali that he would be assisting Azzam in driving a truck filled with explosives. In no uncertain terms, al-Owhali was told that the mission would involve his death, as well as Azzam's. Al-Owhali and Azzam would become, in effect, al-Qaeda's first suicide bombers.[8] KSM then produced a video recorder and told Azzam and al-Owhali to make videotapes celebrating their anticipated martyrdoms, claiming credit in the name of a fictitious organization dubbed the "Army for the Liberation of Islamic Holy Places."

On May 28, Azzam and al-Owhali stood in the background as bin Laden gave an interview to ABC News correspondent John Miller in Khost, Afghanistan. Dressed in a camouflage jacket, sitting on the floor, and cradling a Soviet-made AK-47 assault rifle across his knees, bin Laden railed against the U.S. military presence in Saudi Arabia. He predicted a "black day for America," adding:

> "The continuation of tyranny will bring the fight to America, as Ramzi Yousef and others did. This is my message to the American people: to look for a serious government that looks out for their interests and does not attack others, their lands, or their honor. And my word to American journalists is not to ask why we did that [attack U.S. targets] but to ask what their government has done that forced us to defend ourselves."

Bin Laden concluded that "Our forthcoming victory in Hijaz and Nejd [parts of old Arabia] will make America forget the horrors of Vietnam, Beirut, and other places."[9] Over his shoulder hung a map of Africa, with Kenya and Tanzania in clear view.[10]

Following the press conference, al-Owhali met with bin Laden for the last time. Then on July 31, al-Owhali left Lahore, Pakistan, on a plane bound for Nairobi.

THE EMBASSY BOMBING PLOT: EAST AFRICA, SUMMER 1998

The plans for bombing the American embassies in Kenya and Tanzania were known respectively as Operation Kaaba, after a structure located in the Grand Mosque in Mecca that is the holiest site in the Muslim world, and Operation al-Aqsa, after the mosque in Jerusalem that is Islam's third holiest site.[11] These operations had actually been in the works since late 1993.

It was then that bin Laden—based in Khartoum, Sudan, at the time—sent a controversial figure named Ali Mohamed to Nairobi to conduct surveillance on the U.S. embassy and other American interests in the city. Mohamed, a former Egyptian army major, was first drawn to terrorism in 1981, when he joined the Egyptian Islamic Jihad, the group implicated in that year's assassination of Egyptian President Anwar Sadat. In 1984, Mohamed quit the Egyptian military to work as a counter-terrorism expert for Egypt Air. Then Mohamed moved to California and married a woman from Santa Clara; in 1986 he joined the U.S. Army. Mohamed was posted to Fort Bragg, North Carolina, where he became an instructor in Middle Eastern affairs in the John F. Kennedy special warfare school. In 1988, while on vacation—and in blatant violation of army regulations—Mohamed traveled to Afghanistan where he joined the Islamic guerrillas in their civil war against the Soviets.

After his honorable discharge from the army in 1989, Mohamed became deeply involved in bin Laden's al-Qaeda network.[12] He traveled to camps in Afghanistan and Sudan, where he trained al-Qaeda fighters, and to New York, where he conducted training sessions for the terrorists who would later bomb the World Trade Center. After Mohamed helped bin Laden move to the Sudan in 1991, he became an all-purpose security expert for al-Qaeda. Training bin Laden's personal security guards in the Sudan, he also trained al-Qaeda operatives in Peshawar, Pakistan, where he covered surveillance techniques and focused on bridges, stadiums, and police stations. Mohamed then moved to Nairobi where he cased a number of targets for bin Laden: the American embassy, the U.S. agricultural office, as well as the French embassy and cultural center. These targets were chosen to retaliate against the U.S. intervention in the civil war in Somalia. In late 1993, Mohamed visited bin Laden in Khartoum and presented him with video clips and still photographs of the surveillance. On a photo of the U.S. embassy, bin Laden used a blue pen to mark an area at the rear of the building indicating "where a truck could go as a suicide bomber."[13]

Organization

The East African operation emerged as a result of Ali Mohamed's report. Over the next five years, personnel linked to the plot would go through numerous changes, with operatives using a dizzying array of code names and aliases. (KSM, for example, used thirty different aliases.) By the summer of 1998 al-Qaeda had established a formidable terrorist enterprise in the region, consisting of military and computer experts, bomb builders, weapons specialists, truck drivers, and boatmen. In all, the operation included at least twenty-one men.

The teams assembled in Nairobi and Dar es Salaam were the first in a new constellation of al-Qaeda sleeper cells spread around the world.[14] The cells were comprised of four divisions much like the organizational structure of the IRA: (1) the intelligence section; (2) the administrative section; (3) the planning and preparation section; and (4) the execution section. This was a tiered system in which the chief of intelligence served as the operation's overall commander. His job was to conduct target surveillance; identify points of bomb detonation; assign section deputies to conduct other cell functions; monitor those functions; and communicate coded messages to al-Qaeda planners in Afghanistan. The cells operated on a strategy known in the West as "leaderless resistance."[15] Cell members shared information on a need-to-know basis, including information about one another's identity. As an additional security precaution, the cells were kept geographically apart so that the collapse of one cell would not lead to the collapse of the others.[16] Al-Qaeda's cell structure therefore both limited the potential damage of betrayal from within and safeguarded against potential infiltration from without.

In 1998, the cells in Kenya and Tanzania were led by an Egyptian known as "Ali Saleh." Anonymous makes the point that "bin Laden's senior lieutenants are a talented and experienced group. [Yet those] Islamic leaders in East Africa . . . have so far received little attention from the West."[17] This was certainly the case for Ali Saleh. His true name is Abdullah Ahmed Abdullah, and it is probably safe to say that the United States does not face a more ruthless enemy. Born in Egypt in 1963, Saleh (Abdullah) went on to achieve fame as one of Egypt's most talented soccer players. A Sunni Muslim, Saleh began his involvement with violent extremism in the early 1980s when he joined the ranks of Ayman al-Zawahiri's EIJ, which was then dedicated to the overthrow of the Egyptian government and to violent opposition against U.S. interests in the Middle East. During the Afghan war Saleh trained soldiers in the use of explosives at the Jihad Wal camp in Khost, and in 1993 he joined the fighting in Somalia where he played a role in the murders of U.S. Marines at Mogadishu, an incident immortalized in Mark Bowden's celebrated book, *Black Hawk Down*. A year later, Saleh was instrumental in setting up the original Mombasa cell. By 1998, not only was he commanding the East African operation; Saleh was also one of bin Laden's most trusted associates and a member of al-Qaeda's elite leadership group known as the *shura* council as well as the religious/fatwah committee. During this period, Saleh's associates attempted to purchase uranium from Sudanese black marketers with the intention of building a nuclear weapon.[18] Saleh reportedly slept no more than four hours a night, always with an AK-47 at his side, and never in the same place twice.[19] Today, Abdullah Ahmed Abdullah is atop the FBI's Most Wanted Terrorists list with a $5 million bounty on his head.

In Nairobi, Saleh appointed as his administrative section chief a native Kenyan from the Comoros Islands named Abdullah Mohammed Fazul, code name "Harun"—the same man who had attended Mohamed Odeh's 1994 wedding. A former university honors student, Harun was a computer expert who spoke four languages. And like Saleh and Odeh, Harun was a veteran of the training camps in Afghanistan and the war in Somalia.

Odeh served in the planning and preparation section of the Nairobi cell. An explosives expert, Odeh was also familiar with Nairobi's bustling inner city, having traveled regularly to Nairobi on business with Mustafa Fadhil over the years. Selling their fish to restaurants and hotels, the two men came to know the city, including the area around the American embassy.

The Tanzania cell developed in similar fashion. Central to this development was Khalfan Khamis Mohamed (known as "KK Mohamed"). Mohamed was born in 1973 on the East African island of Pemba and raised in the village of Kidimni on Zanzibar Island. In contrast to the privileged backgrounds of bin Laden and al-Owhali, KK Mohamed's origins were humble. KK's father died when he was young, leaving the family destitute. Yet this was a decent family, and KK developed the human qualities of kindness and generosity. As a teenager, he moved to Dar es Salaam to live with an older brother. After dropping out of high school, he took a job in his brother's dry-goods store. At the local mosque, KK became consumed with the idea that he was part of the worldwide Islamic community and had obligations to fellow Muslims who were suffering in war zones like Bosnia. He would find a means to pursue that obligation in al-Qaeda.[20]

In early 1994 KK Mohamed befriended a mosque member who worked on a fishing boat out of Mombasa owned by a man known as "Mohamed the Fisherman." This was Mohamed Odeh, and thus began KK Mohamed's affiliation with bin Laden's terrorist network. Later that year, KK Mohamed used his own money to travel to Afghanistan where he trained in light weapons, rocket launchers, and surface-to-air missiles at a camp in Manakando. He had hoped to become a warrior for God on a battlefield in the Balkans or Chechnya, but failed to find a way there. Discouraged, Mohamed returned to Dar es Salaam. Then in 1997 he made the first of two trips to Somalia where he served as a weapons trainer for Aideed's militias. Mohamed traveled to Somalia via Mombasa on his second trip, and there he met Odeh's friend Mustafa Fadhil. In March 1998—a month after the fatwahs were issued by bin Laden and al-Zawahari—Fadhil asked if Mohamed wanted to help with "a jihad job." Though he had never met an American, Mohamed signed on to kill as many of them as possible.

Soon thereafter, Saleh established lines of authority for the Dar es Salaam cell. He appointed Mustafa Fadhil (hereafter referred to by his code name "Hussein") as his administrative section chief. A Qaeda veteran, Hussein was known for his compelling personality and excellent leadership qualities. Because Swahili was his primary language and because Dar es Salaam was his adopted hometown, KK Mohamed was assigned to the planning and preparation section, along with Fahid and two others: a Tanzanian named Ahmad Ghailani, and Sheikh Sewedan, a Kenyan. The execution division was led by an Arab called "Ahmed the German."

Strategy

By mid-1998, then, al-Qaeda operatives had woven themselves into the fabric of eastern Africa's Islamic society. Experts claim that hundreds of al-Qaeda members were living normal lives in East Africa, where they had developed support structures for Islamic terrorists headed to the West.[21] In the tiny fishing village of Siyu, Kenya, for instance, al-Qaeda even sponsored its own soccer club.[22] As operatives arrived from Zanzibar, Egypt, Somalia, and Afghanistan, cell administrators in Nairobi and Dar es Salaam helped these men settle into local communities. Some paid cash to local families for the right to marry their women. In this way, the operatives established bloodlines and financial obligations that would serve as guarantees of safe haven.

With the aid of al-Qaeda's international support cells (groups of four or five scattered throughout the world to provide logistical support for the bombing), the conspirators came into possession of a variety of fake passports, cell and satellite phones, laptop computers with internet and e-mail access, and files containing military documents.

Consistent with the information control of leaderless resistance, however, al-Qaeda exercised great caution in the use of this technology. Information about the embassy plot was often passed by couriers and shared in face-to-face meetings held in secure rooms, where instructions were spoken by unwitting middlemen in coded language—a system designed to foil eavesdropping. Aided by the technologically competent Harun, other messages were embedded in innocuous web sites or encrypted e-mail communications. All sensitive information was routed through headquarters in Afghanistan, of course, where bin Laden's experts designed strategy, approved men for the operations, and continued to develop support structures. That included the establishment of additional cells in Baku, Azerbaijan, and London to conduct communications and publicity for the forthcoming strikes. Details of the operations, however, were left to Saleh and his division chiefs.

Enter the Informants

As al-Qaeda progressed with its plans, a parallel effort to break up the bin Laden network was undertaken by the U.S. intelligence community. Back in late 1995, after the Yousef–bin Laden connection became apparent, President Clinton had signed a top-secret order authorizing the CIA to begin covert operations against al-Qaeda; this led to the impaneling of the bin Laden Task Force. By the spring of 1998, some two hundred intelligence specialists working out of a windowless warren of cubicles at the CIA headquarters in Langley, Virginia, were pouring over bin Laden's speeches and written communiqués. Computers with sophisticated "link analysis" capabilities generated diagrams of al-Qaeda's international network. Out of this effort came a covert program to monitor and disrupt small al-Qaeda cells in nearly a dozen countries, including Kenya.[23]

This led agents to Wadih el-Hage, the American jihadist who in 1990 sold Mahmud Abouhalima the assault rifle used to assassinate Meir Kahane, and in 1993 engineered for bin Laden the purchase of a military surplus jet from Davis-Monthan Air Force Base in Tucson, where el-Hage lived at the time. El-Hage, a slight, bearded man with a withered right arm, held a degree in urban planning from the University of Louisiana and was known within al-Qaeda as "The Manager." In 1996, el-Hage became bin Laden's personal secretary, assigned to a rundown charity office in Nairobi where he oversaw a relief organization called Help Africa People.[24] Using the office as cover, el-Hage played a key role in setting up al-Qaeda support cells throughout East Africa.[25] The CIA identified el-Hage's office in August 1997, and for several weeks Kenyan police and visiting FBI agents began harassing el-Hage, searching his files, confiscating his computer disks, and warning el-Hage to leave or face more hassling if he stayed in the country. Meanwhile, according to *New York Times* reporter Judith Miller, the National Security Agency began eavesdropping on telephone lines used by al-Qaeda members in Nairobi. "On several occasions," wrote Miller, "calls to Mr. bin Laden's satellite phone in Afghanistan were overheard."[26] The strategy paid off in the short term: agents discovered a missive on el-Hage's computer entitled "Security Report"; addressed to a senior bin Laden aide, it complained that "the cell is at 100% danger" because of "hostile intelligence agencies."[27] The author of the report was Harun (Abdullah Mohammed Fazul), the administrative section chief of the Nairobi cell. The bin Laden Task Force had found the pulse beating at the heart of the embassy bombing conspiracy. Believing that Harun was only a distant associate of el-Hage's, however, the CIA abandoned the lead. Nevertheless, responding to the pressure, el-Hage returned to the United States and moved with his family to Arlington, Texas, where he went to work in a tire store. "CIA knew there had been an al-Qaeda cell in Kenya," recalled Richard Clarke, "but they had thought that, working with the Kenyan police, the U.S. government had broken it up."[28]

El-Hage might be best described as an informant who got away, owing to the fact that the FBI raid was part of a "counter-terrorism disruption plan" designed to pressure el-Hage into leaving Kenya, rather than to lean on him for more significant information about Harun and his cell. That plan did not apply, however, to several confidential informants with first-hand knowledge of the unfolding plot. In September 1997, al-Qaeda's first known defector, Jamal Ahmed al-Fadl, walked into the Nairobi embassy and claimed that seven Arabs who worked for a local Islamic charity had connections to bin Laden. Not only had al-Qaeda taken aim at the United States, but according to al-Fadl, bin Laden was also attempting to buy a nuclear bomb and other unconventional weapons. Once again, the CIA determined that the intelligence was of marginal value, and al-Fadl's statements were not widely circulated within the government.[29] Kenyan authorities were nonetheless asked to deport the seven Arabs, and CIA officers confiscated and examined documents left behind. The CIA reported to the embassy that bin Laden did, indeed, have an operating cell in the Nairobi, but the evidence confiscated from the Arabs revealed nothing about a planned attack.[30]

A second informant surfaced two months later, in November 1997, when another man walked into the embassy and warned security staff that terrorists planned to car-bomb the building. The informant, an Egyptian named Mustafa Ahmed, laid out specific details of the planned attack (which would turn out to be consistent with what would happen nine months later). After questioning Ahmad, CIA agents (incorrectly) concluded that he was lying. Nevertheless, security staff convinced their ambassador, Prudence Bushnell, to request additional safeguards, causing Bushnell to cable Secretary of State Madelyn Albright with a warning that the embassy was vulnerable to a car-bomb attack.[31]

Taken together, this intelligence established that al-Qaeda definitely had an operational cell in East Africa, but the CIA could not say for certain what bin Laden planned to do with it. "For seven months prior to the bombings," wrote Steve Coll in his book *Ghost Wars*, "neither the Nairobi nor the Dar es Salaam CIA station picked up credible threats of a coming attack."[32] Like Mustafa Ahmed, though, still another informant did know about the coming attack, and this informant was none other than Ali Mohamed.

Since meeting with bin Laden in Sudan in 1993—when he had presented bin Laden with surveillance videos and photographs of the Nairobi embassy, leading bin Laden to identify the *exact location* where a suicide bomber would attack—Mohamed had become an experienced informant for the U.S. government. By the mid-1990s Mohamed had spent several years providing information to the FBI regarding the training of Islamic guerrillas in Afghanistan, Sudan, and New Jersey; informing on Middle Eastern terrorist groups; and helping the FBI build its case against Sheikh Abdel-Rahman. To be sure, he also continued to act on behalf of terrorists during this time. Thus, in the spring of 1993 Mohamed helped Ayman al-Zawahiri enter the United States with a fake passport and tour San Francisco Bay Area mosques, raising money later funneled to al-Qaeda. Moreover, in late 1994 Mohamed returned to Nairobi where he met with an al-Qaeda operative in Wadih el-Hage's office and was directed to survey American and British targets in Djibouti and Senegal, West Africa.[33] All the while, though, Mohamed maintained contacts with the FBI and Defense Department officials.[34] Mohamed met with FBI agents for the last time in 1997—four years after he stood witness to bin Laden's targeting of the Nairobi embassy though Mohamed did not reveal anything about the embassy plot.[35]

Yet the fact of the matter (since nothing was revealed) was that Ali Mohamed was not really a double agent. Rather, he was a high-ranking al-Qaeda terrorist, deeply involved in plotting violence against the United States and its allies. (Mohamed was later arrested in connection with the embassy bombings.) In short, his loyalties were with bin Laden, not the United States.[36]

The Bomb Factories

At the top of Saleh's operations list was the renting of safe houses to build bombs and the buying of vehicles to deliver them. Because these bombs would be weapons of mass destruction, there were two main criteria for the safe houses. First, they had to be large enough to accommodate bomb building, yet secluded enough to conceal the work from public view. Second, they had to be within close proximity of the embassies in order to minimize the risk of accidental explosions en route.

In May 1998, Harun paid cash for a six-month lease on a steel-gated villa in an exclusive section of Nairobi. This villa, at 43 Runda Estates, was surrounded by a high wall and hedges. The main residence had four bedrooms, three baths, and a garage suited for bomb building. Harun moved his wife and two small children into the villa, and purchased a beige-colored Toyota Dyna cargo truck to be used as the bomb vehicle. Using a smaller pickup, Harun then began hauling bomb-making material into the garage.

In June 1998, Hussein instructed KK Mohamed to rent House 213 in the Illala district of Dar es Salaam. Situated in a sprawling low-income neighborhood about four miles from the U.S. embassy, the house was a single-family dwelling in a compound, with a gate and a high wall. It also had a garage large enough to hold a truck. After signing the rental agreement in his own name, KK Mohamed moved into the house with Hussein and his family. Mohamed and Fahid then purchased a white Suzuki Samurai which they used to haul bomb components (hidden in rice sacks) to House 213. Ghailani and Sewedan purchased a 1987 Nissan Atlas refrigeration truck, which would serve as the bomb delivery vehicle. To better accommodate the bomb, KK Mohamed employed a welder to build a seat for batteries and install six metal bars in the bed of the refrigeration truck.

Around this time, evidence of a third embassy plot emerged from the shadows of bin Laden's network, leading to an event that would incur the wrath of Ayman al-Zawahiri. In June of 1998, CIA officers working with Albanian police apprehended four EIJ members who were moving forward with a plan to car bomb the U.S. embassy in Tirana. Washington immediately pushed for the extradition of the four men from Albania to stand trial in Egypt, where they were likely to be tortured. Among those indicted was al-Zawahiri's brother, Muhammad Muhandis al-Zawahiri.[37]

Despite these arrests, the CIA remained unaware of the East African plot. Bomb building began days later. In both Nairobi and Dar es Salaam, Mohammed Odeh supervised construction of two massive, 2,000-pound destructive devices made of 400 to 500 cylinders of TNT (about the size of soda cans), aluminum nitrate, aluminum powder, and detonator cord. Odeh had acquired these explosives from an unidentified source in the seaport of Luanda, Angola, in southwestern Africa. The explosives were shipped from Luanda to Pakistan; from Pakistan to Dar es Salaam and Mombasa (possibly concealed in boxes of lobsters); and from there driven to the bomb factories.[38]

The explosives were packed into some twenty specially designed wooden crates that were sealed and then placed in the bed of the trucks. Once the bombs were built—with the assistance of others, including KK Mohamed who helped grind the TNT—Odeh's former explosives instructor, Abdel Rahman, was brought in to do the electrical work. In both cases, Rahman ran a wire from the bomb to a set of batteries in the back of the truck cab, and then to a detonator switch beneath the dashboard. Perhaps to create the impression that the bombs were built by different people, Odeh used a slightly different configuration in the Dar es Salaam bomb: he attached the TNT to fifteen oxygen tanks and gas canisters—a practice commonly used by Middle Eastern terrorists under the mistaken assumption that they enhance an explosion—and surrounded the weapon with four bags of fertilizer and some sandbags to fill in the gaps.

The operation now moved into the final stages of preparation and planning. The attacks were scheduled to take place on August 7, 1998—

the eighth anniversary of the arrival of U.S. troops in Saudi Arabia—though only Saleh and al-Qaeda planners in Afghanistan were aware of the target date (that being the nature of leaderless resistance with its command to share information only on a need-to-know basis).

The Targets

The embassy in Nairobi was chosen not only because there was a large American presence in the building, but also because U.S. Ambassador Bushnell was a woman and killing a woman would create publicity for the attack. (Bin Laden's communications experts in London were well aware of the fact that Nairobi is a regional hub for the international media.) The presence of Christian missionaries at the embassy would only add to the publicity. Moreover, among the embassy personnel in Nairobi was a large continent of CIA agents who were responsible for work done in Sudan and Somalia that bin Laden opposed.[39] Finally, the Nairobi embassy was an easy target.

Built by the U.S. State Department in the early 1980s, the embassy was a seven-story concrete structure, with five floors above ground and two below. It was situated at the intersection of two of the busiest streets in Nairobi, near two mass transit centers. Consistent with the low-level security concerns of the early 1980s, the building lacked sufficient "setback" from the busy streets and adjacent buildings. To partly compensate for this in the terrorist-prone 1990s, a four-foot high steel bar fence had been constructed around the embassy. Beyond the fence, a line of steel posts had also been added.[40]

Still, the building remained vulnerable to a vehicular assault. (Since her appointment in 1996, Ambassador Bushnell had repeatedly called for security upgrades. She was told that terrorist threats had dissipated.) This was especially so in the rear parking lot off Haile Selassie Avenue. The parking lot, which was sandwiched between the sixty-story Co-op Bank Building and the smaller Ufundi Building, was also the entrance to an underground garage for the embassy. A guard shack sat at the front of the parking lot, manned by a local Kenyan security company whose guards *did not carry firearms*, and it was attached to a "drop bar" (a manually operated gate constructed of a tubular steel framework) that ran parallel to the steel posts.[41]

Security at the embassy in Dar es Salaam was another matter. Originally built by the security-conscious Israelis in the early 1970s, the embassy was a squat three-story concrete building situated on a large lot in a residential suburban area of the city. The building stood at the rear of the lot, and the ambassador's residence was approximately one thousand yards away. In front of the embassy building was a four-story concrete annex (added by the Americans when they acquired the embassy following the 1973 Israel-Arab war, at which time the Israelis were asked to leave Tanzania.) The embassy, the ambassador's residence, and the annex were surrounded by a concrete-enforced metal picket perimeter wall, which provided a twelve-foot setback between the embassy grounds and adjacent streets and properties. The main embassy building was set back twenty-five feet from the roadway.[42]

Reinforced guard booths were located at the two vehicular entryways to the compound; both were manned by an armed security outfit. For years, vehicles had been allowed to enter these gated entryways for security searches. But on July 22, 1998 (as the bombs were being built in Nairobi and Dar es Salaam), the embassy revised its security procedures to insure that vehicles were screened outside the compound before being allowed to enter.[43] In short, security in Dar es Salaam presented Saleh with challenges that he would not face in Nairobi.

After five years of planning, then, al-Qaeda had the on-site intelligence, organization, equipment, technology, and patience necessary to execute a major terrorist attack against the United States. Al-Qaeda certainly had the resources. Bin Laden's network financed the entire East African operation—including money, material, equipment, personnel, communication systems, safe houses, and travel—at an estimated cost of $100,000. These funds were allegedly maintained in accounts at a Saudi-backed bank in Dar es Salaam—deposited via wire transfers from banks in Sudan, Malaysia, Britain, Hong Kong, and Dubai, as well as being funnelled through Islamic charities in Nairobi. But more to the point of this study, al-Qaeda had acquired the criminal trade craft necessary to turn opportunity into terrorism—or, as bin Laden's fatwah read, to strike Americans "in any country in which it is possible."

Yet these skills were not honed to perfection. Although al-Qaeda had the criminal expertise to build weapons of mass destruction, its ability to both deliver the weapons and exploit the routine activities of local communities would fall short of expectations. As al-Owhali later told an FBI agent, "The mission didn't go exactly point for point and time to time the way it was supposed to." That, as we shall see, is an understatement.

COUNTDOWN

August 1

On the morning of Saturday, August 1, Mohamed Odeh was in Mombasa on business, staying with his brother-in-law, Omar, when he received an urgent message from Fahid to contact Saleh, who was also in Mombasa. Rather than doing so right away, Odeh went to retrieve an umbrella he had left at a mosque earlier that day. En route, Odeh ran into Saleh and Fahid on the street. Saleh began yelling at Odeh, clamoring that it was time "for you to get out of here!" Saleh told Odeh that all operatives had to leave Kenya by Thursday, August 6. Odeh, however, had known this for some time.

Four months earlier, Saleh—acting on behalf of bin Laden and al-Zawahiri—had ordered Odeh to get his affairs in order for the impending flight from Kenya. But Odeh had failed to accomplish the simplest of tasks. Now, as they stood on the street, Odeh told Saleh that he was still waiting for his Jordanian passport to be renewed and mailed to his Witu address. Furthermore, he had not yet purchased his plane ticket and lacked money to do so.

Money had been an ongoing problem for Mohamed Odeh. As stated earlier, the East African plot was well financed; those resources were used to pay operatives, including Odeh, a yearly salary. On top of that, Odeh drew revenue from his furniture business with Omar. And on top of that, he still owned the fishing boat purchased for him by al-Qaeda. The problem was that Odeh was a terrible money manager. Even though he lived in a mud hut and apparently had few expenses, Odeh still could not make ends meet possibly because of poor decisions concerning the furniture business. Back on July 14, Odeh had complained to Saleh that he didn't have the funds to travel. At the time, Saleh had given Odeh the cold shoulder and told him to fend for himself. Odeh borrowed some cash from a business associate but by August that money was gone, too.

Exasperated by Odeh's poor money-management skills, Saleh gave him some cash to cover his travel expenses and told Odeh that he (Saleh) would get a passport for him and deliver it to Omar's house that evening.

That night, Saleh and Fahid came to Omar's and gave Odeh a stolen Yemeni passport. It had serious flaws. Not only did the passport have someone else's picture on it, but it had expired. Saleh told Odeh to remedy these problems by going to the Mombasa immigration bureau the next day with an appropriate photograph. Odeh would later tell his FBI interrogators that in his six years as a member of al-Qaeda, he had never experienced the kind of pressure that Saleh was now laying on him.

August 2

Mohammed al-Owhali arrived in Nairobi during the early morning hours of Sunday, August 2—a day late because he had missed a connecting flight between Muscat and Abu Dhabi. Al-Owhali took a taxi to the Ramada Inn in the Iftin district and checked into Room 24. He then called KSM in Pakistan from a phone service near the hotel and advised him of his arrival. KSM told al-Owhali that Saleh would arrange to have someone pick him up. Around sundown, Harun arrived at the hotel, collected al-Owhali and paid the hotel bill, even though the Saudi had not stayed the night. Then they went to the villa at 43 Runda Estates.

Meanwhile, Odeh was making little headway. There was no way he could meet Saleh's demand to get his passport together because the Mombasa immigration office was closed on Sunday, August 2. Moreover, the fact of the matter was that Odeh was in no hurry to leave Kenya. He had family there and had come to respect the Kenyan people in general. Odeh's behavior—and his subsequent remarks made to the FBI—suggest that he did not willingly support the random killing of Kenyans. In his conduct Odeh demonstrates what terrorism scholar Marc Sageman refers to as the "free-rider paradox"—the suggestion that participation in terrorism may not be based on utilitarian ideals for all terrorists. Applied to Odeh's case, this argument implies that even if terrorism is a rational strategy for al-Qaeda as a whole, it is not so for each of its members. Those members would be better off stepping aside and leaving the dirty work to others.[44]

Odeh then decided to go visit his wife's aunt in the town of Malinda, where he hoped to settle some affairs related to his furniture business. In Malinda, Odeh received what he would later describe as "an angry, a real angry phone call" from Fahid, saying: "Where are you? What are you doing?" Saleh wanted to see Odeh immediately, so Odeh hopped a bus back to Mombasa where he planned to meet Saleh at the bus station. The bus was late getting to the station, however, and Saleh had already left by the time Odeh arrived.

August 3

Around 7:30 a.m. on Monday, August 3, Fahid picked up Odeh at Omar's and drove him to the immigration office to get Odeh's passport (using Odeh's alias, "Muhammad Sadiq Howaida"). When they got there, Odeh was reluctant to take care of business. Even though he had a personal photograph with him, Odeh complained to Fahid that he had not yet made living arrangements for his pregnant wife and child while he was to be gone. Odeh walked back to Omar's house to discuss arrangements for his family, while Fahid stayed at the immigration bureau and took care of Odeh's passport for him. Later that day, Fahid met Odeh, and together they went to a travel agency to buy their airline tickets. Yet again, Odeh was having money problems, so Fahid paid cash for both of their fares. As the two men parted company, Fahid told Odeh that Saleh wanted him to leave Mombasa that night on a bus for Nairobi. Saleh expected to see Odeh at Nairobi's Hilltop Hotel within twenty-four hours.

Saleh was already in Nairobi. That morning, he had gone to the villa to meet with al-Owhali. At his side was al-Owhali's companion from Afghanistan, Azzam, who had been in Nairobi for about a week. Saleh then explained the operation's details.

There would be two bombings, Saleh said: one in Nairobi and one 450 miles away in Dar es Salaam. Both were going to occur on the same day, Friday, August 7, between 10:30 and 11:00 a.m. This time-frame had been selected because devout Muslims (who make up approximately one-third of the Kenyan population) would be praying in the shelter of their mosques at that hour. The intention was to kill Americans, not Muslims. Saleh showed al-Owhali some photographs and drawings of the Nairobi embassy and explained that al-Owhali's job was to help Azzam get the truck bomb into the embassy compound. Azzam would drive the truck, and al-Owhali would be the passenger.

Upon arriving at the embassy parking lot, al-Owhali was to exit the truck, brandishing a pistol, and force the guard to raise the drop bar so that Azzam could drive the truck as close to the embassy as possible. Al-Owhali would also be armed with some homemade stun grenades consisting of TNT and aluminum powder wrapped in black tape. Once Azzam had arrived at the embassy building, al-Owhali was to fire his gun in the air and throw several of the stun grenades on the ground to frighten Kenyans out of the area. Finally, al-Owhali was to provide backup in case the bomb failed to explode when Azzam pressed the detonator switch. If that happened, al-Owhali was to go to the back of the truck, unlock it, and toss a stun grenade inside, causing the bomb to manually detonate.

Azzam and al-Owhali were then taken into the garage and shown the truck bomb. Again consistent with the leaderless resistance strategy, Saleh had waited until the last minute to reveal final details of the attack to his suicide bombers—waited, that is, until they had a need to know those details. Saleh bragged that the truck bomb had been built two weeks ago, as had the bomb for the Dar es Salaam operation. He also explained a crucial difference between the two attacks. In Nairobi, two people would be in the truck and both of them (Azzam and al-Owhali) would die in the explosion. In Dar es Salaam, only one person would occupy the vehicle; there would be no gun, no grenades, and no attempt to frighten bystanders. The driver of that truck—also expected to die—would be the Egyptian Ahmed Abdallah, known as "Ahmed the German" because of his blue eyes and fair complexion. (Al-Owhali knew Abdallah from the camps in Afghanistan.) Saleh and Ahmed the German were in regular contact, said Saleh, via cell phones.

August 4

When Odeh arrived in Nairobi at 7:30 a.m. on Tuesday, August 4, he was exhausted from the all-night bus trip. He went to the Hilltop Hotel, a $10-a-night dive in downtown Nairobi frequented by Middle Eastern youth, and registered using the fake Yemeni passport. After checking into Room 102b, Odeh went to sleep.

By this time, at least six—and maybe as many as ten—members of the Nairobi and Dar es Salaam cells were staying at the Hilltop, including Saleh, Harun, Hussein, and Fahid. They all had forged passports and travel documents, and all were intending to leave Nairobi over the next two days on different flights to Pakistan. From there, they planned to travel to Afghanistan where they would be greeted and congratulated by bin Laden.

Waking around noon, Odeh left the room and stumbled into Saleh and Harun, who were just leaving the Hilltop. Saleh noticed that Odeh was *still* unprepared for traveling. How could this be?

During his training in Afghanistan, Odeh had been taught how to travel without attracting attention, as had all of the operatives in the East African plot. Odeh had, in fact, received extensive instruction on avoiding capture and countering interrogation. This training included specific instructions on wearing Western clothing (scented with cologne to prove that the travelers were normal men who were "interested in women" and not religious terrorists whose philosophy is decidedly misogynistic) and carrying modest amounts of cash and cigarettes—all intended to make travelers blend in to large crowds at airports, bus stations, and hotels. Odeh had violated three important tenets of this training: (1) by now he was highly anxious about traveling; (2) he was still dressed as a religious zealot in an Islamic robe and skull cap; and (3) he was still wearing a beard, also associated with fundamentalist religious views.

So Saleh gave Odeh some socks, a shirt, a pair of pants, and a razor. He told Odeh to shave off his beard, so as to avoid the suspicions of Customs officials and others, and to use Saleh's room to do it. Odeh then went to Saleh's room, 107a, where he found Abdel Rahman, who had been staying at the Hilltop for the past two months while the bombs were being constructed. Instead of shaving off his beard, though, Odeh sat down and began talking with his former explosives trainer.

Meanwhile, Saleh had driven al-Owhali and Azzam to the U.S. embassy, and was now pointing out exactly where he wanted the truck bomb to be placed when it exploded: in the parking lot at the rear of the embassy, inside the gate, as close to the building as possible. Al-Owhali suggested that they detonate the bomb in the parking garage directly beneath the embassy, thereby increasing the bomb's lethality. But Saleh was unimpressed, and the plan would remain unchanged. After the reconnaissance, Saleh dropped Azzam and al-Owhali off at the villa. They would never see Saleh again.

Saleh returned to the Room 107a at the Hilltop around 4 p.m. Rahman and Odeh were still there talking. Odeh would later recall that the Egyptian commander displayed a severe demeanor and was "extremely worried," adding that Saleh began saying prayers to calm his nerves. Saleh's apprehension was palpable, and a dark mood descended upon everyone inside the room. Throughout the night, "nobody talked about anything," said Odeh. "Even though the climate was urgent, nobody discussed anything."

August 5 and 6

On Wednesday morning, August 5, a fax arrived at the Cairo office of the *Al-Hayat* newspaper from Ayman al-Zawahiri on behalf of the EIJ, saying that American interests would soon be attacked because the United States had supported the extradition of four EIJ members from Albania to Egypt, where they were expected to be tortured. "We should like to inform the Americans," read the fax, "that, in short, their message has been received and that they should read carefully the reply that will, with God's help, be written in the language that they understand."[45]

Azzam and al-Owhali spent that day and the next—August 5 and 6—at the villa, preparing for martyrdom. Al-Owhali made a series of collect calls to a friend in Yemen named Ahmed al-Hazza, a Qaeda soldier he had fought beside in Kabul, and Azzam made a number of collect calls to his family in Saudi Arabia. During this time, Abdel Rahman came to the villa and made the final electrical connections on the bomb, a procedure that he would repeat at the bomb factory in Dar es Salaam. Finally, Harun brought word from Saleh indicating that everyone associated with the Nairobi bombing—save Azzam, al-Owhali, and Harun–had been instructed to leave Kenya by August 6.

The plot was also progressing in Tanzania back on August 2, before Hussein left for Nairobi. KK Mohamed had been informed of the operation by Hussein. Hussein said that Ahmed the German would drive the truck and that Mohamed would assist him. Both were fluent in Arabic, so there would be no language barrier. Since Mohamed was a native Tanzanian and knew both the local language and the streets of Dar es Salaam, he would direct Ahmed to the embassy. However, Mohamed was instructed to stay in the truck for only part of the drive. Once Ahmed was clearly on his way, Mohamed was to exit the truck, run back to House 213, and clean up any remaining evidence. In preparation for his flight from Tanzania, Mohamed had bought a fake passport from a friend and arranged for transportation to Cape Town, South Africa. Before parting company, Hussein gave Mohamed $1,000 in travel money and three emergency al-Qaeda phone numbers (written backwards), including the Yemen number 415–9123, for Osama bin Laden's satellite phone. Ahmed the German would not be leaving Dar es Salaam. In preparation for his martyrdom, Ahmed gave Ahmed Ghailani a package and asked him to mail it to his family in Egypt.

KK Mohamed and Ahmed the German ran into some last-minute trouble on August 5 when they moved the truck to the rear of the house (in an apparent dry run). The truck, loaded to the springs with two thousand pounds of explosives, got stuck in the sand. After Mohamed and Ahmed dug it out, Mohamed went out and purchased a back-up truck in case the same thing happened on the morning of the attack.

By Wednesday evening, nearly all of the leadership and supporting personnel had left Nairobi. Odeh was one of the last ones out. Before Saleh left, he gave Odeh $500 and instructed him to use the money to bribe customs officials if a problem presented itself at the airport in Karachi. Odeh, who had finally shaved off his beard, spent his last few hours in Nairobi shopping for clothing and getting his shoes shined along Moi Avenue, in anticipation of his 10:00 p.m. flight on Pakistan International Airlines on the night of August 6. Even then, in spite of all the instruction and assistance he had received, the Witu peasant was *still* unprepared for the challenges of international travel.

Meanwhile, anticipating a U.S. retaliation for the events that were about to happen, bin Laden and his advisors left their main outpost in Kandahar, Afghanistan, for the mountains.

THE ATTACKS

In the early morning hours of August 7, faxes were sent to al-Qaeda operatives in London claiming responsibility for the embassy bombings in the name of the "Army for the Liberation of Islamic Holy Places." These faxes claimed that the Nairobi bombing was carried out by two Saudi nationals and that the Dar es Salaam attack was committed by an Egyptian national. Within minutes, the faxes were distributed to news organizations in Paris; Doha, Qatar; and Dubai, United Arab Emirates.

Al-Owhali awoke that morning and dressed in black shoes, blue jeans, a white short-sleeved shirt, and a blue cotton jacket (the August temperature in Nairobi is cool). At 9:20, he phoned his friend Ahmed al-Hazza in Yemen. Then al-Owhali shoved a 9mm Beretta pistol into his jacket pocket and wedged four of the stun grenades into his belt. Twenty-five minutes later, Azzam and al-Owhali boarded the bomb truck and pulled away from the villa. Because they were unfamiliar with the route to the embassy, Harun drove ahead of them, leading the way in a white Datsun pickup.

From behind the wheel, Azzam noticed that al-Owhali's jacket was tightly covering the stun grenades in his belt. So Azzam told al-Owhali to take the jacket off because it could create problems when he reached for the grenades. Al-Owhali took the jacket off and placed it on the seat next to him. As they continued toward the embassy, Azzam and al-Owhali listened to an audio cassette of Islamic poems in order to psych themselves up for the violence ahead. Once they reached a traffic circle near the embassy, Harun pulled off to the side and waved Azzam on. Azzam pulled into the traffic flow along Haile Selassie Avenue, headed toward the embassy, chanting poems with al-Owhali.

The streets and sidewalks around the embassy were bustling with cars and people when the terrorists arrived shortly before 10:30. Azzam drove to the rear parking lot and approached the drop bar. A mail van was leaving the lot, so Azzam pulled to a stop and waited for it to pass. Once the path was clear, Azzam pulled up to the drop bar, as al-Owhali sprang from the passenger seat and started walking toward a lone guard standing next to the shack.

Suddenly al-Owhali realized that his 9mm Beretta—which he was supposed to use to confront the unarmed guard—was still in his jacket on the seat of the truck. Al-Owhali froze for a moment, trying to decide whether to go back to the truck and retrieve the gun, or to improvise. Thinking that the first option would take too long, al-Owhali pulled a stun grenade from his belt and began yelling at the guard in English, demanding that he unlock and raise the drop bar. But the guard refused. So al-Owhali pulled the pin on the grenade and threw it at him, causing a loud explosion. The guard ducked the grenade and ran away, yelling "Terrorism! Terrorism!" This left the drop bar down, denying Azzam access to the target area.

As pedestrians fled the area, people inside the embassy came to the windows to see what was going on—thus exposing themselves to the glass and steel encasing the offices. Azzam moved the truck in a position parallel to the embassy—still outside the drop bar zone, but close enough to accomplish the mission. Azzam then drew the Beretta from al-Owhali's jacket and started firing at the embassy's windows. Now even more people scattered from the area, leaving both the truck where it should not have been and al-Owhali standing alone at the drop bar with nothing to do.

Al-Owhali started running, following the others to safety. A moment later, Azzam pressed the detonator switch.

With a deafening roar, a red-orange fireball lit the sky as the pay-load tore upward at 21,000 miles an hour, ripping a huge crater from the ground to the roof of the building. The blast hurled people through the air, crushing them under falling walls and ceilings as the gouged rear face came down in a cascade of concrete, steel, and shattered glass.

Meanwhile, in Dar es Salaam, KK Mohamed did just as he was told. At about 10:00 a.m., he left House 213 with Ahmed the German. When the Nissan Atlas stopped at Uhuru Street, Mohamed got out and began running back to the safe house to pray as Ahmed continued on his own.

Around 10:30, Ahmed pulled up to one of the vehicular gates at the embassy. In front of him was a huge water tanker driven by an African named Yusufu Ndange, husband and father of six children. Ndange was making his weekly stop at the compound to replenish the em-bassy's water supply (a routine activity that was obviously overlooked by Saleh's operatives in their surveillance runs). One guard was stand-ing behind the water tanker, two guards were standing inside the nearby guard booth, and two more were in the pedestrian entrance screening area near the annex. Inside the screening area was a small crowd of young Tanzanians waiting to be admitted to the annex to process their student visas for the upcoming fall semester at U.S. col-leges and universities.

No one really knows what happened next, but a leading theory is this: because of the recent change in security procedures at the embassy, Ahmed was forced to stay outside the perimeter (again, this routine ac-tivity was overlooked by Saleh) where he was next in line to be searched after the guard had finished searching the water tanker. Unable to pen-etrate the embassy's outer security, and with time running out on the plan to simultaneously attack the embassies in Nairobi and Dar es Salaam, Ahmed went ahead and pressed the detonator switch from where he sat—some thirty-five feet from the outer wall of the embassy building.

The force of the blast propelled the water tanker over three stories into the air. By the time it came crashing down against the embassy building, all five guards were dead along with Yusufu Ndange and five students near the annex. In all, the explosion killed eleven people, all Africans, and injured eighty-five others. Ahmed the German was evis-cerated along with the bomb truck.

AFTERMATH

Immediately after the attack in Nairobi, Al-Owhali was laying face-down on the pavement, bleeding from the head. The bomb's concussion had knocked him down a short distance from the embassy. Haile Selassie Avenue was strewn with hunks of concrete, twisted steel, and broken glass. Several buses lay burning, with corpses hanging from the windows. The Co-op Bank Building had collapsed into the embassy's emergency generator, spilling thousands of gallons of diesel fuel into the embassy basement. The diesel fuel ignited, and huge plumes of black smoke and fire were now billowing from the gutted building. Burning bodies were spread around the area; others were buried under a mountain of debris. The vast majority were Kenyans.[46]

As sirens shrieked by, al-Owhali picked himself up and walked to a nearby clinic, which was just beginning to receive its first wave of victims. As he waited for treatment, al-Owhali realized that he still had a stun grenade tucked into his belt, so he removed the device and threw it into a trash can.

Al-Owhali received some first aid and was taken by ambulance to the MP Sha Hospital. After registering in the name of "Khalid Saleh," he received stitches to his forehead, right hand, and wrist. Upon being discharged, al-Owhali walked to the street and weighed his options.

They were few. Since he had failed to complete his martyrdom mission, al-Owhali was stuck without a plan. He was in a foreign city with no money, no plane ticket, no passport, and no official identity documents. He knew no one in Nairobi, nor did he speak Swahili. He had only the blood-stained clothes on his back and, in his pockets, three bullets and a key to the padlock on the back of the now-destroyed truck bomb. Since these items could incriminate him in the attack, al-Owhali went back inside the hospital and entered the men's room where he washed the keys and bullets in the sink to remove his fingerprints. Then he tried to flush them down the toilet; but that failed, so al-Owhali retrieved the items and hid them on a window ledge inside the men's room. Then he left the hospital.

Al-Owhali walked the streets trying to find his way back to the villa, where he had left his passport and cash. But he had not taken the time to familiarize himself with the city, so he couldn't find Runda Estates. The only other place he knew was the Ramada Inn where he had briefly stayed upon arriving in Nairobi on August 2. So al-Owhali hailed a cab and took it to the Ramada, where he asked the driver to wait for his fare. Al-Owhali went inside and spoke to the clerk who had checked him in days earlier, explaining that he had been injured in the embassy blast and had lost his money and travel documents as well. The clerk took sympathy on al-Owhali and agreed to advance him cab fare and a room for the night, with the understanding that al-Owhali would repay him once he could contact "people from Yemen" who would assist him. Al-Owhali then checked into Room 7.

The clerk left the hotel and went to the home of someone he knew from Yemen, seeking help for the man who had been injured in the bombing. Later, the clerk returned to Room 7 with a change of clothes. Al-Owhali showered, put on the new clothes, and threw the old ones in a drawer. These items would later be found by police, but already before that, law enforcement officials had made a major break in the case by taking advantage of a simple routine activity and an amazing display of criminal incompetence, arrogance, and sheer stupidity.

Meltdown in Karachi

Mohamed Odeh checked through the immigration section at Karachi airport on the morning of August 7, shortly after the attacks. The first immigration officer who looked at his passport saw no problems and waved Odeh through. But then a supervisor took a second look at the passport and noticed that something wasn't right. Although Odeh's Yemeni passport appeared to be legitimate, the photo did not match. It showed a man with a beard, which Odeh no longer wore, having shaved it off on Saleh's orders.

Odeh tried to bribe the immigration officers, but there were no takers. Instead, the officers took Odeh aside and put him in a room where they planned to conduct further questioning when time allowed. Over the next several hours, the officers heard news of the bombings on the BBC. Approaching Odeh, an officer asked: "Are you a terrorist?" Odeh did not reply. When the officer specifically asked whether he had been involved in the Nairobi bombing, Odeh attempted to persuade him that the attack was justified. In the name of Islam, it was the right thing to do, he told them. This captured the officer's attention, at which point Odeh was turned over to Pakistani intelligence. Over the next three days, Odeh made a full confession.

Odeh admitted to his participation in the embassy attacks, boasting of his expertise in explosives and intelligence gathering. He went on to describe the meeting at the Hilltop Hotel in Nairobi, telling interrogators that six other conspirators had left Kenya before the explosion and had arrived at the Karachi airport on different flights between August 5 and August 7. Odeh admitted that even he, a senior operative, did not know about the involvement of certain individuals in the bombing when they met on the same flight from Nairobi to Karachi. He told interrogators that the bomb had been built at 43 Runda Estates, and gave the names of others, including Saleh and Abdel Rahman, who had participated in the Dar es Salaam attack. (Later, upon searching Odeh's hut in Witu, agents would find a drawing of the entryway to the Nairobi embassy and a configuration of the planned bomb blast.) But most importantly, Odeh confessed to being a member of al-Qaeda, under the leadership of Osama bin Laden.

This information was immediately passed on to the FBI, thereby giving the bureau its first solid lead connecting bin Laden to the embassy bombings.

Loose Ends

Successful terrorism conspiracies are characterized by criminal competencies and organizational contingencies. After August 7, al-Qaeda had neither. Al-Owhali was stuck in Room 7 at the Ramada Inn with no money and no plan to get out of Nairobi. What's more, he had no support system. Beginning on the morning of August 8, al-Owhali began making collect calls to al-Hazza in Yemen, seeking money transfers and false travel documents. He also asked his friend to contact KSM and relay the message that al-Owhali "did not travel"—a code meaning that he did not die in the bombing. (Later intelligence would suggest that KSM flew into Nairobi before the attack.)

Al-Hazza eventually wired a $1,000 transfer to al-Owhali, which he picked up at a jewelry store near the Ramada on or about August 11. Still, there was no word from KSM. Essentially, al-Owhali had been hung out to dry. After reimbursing the Ramada clerk for the money he owed him, al-Owhali relocated to the Iftin Lodge in the Eastleigh district. With no identity documents in his possession, al-Owhali used the hospital form he had acquired on August 7 and registered at the lodge as "Khalid Saleh."

By now, the FBI and Kenyan law enforcement were deeply involved in the bombing investigation. On August 12, Nairobi police received a tip that one of the bombers might be among the injured. The police tracked the information to the MP Sha Hospital and discovered the record of "Khalid Saleh" who had been treated and released hours after the explosion. The Kenyan Criminal Investigation Division (CID) then tracked "Saleh" to the Iftin Lodge. Because he could produce no official identification, the CID agents took him into custody.

For two solid weeks, al-Owhali maintained his front. He told investigators that his name was Khalid Saleh. He said that he was a Yemeni who had travelled to Nairobi to visit his uncle and that he was simply walking by the embassy when the bomb exploded. Later, after being turned over to the FBI, al-Owhali broke down and confessed his role in the affair. In explaining his ties to al-Qaeda, al-Owhali gave up the names of the other members of his cell, along with their physical descriptions and an account of their activities.

IMPLICATIONS FOR U.S. COUNTER-TERRORISM POLICY

The embassy bombings provide several important lessons about al-Qaeda's terrorist-oriented criminality. First, like the 1993 World Trade Center bombers, the East African operatives demonstrated variable competencies ranging from highly sophisticated methods of surveillance, financing, communications, and bomb-building to highly unsophisticated techniques of seizing buildings, coordinating points of bomb detonation, and executing effective getaways. Much like the World Trade Center attack, the embassy bombings were technical failures inasmuch as they did not accomplish their primary goal: to kill Americans on a vast scale. Because of al-Qaeda's inability to capitalize on routine activities surrounding embassy security—due to poor planning and an inability to adapt to changing conditions—neither truck bomb ended up where it was supposed to be.

Second, both training and its implementation matters. Every one of the East African operatives attended al-Qaeda camps in Afghanistan where they honed skills that made the terrorist attacks possible. Some of these men, however, were vastly over-trained relative to their assignments, while others, though also highly skilled, exhibited nothing less than a singular stupidity in criminal affairs. Mohammed al-Owhali attended no less than five different al-Qaeda camps where he was trained in tactics ranging from weaponry, explosives, and communications to hijacking, seizing buildings, kidnapping, and cell management. Yet his assignment in Kenya involved little more than using a pistol to subdue an unarmed guard. And at that, he failed miserably. Similarly, not only was KK Mohamed trained by al-Qaeda in the use of weapons, rocket launchers, and surface-to-air missiles, but he also did two tours of duty as a weapons trainer in Somalia. Yet Mohamed was little more than a low-level "gofer" in Tanzania—he rented a house, bought a truck, crushed some TNT, and rode part way to the target site. On the other hand, despite his vaunted status as one of bin Laden's most acclaimed military commanders, Saleh failed to detect some easily observable security changes at the embassy in Dar es Salaam. He also defaulted on his responsibility to manage the operation's most audacious loose canon, Mohamed Odeh. And while Odeh may have effectively applied his explosives training to constructing the bombs, when it came to acquiring travel documents, managing money, concealing incriminating evidence, and crossing international borders, his performance was dreadful. Such behavior is not unusual for a common criminal, nor is it unusual for a terrorist who has spent years in a training camp. Terrorists *are* criminals, and their criminal skills will vary depending on individual characteristics.

The United States implemented an array of responses to the embassy bombings; some were successful, but most were not. The successful responses, which received little media attention, drew on the criminal vulnerabilities of al-Qaeda and included the vast international law enforcement manhunts that led to the arrests of KK Mohamed and Ahmed Ghailani. Like all operatives in the embassy plot, Mohamed had been instructed not to leave anything behind connecting him to the attacks. Odeh's confession had led agents to the Dar es Salaam bomb factory, however, and that investigation led them to Mohamed's family home in Kidimni on Zanibar Island where they discovered a TNT grinder. Interrogations of Mohamed's family led agents to Cape Town, South Africa, where they arrested the terrorist in October 1999 while he was working at a Burger World restaurant. Several years later, Ahmed Ghailani was taken into custody following a dramatic gun battle with police in the eastern Pakistan city of Gujrat. Ghailani had come to the city to obtain false travel documents as part of a plan to flee the country. Gujrat was chosen because it is a notorious hub of illegal human trafficking.[47] Two conspirators who helped with public relations in London—the Egyptians Abdel Bary and Ibrahim Eidaros—were arrested by British authorities after their fingerprints were found on documents related to the East African bombings.[48]

Actions taken by the United States that disregarded these sorts of routine activities and poorly developed criminal skills would lead to even deadlier forms of terrorism in the future. This finding concurs with the CIA inspector general's assessment of the agency's performance before September 11, 2001. That report criticizes CIA management for focusing on al-Qaeda's leadership, rather than looking for ways to attack the terrorist network at lower levels. "By going after Osama bin Laden," the report concludes, "the agency missed opportunities to recruit low-level agents on the margins of al-Qaeda who might have eventually provided access to its inner workings."[49]

After the bombings, the immediate goal of U.S. policy toward al-Qaeda was to kill bin Laden and his top lieutenants. On August 8, the CIA determined that bin Laden and several hundred al-Qaeda members were expected to gather at three training camps near Khowst to plan their next wave of strikes. Nearly two weeks later, on August 20, navy ships in the Arabian Sea fired eighty Tomahawk cruise missiles at the camps. Bin Laden was not there, however, nor were any other terrorists. The missiles killed twenty-six Afghan-Arabs, leading al-Zawahiri to call a Pakistani reporter and declare: "The war has started. The Americans should wait for an answer."[50] On the same day, the United States bombed the al-Shifa pharmaceutical plant in Khartoum, Sudan, which intelligence reports said was producing a precursor ingredient for VX nerve gas with bin Laden's financial backing. Yet subsequent analysis found no trace of the VX precursor, EMPTA, and the attack created a firestorm of criticism in the international press.[51]

These ineffective responses to the bombings only increased bin Laden's popularity in the Muslim world and encouraged al-Qaeda to carry out more audacious operations. The response also set off a debate about the efficacy of U.S. counter-terrorism policy. It would be years, though, before that debate would extend to the matter of al-Qaeda's training camps in Afghanistan. *The 9/11 Commission Report* makes the points abundantly clear in its analysis of the embassy attacks:

Defense Secretary William Cohen told us Bin Ladin's [sic] training camps were primitive, built with "rope ladders"; General [Hugh] Sheldon called them "jungle gym" camps. Neither thought them worthwhile targets for very expensive missiles. President Clinton and [White House Chief of Staff Sandy] Berger also worried . . . that attacks that missed Bin Ladin could enhance his stature and win him new recruits . . . [Moreover,] attacks in Afghanistan offered "little benefit, lots of blowback against [a] bomb-happy U.S."[52]

Hence, bin Laden's training camps would remain unmolested, due primarily to the hesitation of the U.S. military. According to Richard Clarke's recounting of events, both he and President Clinton had, in fact, pressed for the elimination of bin Laden's camps after the embassy attacks. "'Hugh,'" Clinton had said to the Chairman of the Joint Chiefs in Clarke's presence, "'what I think would scare the shit out of these al-Qaeda guys more than any cruise missile . . . would be the sight of U.S. commandos, Ninja guys in black suits, jumping out of helicopters into their camps, spraying machine guns. Even if we don't get the big guys, it will have a good effect.'"[53] Shelton balked at the plan, however, claiming that the United States had no staging area from which to launch the raids.

It is doubtful, though, that the helicopter raids would have made much difference in the long run. At the time, the United States lacked a coherent policy on Afghanistan; therefore, taking out the camps, independent of an overall counter-terrorism strategy in the region, would have produced few meaningful results. The FBI also lacked a plan to collect intelligence on al-Qaeda. Even though the embassy bombings prompted the bureau to envision the creation of a cadre of experienced and trained agents, analysts, and linguists, that plan, in the trenchant words of *The 9/11 Commission Report*, "did not succeed."[54]

The period after 1998 marked a new milestone in the evolution of al-Qaeda, eventually leading to a series of terrorist attacks spanning the globe. According to the *Report*, upon his capture in 2003, KSM told interrogators that the embassy bombings convinced him that bin Laden was "truly committed to attacking the United States."[55] And in early 1999, bin Laden gave KSM the green light for organizing the 9/11 attacks. Later that year, the muscle hijackers began training at the al Faruq camp near Kandahar.

PART II

DOMESTIC CRIME AND TERRORISM

3

The Legacy of Lost Causes

The Covenant, the Sword, and the Arm of the Lord

As stated at the book's outset, my goal is to identify the distinguishing features of terrorist-oriented criminality. In order to do this, the social learning and routine activity theories must be tested against the criminological evidence on terrorism in different countries and at different points in history. Only by scrutinizing these theories under diverse social circumstances is it possible to make generalizations about terrorism common to different times and places. Stated another way, our understanding of terrorism is enhanced by a systematic comparison of the phenomenon in various cultures using the same set of criteria. Absent these sensitive global comparisons, theories of terrorism become ethnocentric; that is, they offer concepts that apply to only one particular society during a specific historical era. It is necessary, then, to compare international jihad groups with domestic terrorist organizations in order to understand not only the criminology of terrorism, but also to gain an accurate picture of the terrorist threat facing America, both yesterday and today.

As we have seen, jihad criminality was forged by the mujahdeen in the fires of the Soviet-Afghan civil war; later, it was perfected by bin Laden's forces in the Qaeda training camps. The criminality of domestic terrorists in America arose, of course, from an entirely different state of affairs. Historically, terrorism in the United States has taken two forms: vigilante terrorism and insurgent terrorism. Vigilante groups have attempted to defend the status quo by using terrorist tactics on a local level. The Ku Klux Klan's reign of terror following the Civil War is a prime example. Insurgent groups, on the other hand, have attempted to change public policies by taking direct action against the state. Groups like the Black Panthers and the Weathermen of the late 1960s were the antithesis of vigilantism because they aimed to destroy the status quo.

This trend began to shift in the early 1980s due to the criminal activities of a secret collective of paramilitary survivalists, tax protestors, bankrupt farmers, skinheads, and ex-convicts motivated by an extreme right-wing ideology. Rather than maintaining the status quo or influencing public policy, their sole objective was mass murder. Driven by rage over a series of legal battles involving tax resistance, land rights, and gun control, their goal was to foment a white paramilitary rebellion capable of bringing down the federal government and catalyzing social upheaval. Toward that end, they would assassinate federal officials, politicians, police officers, minorities, and Jews. They would threaten federal judges and attempt to assassinate governors and presidents. They would sabotage gas pipelines, blow up bridges and electrical power grids, and derail passenger trains. They would rob liquor stores, banks, armored trucks, and military installations. They would burn churches and synagogues. They would attempt to poison municipal water supplies with chemical agents. And they would bomb federal buildings, including the Alfred P. Murrah Federal Building in Oklahoma City. Their story begins with a racist terrorist organization called the Covenant, the Sword, and the Arm of the Lord (CSA).

BACKGROUND

On April 19, 1985, the FBI attempted to serve a warrant on the CSA at its fortified compound in rural Arkansas. After a four-day standoff between two-hundred law-enforcement officers and the CSA's "Home Guard," agents entered the encampment and discovered a stockpile of illegal weapons and ammunition, including thirty-five machine guns, fifteen automatic rifles, silencers and hand grenades, three anti-aircraft rockets, fifty pounds of military plastic explosives, three-hundred blasting caps, a thousand rounds of ammunition, and two thousand feet of detonator cord. Agents also found thirty gallons of cyanide which the CSA planned to unload into the water supply of Washington, D.C. The purpose of the CSA's immense stockpile of weaponry, including its weapon of mass destruction, was to wage a holy war against the United States government. Although the CSA was part of a larger conspiracy involving dozens of extremists, three men were primarily responsible for its criminality.

The Preacher

The first was CSA founder James D. Ellison.[1] Ellison was born in 1940, somewhere in Illinois, to parents of Caucasian and Cherokee heritage. When Ellison was fourteen years old, his father was killed in a traffic accident, leaving the teenager to care for his mother and younger siblings. His father's untimely death also coincided with Ellison's conversion to fundamentalist Christianity. Ellison matured quickly and avoided the temptations of alcohol and drugs. After graduating from high school, he married a woman named Cheryl and enrolled in Lincoln Bible College, a seminary affiliated with the Church of Christ in Lincoln, Illinois. But Ellison was expelled prior to graduation for questioning church doctrine. Nevertheless, in 1962, when Ellison moved to San Antonio, Texas, he somehow became an ordained minister in the Church of Christ.

Evangelists often claim that they have been "slain in spirit"—possessed so completely by Jesus' love that they've died themselves—but Ellison *did* nearly die in 1970. In later sermons, Ellison claimed that he experienced an epiphany in April of that year following a construction accident. While working on a building as an iron worker, Ellison fell to the ground and was struck by a steel beam. The young minister broke his back and both legs, as well as all of his ribs and left ankle.

Doctors did not expect Ellison to live. Two weeks later, however, he was back on the pulpit declaring that God had spared him for a reason. For the next nine months Ellison preached feverishly about the accident in the context of God's judgments in the Book of Revelation. One by one, Ellison began to draw a following, and in 1971 the Ellisons and seven other families moved to a farm in Elijah, Missouri, where they established a Christian commune. "While I was praying," Ellison later explained to an Oklahoma grand jury, "God directed me to come to this part of the country, and acquire land, and establish a place of refuge for people that needed a place to live." Over the next few years, though, one by one Ellison lost his following. Cheryl also abandoned him after years of physical abuse, leaving the preacher to raise five children by himself.

In 1972, Ellison met Ollie Stewart, an attractive twenty-two-year-old bank employee from Lewis Springs, Missouri.[2] The daughter of a Church of Christ minister, Ollie was on the mend from an abusive relationship with her former husband, who had left her with a mountain of debt and sole custody of their mentally retarded two-year-old daughter. "She enjoyed spending time with men," said Ellison's confidant, Kerry Noble. "Ollie found strength in Ellison. He was a handsome and charismatic pastor. He gave her safety."[3]

In 1976, Ellison bought a 224-acre plot of land from the Fellowship of Christian Athletes on the shores of Bull Shoals Lake in the Ozark Mountains of northern Arkansas, just south of the Missouri line. Soon Ellison began to attract fundamentalists who were unhappy with mainstream churches and looking for a more authentic Christian experience. Consisting of mostly poor and rootless young couples in their early thirties, Ellison's flock also included a smattering of ex-convicts and ultimately some four hundred recovering drug addicts, primarily young and destitute.

The layout of Ellison's property provided a natural parceling into three settlements. On the "main compound," Ellison and his followers constructed primitive housing, barns, sheds, a machine shop, and a large stone building—called the Sanctuary—which served as a combination church-school. Also on the main compound were a saw mill and a salvage business that generated modest revenues for the community. Adjacent to the lake was the "plateau compound," and further inland was the "valley compound." In these areas, the commune's men, women, and children worked a large garden which provided an abundance of fresh vegetables. Cows, goats, hogs, sheep, chickens, and horses grazed nearby. Ellison christened his idyllic setting the Zarepath-Horeb Church. In the Old Testament, Zarepath was a Phoenician seaside village; Horeb was the Old Testament name for Mount Sinai, where God appeared in the burning bush to Moses. Ellison's group had little interest in politics, left or right, and discussions about race and anti-Semitism were virtually non-existent. "Our objective," Ellison said at the time, "is to simply be free to exercise our rights the way we want to."[4]

Daily life inside Zarepath-Horeb was highly regimented by Ellison and six elders. Smoking, drinking, and swearing were strictly prohibited. Work was mandatory, and all material property (wedding rings, family heirlooms, vehicles, and the like) were turned over to the "Body"—or the organization as a whole. In prayer services, Ellison used the scriptures to warn his flock about America's imminent social and economic decline. Because of this, Ellison asserted that Christians must develop the capacity to survive.

Then, in early 1978, Ellison claimed to have a vision of a coming apocalypse. In sermons he began to prophesy that the end of the world would come on August 12, 1978—the ninth of Ab on the Jewish calendar, when Jews celebrate the destruction of both the First and Second Temples.[5] Following the Tribulation—fires, famine, pestilence, and earthquakes—criminal gangs would spill out of American cities into the countryside like a swarm of locusts, plundering, raping, and killing. "It will get so bad," Ellison warned, "that parents will eat their children . . . Maggot infested bodies will lie everywhere." Christians would be unable to defend themselves against this cataclysm, and millions would die. To defend themselves against the catastrophe, the residents of Zarapeth-Horeb were required to study paramilitary tactics.

Accordingly, during 1978 and1979 Ellison and his followers spent an estimated $52,000 on weapons, ammunition, and military equipment. Most of the firearms were purchased without paperwork at gun shows in Arkansas and Missouri, using money generated from the commune's businesses. They included an array of 9mm and .38- and .45-caliber pistols, assault rifles, and 12-gauge shotguns. To train his congregation in the use of these weapons, Ellison appointed as his "defense minister" a young man named Randall Rader.

The Rock Star

Rader would play a crucial role in taking Zarepath-Horeb from a peaceful commune of pious Christians to a violent paramilitary sect. Yet he was an unlikely candidate for that calling. Randall Rader was born in the farming community of West Plains, Missouri, in 1951. Upon graduating from high school in 1969, Rader moved to Los Angeles where he became a guitar player in several fledgling rock bands. Catching the final flames of California flower power, Rader became a regular user of LSD, marijuana, speed, and downers. After four years of this, Rader experienced an epiphany of his own.

In 1974, on a visit back home to West Plains, Rader attended a fundamentalist religious revival. Something in the preacher's message moved him deeply. Repentant for his decadent lifestyle, Rader proclaimed his sorrow and accepted Jesus as his personal savior. It was a miraculous conversion. Rader became a devout Christian and began to envision the destruction of Western civilization and the epic role he might play in preventing it. Then, at a 1975 meeting at the Methodist Church in West Plains, Rader met Pastor Ellison.[6]

In 1976, Rader married a woman from Chicago named Kathleen Bator. The couple settled into a dwelling on the main compound, and in the fall of 1977 Rader became a church elder. He began his work as Ellison's defense minister a year later. Little in the once-aspiring rock star's background prepared him for commando training. While he had hunted with his father as a boy, Rader had no formal military training. Yet as he had done first with his music career and then with his religious conversion, Rader became devoted to his assignment, presiding over weekly military meetings and compiling a library of books on military tactics and firearms. He even learned to decipher gun manuals written in Chinese and German.

In the summer of 1979, to supplement income from the logging and salvage businesses, Ellison moved to Missouri where he took a job building Minuteman missile silos for the military—then the biggest weapons in America's nuclear arsenal. By this time, with the summer of 1978 come and gone, some of the residents had become disappointed with Ellison's prophecies. Rader was one of them. In Ellison's absence, Rader tried to take over the group and steer it into a more forceful direction. This began when he brought a double-edged sword to the Sanctuary services one night. Taking the platform, Rader struck a post with his weapon and threatened to do the same to another member's head. In his memoir, *Tabernacle of Hate,* fellow CSA elder Kerry Noble recalls that "Randall turned into a dictator, wanting to rule by fear and intimidation . . . Suddenly he was wearing a Nazi-like uniform, often carrying a German bullwhip and even wearing a monocle."[7] Angry with Ellison's failed prophecy about the apocalypse, and in accordance with his role as a Christian crusader who feared an impending onslaught by urban gangs, Rader took matters into his own hands. His first step was to convert the group's legal semi-automatic weapons into illegal automatics—essentially machine guns.

When Ellison returned at the end of the summer, he brought something with him that only fueled Rader's extremism. While in Missouri, Ellison met Dan Gayman, pastor of the Church of Israel near Schell City. Gayman had introduced Ellison to the odd religion known as Christian Identity, a theology that gives the blessing of God to the racist cause. (Also attending Gayman's church during this period was the young Eric Rudolph who would later use his Identity teachings as justification for a series of bombings throughout the South, including the 1996 Centennial Olympic Park bombing in Atlanta.) The Identity creed proceeds from the notion that Jews are the children of Satan, while white "Aryans" are the descendants of the biblical tribes of ancient Israel and thus are God's chosen people. Identity further holds that the world is on the verge of a final, apocalyptic struggle between good and evil and that Aryans must do battle with the Jewish conspiracy and its allies so that the world can be saved.[8]

After hearing a tape of Gayman's preaching combined with patriotic music, Ellison's congregation began a gradual transformation toward the religion. Although Ellison took the reins away from Rader and berated him for converting the firearms to machine guns, Ellison nevertheless adopted his defense minister's reasoning for doing so: namely, that sophisticated weaponry would be needed for protection against rioting hordes once the federal government collapsed under the weight of its own Jewish-inspired deceptions. The machine guns stayed, and the commune became a criminal enterprise.

Over the next six months, the residents of Zarepath-Horeb engaged in intense study of Christian Identity. They prayed about it with passion. And, ultimately, they embraced the doctrine without reservation. Ellison then used the Identity philosophy to rename his commune the Covenant, the Sword, and the Arm of the Lord. Ellison designed an emblem for the CSA featuring a rainbow for the *covenant*, pierced by a flaming *sword*. Devotees were the *arm of the Lord*. Ellison insisted that every commune member sign a "Declaration of Non-Surrender," in which they vowed to fight to the death for Jesus Christ. He also insisted that they donate their individual salaries for the logging and salvage work to the Body and burn any remaining vestiges of their pre-Identity lives, including keepsakes and high-school yearbooks. They destroyed their radios, televisions, and any other reminders of the outside world. Yet the greatest change came in the build-up of paramilitary forces.

Ellison instructed the men to shave their beards and cut their hair short. They were issued camouflage uniforms with the CSA logo on shoulder patches, along with red berets and combat boots. Every man was given a pistol and rifle. Concrete-enforced bunkers, hedgehogs, pillboxes, razor-wire fences, a communications center, and a military storage unit were added to the main compound. Tunnels were dug between the houses and the bunkers. Shooting portals were built into the Sanctuary. A sixty-five foot radio tower went up. Next to the creek across from the valley compound, Rader constructed a firing range. Lookouts and foot patrols were posted throughout the area. Klansmen appeared at the commune, and to supplement the group's income in order to pay for the improvements on the land, the CSA began a mail-order service for such neo-Nazi hate literature as the *Protocols of the Learned Elders of Zion, The Holy Book of Adolf Hitler,* and *Great Accomplishments of the Negro Race* (which was full of blank pages).

And Ellison's sermons became absolutely electrifying. In a late 1979 service, he stood before his armed warriors and proclaimed:

> The Jews have declared war on our race, promoting race-mixing and thereby polluting the pure seed of God. This ZOG, this Zionist Occupied Government, is killing our white babies through abortion! It is destroying white minds with its humanistic teaching of evolution! I tell you this—niggers may be descended from apes, but my ancestors never swung from trees by their tails. In order to preserve our Christian heritage and race, it is our right, our patriotic duty, to overthrow the Anti-Christ government. . . . Prepare for war, O Israel! Wake up the mighty men! Let the men of war come near. Beat your plowshares into spears and your pruning hooks into swords. Let the weak say, "I am strong"![9]

In the spring of 1980, the CSA sold their hogs, believing them to be unclean. They celebrated their first Passover complete with a slaughtered lamb and blood sprinkled on the door posts of Ellison's house. Ellison's men of war were now the true children of Israel. "Now we were no longer Christian survivalists," recalled Noble, "but we were white supremacists!"[10] Around this time, Ellison replaced his failed prophecy with a new forecast: God had warned him that a war against the forces of ZOG was imminent. To further prepare for the struggle ahead, the CSA would need to fortify its resources.

The CSA's first felony took place on April 18, 1980, when Ellison directed Rader to help Ellison's sister, Jean Troxell, with an insurance scam by burning down her house located near the CSA property. With several others, including Ellison's teenaged son, Rader assisted in the arson which resulted in an $11,000 settlement.

Rader's criminal skills were also developing in the area of weaponry. Working out of the machine shop, Rader specialized in converting Chinese AK-47 and German Heckler & Koch assault rifles into fully automatic weapons. He did so by modifying the bolt carriers, trigger packs, and trigger housings—a process that allows the trigger hammer to follow the bolt carrier forward when the rifle is fired. (The hammer follow-down results in automatic fire.) The modification was completed by adding flash suppressors to the firearms, or devices that swallow flames spit out by a gun's firepower. Kent Yates, a Vietnam veteran and former Green Beret who had been trained as a demolitions expert during the war, assisted Rader by manufacturing silencers—made from aluminum tubing, rubber, and Allan bolts—as well as land mines and hand grenades made from C-4 explosives and dynamite.

Rader also began to fashion exotic weaponry. This included a firearm that eventually become legendary among right-wing activists of the era. Back in 1979, on a visit to a gun shop in nearby Mountain Home, Arkansas, Rader had purchased an Ingram MAC-10 machine pistol. As manufactured by Military Armament Corporation (MAC), the gun was a legal semi-automatic. Once converted to a machine gun, the MAC-10 was one of the most gruesome weapons ever made. The gun resembled a small metal box mounted lengthwise on its side, a trigger on the underside, with a slot for the ammunition clip serving as the grip. It had a short barrel which Yates threaded for a silencer. Rader then added a takedown pin, enlarged the bolt handle, and wrapped the pistol grip with camouflage tape. The result was a weapon that was worthless from a distance, but at close range it was a meat grinder. Rader's MAC-10 could fire more than nine hundred rounds per minute, fifteen bullets a second.[11] It had only one purpose: to kill another human being with extreme prejudice.

But Rader's pride and joy was a paramilitary training school he built next to the firing range and called Silhouette City. Modeled after the FBI's shooting range at Quantico, Virginia, Silhouette City was designed to resemble an urban intersection, complete with buildings arranged along four streets, abandoned automobiles, and silhouettes of a state trooper wearing a Star of David and of the Israeli leaders Menachem Begin and Golda Meir. Trainees were drilled in "Christian martial arts," rifle and pistol marksmanship, and wilderness survival. Specialized instruction involved capturing buildings, repelling facades, and planting bombs, all of which was spelled out in Rader's *Christian Army Basic Training Manual* (which remains to this day the most comprehensive guide to guerrilla operations ever printed in the United

States). The school charged $500 tuition, and it was a resounding suc-
cess. By early 1982, Silhouette City was known throughout the racist
right, as applications poured in from white activists across the nation.

By now, Rader had matured into a supremely competent leader
who commanded some forty men. "Randall Rader was not someone
you would call 'Randy,'" said Noble. "He was six-foot-two, muscular,
with brown hair cut short, and good looking."[12] He was also cold and
ruthless. Noble recalls times when Rader would use his bullwhip to
strike men under his command for not working hard enough. He took
survivalism to its limits. Once Rader killed and skinned his own dog
and then ate its raw meat to demonstrate his commitment to the cause.
In their authoritative book on the radical right, *The Silent Brotherhood*,
Kevin Flynn and Gary Gerhardt write that "It was Rader who was most
responsible for the CSA's enjoying the reputation it had throughout the
right wing for militant survival training."[13] As a result of his reputation,
Rader ultimately attracted one of the most violent men the right has
ever known.

The Predator

In 1980, to advertise the group's elite training and spread the news
about its Identity ministry, Ellison began publishing a monthly newsletter called the *C.S.A. Journal*. Along with hundreds, maybe thousands, of
Americans, Richard Snell became a subscriber. And after meeting Ellison and Rader at a 1981 Christian-Patriot Defense League meeting,
Snell and his wife, Mary, became regular visitors at the CSA compound.

Born in 1931, Richard Wayne Snell spent his entire adult life in
southern Oklahoma. Snell was a burly, white-bearded racist who
worked as an international importer when he came to the CSA. He was
also a man with profound personal problems. A court-appointed psy-
chiatrist would later diagnose Snell as suffering from a "paranoid personality disorder" that manifested itself in a conspiratorial view of history. Specifically, Snell believed that the U.S. government had fallen
prey to a shadowy group of conspirators known as ZOG—Zionist Occupied Government—and that members of this cabal had persecuted
him personally. This persecution was first displayed in Snell's loss of his
photography business in the 1960s, with Snell believing that he had
been driven from the business by agents of ZOG. Snell's paranoia was
exacerbated by the December 1978 suicide of his son, Ken, due to a self-

inflicted gunshot wound while in the throws of drug addiction.[14] Again, Snell saw his son's suicide as the fault of ZOG—the government entity ultimately responsible for the proliferation of drugs in America.

Snell's affiliation with the CSA was concurrent with yet another devastating personal loss. By 1982, after years of financial setbacks, Snell had become impoverished. Unable to pay back taxes he owed to the Internal Revenue Service, Snell was served an arrest warrant and the IRS took Snell to court, where they obtained an order to seize all of his personal property. A combined IRS and FBI task force raided Snell's property, impounding his home, land, and vehicles. This was the event that pushed Snell over the edge. Snell would never forget the agents who had humiliated him. Nor would he forget where they worked—at the Murrah Federal Building in Oklahoma City.[15]

THE PLOT

The Covenant, the Sword, and the Arm of the Lord did not emerge in a social vacuum. By the early 1980s, mainstream American culture had become anchored in conservatism, patriotism, and traditional family values that were at the heart of a growing religious revival waged by the fundamentalist Christian Right. These were the days of the Reverend Jerry Falwell's "moral majority," a 6.5-million member political action group, which was waging a well-heeled campaign for the acceptance of Christian education in public schools and of legal sanctions against abortion, pornography, homosexuality, and other forms of "immorality." Of the 80 million television sets studied by the Neilsen rating service during this period, 68 million were tuned at least once a month to such fundamentalist programs as Pat Robertson's *The 700 Club, The Jimmy Swaggart Ministry, The Oral Roberts Ministry,* and Jim and Tammy Faye Bakker's *PTL Club.*[16]

Terrorism scholar Jeffrey Kaplan argues that "Ellison's compound [exhibited a] complete alienation from the surrounding culture."[17] That is true, but only up to a point. The CSA was certainly isolated physically from the surrounding culture. There were no telephones, radios, or TVs at the compound. The nearest town was forty miles away and the nearest paved highway was nine miles away. Yet despite these obstacles, the CSA managed to stay connected with the local culture by marching in lockstep with the Reagan-era zeitgeist.

"We *were* isolated, but in '80 we started going public with our beliefs," said Noble.[18] Himself a former counselor for *The 700 Club* and a father of six children, Noble recalls that the CSA was the focus of extensive media coverage in the early 1980s. The *Los Angeles Times*, the *Arizona Republic*, the *Dallas Morning News*, ABC News, the British Broadcasting Corporation, along with television reporters from St. Louis and Chicago—all visited Bull Shoals Lake and filed favorable reports about the one hundred men, women, and children who lived there. "Although our doctrine was extreme," writes Noble, "we were considered hard workers by neighbors [and] we didn't cause problems. . . . We had our own private school, with children unaffected by drugs, violence, abusive parents, child molesters, or kidnappers."[19]

The CSA operated not as a cult, therefore, but as an open religious community with strong conservative values that resonated deeply with the mainstream political establishment. Ellison's flock did not conceal their contempt for the federal government—or for what President Reagan derisively called "big government"; instead, they disseminated their views widely in the *C.S.A. Journal*. Along with its editorials, the *Journal* regularly carried instructions for the use of fully automatic weapons, as well as detailed guides for hand-to-hand combat (one article describes how to slit the throat of an enemy with a buck knife). For a while, the CSA ran a health food store in Mountain Home. Noble wrote letters to the editor of the town's *Baxter Bulletin*, urging Christians to follow biblical teachings rather than obey secular laws. Ellison held an annual convention at the CSA, and his advertisements for these gatherings were carried in such publications as the *Eagle*, a nationally distributed survivalist magazine, and they included opportunities to participate in guerrilla training at Silhouette City. Randall Rader felt comfortable enough in the local community to once contemplate a run for the elected office of county constable. Ellison remained on good terms with the Marion County sheriff, Roger Edmondson. Their relationship was so agreeable, in fact, that at Ellison's request Edmondson periodically ran background checks on individuals seeking refuge at the commune.

Spurred by the positive media attention and the favorable relationships CSA enjoyed with the locals, Ellison continued his pattern of reforecasting doomsday prophesies. In his next vision, Ellison received word that he was sinless and invincible. He was nothing less than the reincarnation of the biblical King David. This led Ellison to proclaim in

1982 that he was "King James of the Ozarks." Ellison underwent an elaborate coronation in a Christian Identity ceremony presided over by Pastor Robert Millar, who headed the four hundred-acre Identity commune near Muldrow, Oklahoma, called Elohim City (*Elohim* is the Hebrew word for God). Ellison said that God had warned him that war was imminent, and that he must prepare to defend his congregation against the onslaught of urban infidels. In order to finance the resources necessary to defend against that invasion, Ellison preached that it was proper to steal from non-Identity believers, a concept he termed "plundering the Egyptians."

Ellison's proclamation was met with disapproval by the commune's more law-abiding members. Nevertheless, he made an even more unpopular decision in 1982: because he was above sin, he had been told by God to take a second wife.

Women play an important role in the racist right. More than anything, racist groups emphasize women's familial roles. According to terrorism scholar Jessica Stern's interview with Kerry Noble's wife, Kay, this was taken to an extreme at the CSA. "Women called their husbands 'lord' as a sign of respect," she said, "in imitation of the way the biblical Sarah referred to her husband, Abraham."[20] First and foremost, CSA women were expected to fulfill their obligations to their husbands—and to the movement—by bearing Aryan babies. The women were also expected to act as social facilitators by "going along with the program," as it were. According to sociologist Kathleen Blee, when social ties are strengthened, individual racists come to view themselves as part of a larger social movement, thereby giving them a collective identity. In this way, women help create what Blee calls "the 'oppositional subculture' by which organized racism is sustained over time."[21]

Ollie Ellison had done much to fulfill these obligations. By 1982, she had provided her husband with hearth and home and borne him six children. But Ollie could not go along with the program inspired by Ellison's prophesy on polygamy. Instead, she became despondent over Ellison's decision to take a twenty-nine-year-old minister's daughter from Minnesota, named Annie, as his second wife.

Shortly after this, Ollie started wandering the woods at night, praying to be saved from the Identity philosophy that had so profoundly changed her life. "Ollie was a great woman," said Noble. "But Ellison brought her shame and guilt when he took another wife. She also hated Identity and the paramilitary [training] was a problem for her. It was all over male dominance. She was not a hateful person."[22] Ollie was not alone.

Unwilling to commit crimes for Ellison, and unhappier still with his edict allowing polygamy, dozens of families fled the CSA settlement between 1982 and 1983. This left only the hard-core extremists, as evidenced by Noble's description of life inside the compound:

> Ellison had begun letting people move to CSA that we wouldn't have let in years earlier. Where cigarette smoking had once never been allowed, butts littered the grounds. Where beer drinking had previously not been tolerated, bottles cluttered the trash cans. Where years before a single cuss word was never uttered, foul language flowed steadily. Where once praise meetings were frequent and all were anxious to attend, we seldom had meetings. Ellison was no longer looking for spiritual leaders. Now, he just wanted to build an army.[23]

That suited Rader just fine. In early 1982, he made plans to bomb a dam that controlled the water supply for a three-county area of northern Arkansas. Around the same time, while attending a survivalist seminar in Detroit, Rader and Ellison took possession of a thirty-gallon barrel of cyanide from Pastor Robert Miles, a Michigan Klan leader who had recently served time in Marion Federal Prison for firebombing ten empty school buses. "The purpose of the cyanide," Nobel confessed, "was so that in the future, when the judgment time had arrived, we could dump the cyanide into the water supply systems of major cities, condemning hundreds of thousands of people to death for their sins."[24]

Organization

In July 1983, Ellison was invited to give the closing address before the Aryan World Congress. The event, scurrilously billed as the "Annual Summer Conference and Nigger Shoot," was hosted by the American neo-Nazi Identity preacher Richard Butler at his rural compound near Hayden Lake, Idaho. In his speech, Ellison announced that the FBI's recent killing in southern Arkansas of tax protestor Gordon Kahl was a call to arms. Kahl was a member of yet another paramilitary group—the Posse Comitatus—with a sense of living in apocalyptic time. "Kahl was the catalyst," Ellison said later, "that made everyone come forth and change the [various neo-Nazi] organizations from thinkers to doers."[25]

That process began with a series of late-night meetings in which Ellison, Butler, Miles, Louis Beam ("ambassador-at-large" for the Aryan Nations), and other Identity leaders discussed how to overthrow the United States government and create a separate Aryan homeland in the Northwest. These discussions centered on William Pierce's *The Turner Diaries*, an extremist novel that envisions the government's overthrow by a white-supremacist guerrilla force known as the Order. In the book, the group systematically kills Jews and blacks, and then wages war against the U.S. government through the bombing of FBI headquarters in Washington. From these discussions emerged a sort of specialization within the radical Right.

Because Butler's organization served as the annual mecca for movement gatherings, Aryan Nations would become the public face of the campaign. The organization would issue press releases, recruit new members, and establish communications systems, including a computer bulletin board. The CSA would arm the movement and serve as its training center. Finally, an elite cadre of "Silent Warriors" would mount attacks against the government and its agents, including armed robberies to finance the revolution. This group would be composed of select CSA members, along with a new contingent of racists called the Order.

THE ATTACKS

Ellison returned from the Aryan Congress with more enthusiasm than he'd had in years. He called his elders together and told them that it was finally time to make war. "If the left wing could do it in the sixties," he said, "the right wing can do it in the eighties."[26] In a symbolic gesture of this new campaign, Ellison delivered his sermons wearing camouflage gear and carrying a gun. He also placed a swastika over the cross in the Sanctuary and ended his prayers with the straight-arm salute. The war, as Noble recalls Ellison's telling of it, involved "dumping cyanide into the reservoirs of major cities, killing federal agents, blowing up an [Anti-Defamation League] building or overpass in major cities; maybe even blowing up a federal building."[27]

In early August 1983, at Ellison's command, CSA member James Morris stole a load of helmets, uniforms, and other military equipment upon his discharge from the Marines. Although this was just the beginning of Ellison's war on ZOG, in many ways it would be the CSA's most successful crime. Though long on ideology, the group was short on criminal skill. "The CSA was not very successful," said Danny Coulson, then head of the FBI's counter-terrorism unit, "but they were very dangerous."[28]

On August 9, 1983, Ellison drove CSA elder Bill Thomas to Springfield, Missouri. As Ellison waited in the car under the cover of night, Thomas approached the Metropolitan Community Church, which openly supported gay rights, carrying a gallon of gasoline. Thomas shoved the gas can into the mail slot of the front door and ignited it. The attack was an abject failure: beyond charring the door, no major damage was done.

Six days later, Ellison and Thomas drove to Bloomington, Indiana, where they cased banks for a robbery. Unable to locate a suitable target, they firebombed the Beth Shalom synagogue. The small explosion destroyed an old Torah and burned a curtain. Beyond that, there was no major damage.

Richard Snell made his debut as an Aryan warrior on November 2 when he, Thomas, and CSA member Steve Scott strapped twenty-three sticks of dynamite to a natural gas pipeline where it crossed the Red River between Mena and Texarkana, Arkansas. Snell and his confederates believed that the pipeline was the major feeder from the gas fields in the Gulf of Mexico to the metropolitan arteries of Chicago, with its vast African American and Latino populations. "It was winter [sic]," Noble remembered. "We thought people would freeze, that they might start riots."[29] The dynamite dented the pipe but failed to rupture it. Once more, the CSA had failed to kick off its holy war.

By this time, with most of the hard-working timber and salvage workers gone from the CSA, money had become a serious problem for Ellison. So he ordered his men to step up their efforts to plunder the Egyptians. Small groups were dispatched to nearby towns on shoplifting sprees, concentrating on CB radios, car stereos, portable TVs, and jewelry. (Several vehicles were also stolen and driven to the CSA.) Members would later pawn this stolen merchandise for cash. Ellison himself participated in the crime spree, though he was not much of a criminal. On one trip to Forth Smith, Arkansas, Ellison was caught shoplifting at a grocery store; the manager simply threw Ellison out without calling the police. Some CSA members planned to rob a pawnshop in Springfield, Missouri, but the robbery never took place. Others planned a jewelry heist in Las Vegas, but it was canceled, too.

The only successful CSA robbery that was committed was marked by a ruthlessness that far exceeded its benefit. On November 11, Snell and Thomas robbed a pawnshop in Texarkana. During the holdup, Snell put a Ruger .22-caliber semi-automatic pistol to the head of the proprietor, William Strumpp, assuming him to be Jewish (he was not), and fired three times, killing him. After stealing guns, jewelry, and several thousand dollars in cash, Snell reported back to Ellison and proclaimed that Strumpp was "an evil man, he was a Jew, and he just needed to die." Later that evening, overcome with guilt, Bill Thomas fled the CSA commune.

By this time—the fall of 1983—Richard and Mary Snell had purchased a small plot of land in Muse, Oklahoma (population 306), where they lived in a house trailer. Snell's daughter had recently moved to Robert Millar's Identity enclave up at Elohim City, so there was just the two of them. Out back, Snell and Steve Scott had built a crude survival training camp, and the two had begun to attract a small following. They recruited their men through the usual methods: gun shows, Klan breakfasts, and the like.

Around this time, Snell took a step toward avenging his personal hatred of the federal government. Consistent with the plot of *The Turner Diaries*, this one called for mass murder. According to court documents, in October 1983, Snell came to Ellison and asked him if "in his opinion . . . it [would] be practical to blow up a federal building in Oklahoma City, or possibly a federal building in Dallas or Fort Worth, Texas." This discussion evolved into a plan to park a vehicle in front of the Oklahoma City Federal Building and blow it up with rockets detonated by a timer. Snell, Ellison, and Scott subsequently traveled to Oklahoma City where, posing as maintenance workers in brown uniforms, they entered the Murrah Federal Building and assessed what it would take to destroy it. Ellison carried a notepad on which he made sketches showing where the building was most vulnerable to collapse from the explosion of rocket launchers that were to be placed in a van. Ellison said: "[The van] could be driven up to a given spot, parked there, and a timed detonating device could be triggered so that the driver could walk away and leave the vehicle in a position and he would have time to clear the area before the rockets launched."[30]

As these plans progressed, the CSA continued its bleak crusade of terror. In December, sixty-eight-year-old William Wade approached Ellison with a plan that also came from the pages of *The Turner Diaries.* Wade owned the land where Gordon Kahl had been killed by federal agents a year earlier. Still bitter over the affair, Wade solicited the CSA's help in assassinating the judge, U.S. attorney, and federal agent who were involved in the prosecution of those who had harbored Kahl. Accordingly, on December 26, Richard Snell along with CSA members Ivan Wade, Lambert Miller, and David McGuire set out for Fort Smith to kill FBI special agent Jack Knox, U.S. District Judge H. Franklin Waters, and U.S. Attorney Asa Hutchinson. But a snow storm prevented the group from reaching Fort Smith, and the assassinations never occurred.

Shortly thereafter, Noble began pleading with Ellison to abandon violence and return to spiritual matters. After Ellison accused his top lieutenant of being a traitor, Noble made a desperate bid to prove his loyalty. He traveled to Kansas City, Missouri, with a briefcase full of C-4, dynamite, and a .22 pistol equipped with a silencer. Noble had been given orders to blow up an adult bookstore and then go on a shooting rampage at a "queer park." When the bookstore owner wouldn't let him in with his briefcase, Noble decided to bomb a church that ministered to homosexuals. When it came time to set the switch, however, Noble picked up his briefcase and walked away.

Meltdown: "War of '84"

By end of 1983, Ellison had begun to envision himself as a founding father of the second American Revolution, even though his campaign of terror had produced nothing of the kind. In a four-page declaration entitled the "War of '84," Ellison avowed, "It is inevitable that war is coming to the United States of America . . . It is predestined!" He implored his warriors "to attack the enemy at every opportunity." For Ellison, this was judgment day, the beginning of the great apocalyptic battle itself. The "War of '84" would prove to be one more example of Ellison's delusions of grandeur. Instead, 1984 saw the CSA spiral downward in a series of events distinguished only by their rapacious violence and criminal ineptitude.

First was the absurd plan to strike the Oklahoma City Federal Building with rocket launchers. After casing the Murrah Building, Ellison designed a remote-controlled bomb and asked Kent Yates to put it together for him. In early December 1983, Yates began preparing and testing rockets for the attack. In one of his first test runs, however, a rocket blew up in Yates's hands, burning them severely. With Yates unable to handle anything, let alone a rocket, his tenure as the CSA's munitions expert came to an end. And with it came an end to the CSA's plan to bomb the Murrah Building—at least for the time being. Yates's accident "was interpreted as a sign from God," Noble warned, "that another plan was to be implemented [at a later date]."[31]

Next was the equally preposterous plan to poison municipal water supplies with thirty gallons of cyanide. As Jessica Stern observes, potassium cyanide is *not* a sophisticated weapon of mass destruction. It is commonly found in rat poison, silver and metal polishes, photographic solutions, and cleaning products. Although cyanide is highly toxic, it is not a simple task to deliver it in a fashion capable of killing large numbers of people. Citing a United Nations study, Stern shows that the amount of potassium cyanide required to poison an untreated reservoir is ten tons. The effects of water dilution on thirty gallons of cyanide would have rendered it completely ineffective.[32] Even if the CSA had dumped the cyanide into the reservoir of a major city—the most frequently mentioned target was the nation's capitol—reservoir water is routinely tested and treated.

"At one point we put some of the cyanide into hollow point bullets and sealed them with hot wax," Noble said in 2005. "But other than that, we kept it locked up. Back then there were no books on [chemical warfare], we didn't have the Internet, and we didn't really know what we could do with it [the cyanide]. We were ignorant on that kind of thing."[33] Contributing to this ignorance was the fact that Ellison had failed to recruit a specialist in the area of chemical weaponry. In fact, by 1984 the CSA had lost all of its specialists.

That included Randall Rader, who had been gone since late 1982. It was then that Rader had been ostracized by the CSA following the tragic death of his thirteen-month-old daughter, who drowned in a basement full of water at the main compound while Rader was supposed to be watching her. Rader drifted aimlessly until he was invited to Idaho to run paramilitary training operations for the Order. "After Rader left," Flynn and Gerhardt write, "CSA went over the edge."[34] That became clear with Richard Snell's final act as a serial predator.

On the morning of June 30, 1984, Snell and Scott were pulled over for a routine traffic violation by state trooper Louis Bryant, a black officer, in DeQueen, Arkansas. Snell opened his door, got out of the vehicle, and drew a .45-caliber pistol that he had previously stolen in the pawnshop robbery. As Bryant approached, Snell shot him in the mid-section, then shot him again as he lay on the ground, killing him.

A trucker saw the incident and called the police. Roadblocks immediately went up twenty-five miles away in Broken Bow, Oklahoma, in the direction that Snell would likely be traveling. When Snell reached the roadblock forty minutes later, he again rolled out of his van, pulled a Ruger Mini-14 assault rifle on dozens of officers, and starting firing. The officers shot back, and Snell took seven bullets.

The fifty-four-year-old racist was loaded into an ambulance and rushed to the hospital. His heart stopped beating twice along the way, but he was revived both times. When Bureau of Alcohol, Tobacco, and Firearms agent Bill Buford arrived in Broken Bow to examine the cache of weapons found at the roadblock, he found the Ruger Mini-14 used in the shootout, along with several hand grenades, a silencer for a MAC-10, and a Ruger .22-caliber semi-automatic pistol. Buford also found a crude sketch of his own home. Agent Buford, it seems, was to have been Snell's next victim.

After running a firearm trace, Buford learned that the Ruger Mini-14 had been purchased in Jacksonville, Arkansas, by one James D. Ellison back in 1979. And the .22 Ruger semi-automatic—which subsequent ballistics tests determined was the weapon used in the killing of pawnshop owner William Strumpp—had been purchased several months earlier by Ellison in Marshville, Missouri.

This was the beginning of the end for Ellison and the CSA. At the request of Arkansas Governor Bill Clinton, Snell was extradited to Arkansas and charged with capital murder in the Strumpp case. Later that month, Kent Yates was arrested at the compound on an outstanding New Mexico warrant for federal firearms violations. Bill Thomas was later arrested in Missouri on charges stemming from the pawnshop murder. Facing the death penalty, he turned state's evidence against Snell and revealed information about other illegal activities at the CSA. Then, in late August, Ellison received a summons from a federal grand jury in Muskogee, Oklahoma, investigating the murder of trooper Bryant. The grand jury wanted to question Ellison about the guns found in Snell's van at the Broken Bow roadblock.

Ellison had no intention of cooperating and sent a letter back to the grand jury, saying that he was unable to appear due to problems with the mortgage on his property. A misdemeanor warrant was issued for his arrest, and a federal marshal, accompanied by state and federal officers, eventually tracked Ellison to his attorney's office in Yellville, Arkansas. Accompanying Ellison was his "spiritual advisor," Robert Millar. As the agents questioned Millar about his relationship with Ellison, Ellison slipped out the back door, jumped off a thirty-foot cliff, and escaped into the pines. Two days later, however, Ellison was taken into custody in Harrison, Arkansas.

Ellison made his grand jury appearance on September 26, three months after the murder of trooper Bryant. Ellison presented himself as a humble "woodcutter" with an interest in the religious lives of wayward youth, especially those with drug and alcohol problems. When asked about the firearms, Ellison claimed that he had traded the Ruger Mini-14 semi-automatic rifle to Richard Snell for a load of scrap automobile alternators. Ellison said he had no knowledge of Snell's involvement in the killing of Bryant, nor did he know anything about the .22-caliber Ruger used in the Strumpp murder. Ellison went on to say that while Snell was a frequent visitor to CSA, Snell was not a member of his congregation, nor did he live at the commune. And with that, Ellison was dismissed.

Yet the federal government was not through with James Ellison. In fact, Bill Buford had been gathering intelligence on the CSA since 1978. Over the years, Buford had developed a total of seven confidential informants, all of whom had first-hand knowledge of the CSA's criminal activities from having lived, often for many years, inside the compound. Buford flipped several of these people while they were in jail for non-CSA related offenses; others were enticed by financial considerations.[35] Through these informants, Buford learned that Ellison's organization was preparing for a confrontation with federal agents by stockpiling food, supplies, weapons, ammunition, and explosives. Inside his house, Ellison was said to have hidden thirty to forty pounds of C-4 plastic explosives and a .90-caliber automatic weapon. Also hidden on the property were another two hundred pounds of C-4 and C-3 explosives, hundreds of assault rifles, enormous quantities of ammunition, infrared night-vision devices, various types of hand grenades, four anti-aircraft weapons, and a military rocket launcher with a C-4 hand grenade in place and ready to fire—a weapon capable of destroying an armored personnel carrier. Claymore mines surrounded the camp, informants said, and the trees were rigged with trip wires and booby traps. In addition to these dangers, Buford's sources said that the CSA had kidnapped a number of children who were being "kept for Elohim City."

Around the time of Ellison's grand jury appearance, Buford started sharing his intelligence with Jack Knox of the FBI's Fayetteville office. (His office was *not* in Fort Smith as Snell and the others thought when they set out to assassinate him in late December.) This was mainly a bureaucratic strategy: if ATF agent Buford could prove that the CSA was involved in terrorist-related activities, then Ellison could be prosecuted under the Department of Justice's racketeering law, which demanded FBI participation in the case; hence, Buford's collaboration with Knox.

Also around this time, the physically imposing Ellison (he stood 5' 10" with wide shoulders, a thick chest, and large forearms) began to beat Ollie—sending her into an even deeper state of depression. "The abuse started after Ellison took his second wife," said Noble. "It was both physical and psychological."[36] Then another shoe fell: after months of Ellison's having failed to make payments, the bank foreclosed on the CSA property, and a judge ordered Ellison to get out within ten days.

With his paranoia at an all-time high, Ellison ordered Noble to prepare CSA's Home Guard for a possible incursion by ZOG. Far from a formidable threat, the Home Guard included such inexperienced and troubled young men as Mike McNabb. Due to a gunshot blast to the face at age thirteen, McNabb had only one eye and a damaged brain. McNabb was stabbed in the stomach two years later, causing even further harm to his system. Indeed, Noble described the Home Guard as "a unit that had a man fifteen years older than me that had an artificial leg; . . . an epileptic, retarded man; two half-blind, fat, young men; and two men who could care less about the military than I did."[37]

THE SIEGE

Ellison received an eleventh-hour reprieve on the foreclosure when a CSA sympathizer paid off the bank note on Ellison's property from monies obtained in an insurance settlement on a house fire. The reprieve, however, did little to quell his paranoia, which was fueled primarily by Governor Clinton. Following the murder of trooper Bryant, Clinton had taken steps that would make available to law enforcement a list of suspected or known members of Arkansas's numerous white supremacy groups. As part of that effort, in early 1985 Clinton convinced the state legislature to pass an anti-paramilitary training law designed by the Anti-Defamation League. These efforts placed the CSA squarely in the bull's eye. Then the unexpected happened.

In March 1985, the FBI received a tip that Order member Randy Evans, along with several other members of the group (Thomas Bentley, James Wallington, and Jefferson Butler), had moved into the CSA encampment to avoid arrests on outstanding warrants out of Washington, Idaho, and Colorado. Also with them was Sue West (a.k.a. Jean Carrigan), wife of one Walter West, who had been killed by the Order a year earlier. On March 19, Oklahoma state police found Sue West's body under a bridge on the Turner Turnpike. Her throat had been slit with a nine-inch knife. Over the next month, Buford's intelligence would lead the FBI to believe that the homicide was committed by an obscure CSA figure named James Rolston.

Back at the compound, Ellison bleached his black hair white to disguise his identity and designed an escape plan from Bull Shoals Lake. This plan involved a steel-plated personnel carrier that had been constructed on the chassis of a four-wheel drive truck. Mounted on top was an English-made anti-aircraft machine gun.

The stage was now set for the event that would trigger the siege.[38]

On Monday, April 15, Missouri state trooper Jimmie Linegar was conducting random traffic checks along a lonely stretch of highway between the tourist town of Branson, Missouri, and the Arkansas border. At 1:45 p.m., Linegar pulled over a brown 1975 Chevy van and asked the driver for his license. The young man behind the wheel complied, and Linegar returned to his cruiser to run a background check. The name on the license, Matthew Mark Samuels, corresponded to an alias used by a twenty-two-year-old neo-Nazi from Athol, Idaho, named David Tate. Coincidentally, earlier that day, federal authorities in Seattle had identified Tate as one of twenty-three people indicted on racketeering and conspiracy charges in connection with the terrorist activities of the Order. Specifically, Tate was wanted for the murder of Walter West.

Sensing trouble, Linegar radioed for backup, and trooper Allen Hines rolled up minutes later. As the two officers approached the van,

Tate opened the door and lurched onto the ground, clutching a .380-caliber Ingram MAC-11 automatic machine pistol. As Linegar reached for his service revolver, Tate opened fire. The bullets slammed into Linegar's side, killing him instantly. Tate ran to the back of the van and fired three shots at Hines, hitting him in the arm, hip, and neck. Then Tate fled into the heavily-wooded terrain.

A massive manhunt was launched involving a combined force of FBI SWAT teams, Missouri state police, and local deputy sheriffs. Armed Cobra gun-ship helicopters from the Missouri National Guard flew over the Ozarks while bloodhounds tore through the dense underbrush. FBI agents tried to pick up Tate using sensors aboard a bureau spy plane capable of detecting living humans in total darkness by their body heat. Roadblocks were set up, and Tate's picture appeared on television and was posted in local stores. During the sweep, agents stumbled onto twenty-six-year-old Frank Silva, another Order fugitive, and arrested him at the Safari Campground near Beaver Lake in Benton County, Arkansas. But Tate eluded the dragnet.

Meanwhile, a search of Tate's abandoned vehicle had turned up a veritable arsenal, including six machine guns, three handguns, a sniper rifle, two assault rifles, dynamite, hand grenades, a pint whiskey bottle filled with nitroglycerine, boxes of silencers, and thousands of rounds of ammunition. Officers also found police scanners, knives, camping gear, ski masks, and four birth certificates for Tate aliases. Along with evidence gathered for the indictment against the Order, these discoveries led agents to believe that Tate was making his way on foot to the CSA compound at Bull Shoals Lake (an hour and a half drive from Branson), where he would find sanctuary among the Identity Christians. Buford's intelligence indicated that Tate had visited the compound back in 1981. "Tate was just a punk kid then," said Noble. "He came for our national convention with Richard Butler from Aryan Nations."[39]

News of these events, monitored by Ellison and his followers back at the CSA communications office, sent the group into a state of panic. "By then we had TV," Noble recalled, "but we had no idea that he [Tate] was coming to CSA. We were already nervous because we had seen federal cars in Mountain Home and the media was on the road outside the compound everyday."[40] The paranoia was especially acute among the four Order fugitives who expected the police to use the search for Tate as a pretext to raid the encampment. The Home Guard may not have posed much of a threat to outsiders, but the Order did. Consequently,

Ellison vowed not to leave his house until the commotion over Tate had died down. In the meantime, the CSA began to destroy some of their weapons in anticipation of a raid.

On Tuesday, April 16, Jack Knox took the FBI's case to the United States magistrate in Fort Smith, seeking a search warrant to allow agents to enter the CSA camp. Knox got his warrant, charging Ellison with racketeering, kidnapping, bombing, arson, attempted murder, and a raft of federal firearm violations. The warrant also listed a knife that may have been used in the murder of Sue West. The next day, United States Attorney General Edwin M. Meese arrived in Fort Smith to oversee the government's unfolding case against Ellison.

On Thursday, April 18, Sergeant Gene Irby, an Arkansas State Police officer who was well-known to the CSA residents, appeared at the front gate of the compound and informed Kerry Noble that a federal warrant had been issued for Ellison. After delivering the news to Ellison, Noble returned to the gate and told Irby that Ellison wanted to pray about it overnight. The request was granted.

Around ten o'clock the next morning—Friday, April 19—Irby returned to the front gate only to be told by Noble that Ellison was refusing to surrender. The FBI then set up roadblocks, established a siege perimeter, and surrounded the encampment with a massive contingent of two hundred heavily armed agents. A Huey helicopter and an armed personnel carrier were brought in. "At this point," said Danny Coulson, "the FBI was contemplating the biggest shoot-out in its history."[41]

TERRORISM, FEMINISM, AND CONFLICT RESOLUTION

As helicopter gun ships hovered near the compound, negotiations began between Noble and Coulson, the FBI's Hostage Rescue Team commander. "April 19 was our D day," Coulson would later write in his penetrating account of his negotiations with the CSA. "They expected ZOG to come in and shoot the place up . . . We had to convince them that we weren't the devils they were waiting for, and that we were patient and that we weren't going away."[42] Of special concern to the FBI were the sixteen women and at least two dozen children inside the camp.

By Saturday morning, April 20, the siege was receiving extensive coverage by local and national media. One of the reporters, James Coates of the *Chicago Tribune*, filed this account:

A solid chain link gate closed off the dirt road leading up to the CSA compound, and all visitors were greeted by a group of roughly a half dozen obviously frightened and surly young men carrying Mini-14s, MAC 10s, and other automatic and semi-automatic weapons. Other armed CSA soldiers were clearly visible in a fifty-foot-tall guard tower overlooking the front gate, from which they pointed machine guns at reporters. . . . [A] large number of buzzards . . . circled lazily overhead, almost as if they had some foreknowledge that blood soon would spill. . . . FBI commandos congregated on the fringes of the compound. Trim men in spit-shined paratroop boots sat around assault helicopters just out of sight from the CSA guard tower and painted one another's faces in camouflage makeup.[43]

Ellison was still refusing to surrender, primarily because of a drama being played out inside the compound. Early in the day, Randy Evans tried to marshal the CSA forces into a shoot-out with the FBI because it was Adolf Hitler's birthday. Ellison stifled this Aryan bravado by punching Evans in the eye, knocking him down and shutting him up. After that, the negotiations began in earnest. This was due to several key events that transpired over the next two days.

First, on Sunday, April 21, Ellison allowed four women and twelve children to leave the camp, thus removing a major source of concern on both sides. Second, later that day, a filthy and exhausted David Tate was captured in a city park near Branson without a shot being fired (he had simply laid down his MAC-11), thereby eliminating another source of concern for both Ellison and the FBI. Finally, and most importantly, Coulson allowed Ellison to bring in two third-party negotiators.

The first was Ollie Ellison. Appreciating the social role of women in Identity circles, Coulson remarked: "In that culture, women are honored for their intuition. Our meeting was very brief. Her purpose was to size us up. To see if I was a man of honor."[44] In his memoir, No Heroes, Couslon is almost rhapsodic in his description of their meeting at the siege perimeter on April 21:

Ollie Ellison gave me a Mona Lisa smile and a slight nod. . . . This was not the terrified, beaten-down gun nut's wife I had envisioned. Ollie was a true beauty, five feet seven or five feet eight inches tall, with long dark hair, and high cheekbones that reminded me of Emmylou Harris or Rita Coolidge. In a modest sleeveless print dress that hung loosely below her knees, she might have been a flower child or a Berkeley grad student . . . The lives of every man, woman, and child depended on her, including eleven children under her own roof. We had to be her worst nightmare, ZOG warriors, men poised to launch an attack upon her home. Yet her eyes were cool and intelligent. She stood ramrod straight, shoulders back, chin up.[45]

After Coulson assured Ollie that only Ellison would be arrested, though others inside the compound could be arrested in the future, and that the agents would not bust up CSA homes during the search for evidence, Ollie convinced her husband to surrender. Never has a woman in the American racist right played such a defining role in mediating a conflict. "She was totally unique," said Coulson, who had managed dozens of hostage situations during his acclaimed career. "I was very impressed with her. Our meeting was the first place for failure, and we had a lot of stigma to break through. I play for breaks, and I got one with Ollie."[46]

But Evans and the other neo-Nazis were still inside, and they had no intention of laying down their weapons. Seeking to accomplish that end, Coulson permitted Ellison to call in the second third-party negotiator: Robert Millar. Coulson dispatched a plane to Oklahoma to pick up the Identity patriarch. He arrived around noon and was permitted to join Ellison for a prayer meeting with Evans and the others. At 3:30 p.m., Millar radioed Coulson with the bad news: while he was making progress, Millar needed to stay overnight. The request was granted.

At 10:05 a.m. on Monday, April 22, Ellison, Millar, and Noble came to the perimeter with a document listing the CSA's terms of surrender. Most of the twenty-three items in the document dealt with Ellison's legal counsel and the conditions of his incarceration. Before surrendering, though, Ellison demanded that he be able to return to his house so that he could comb his hair for the media photographers at the roadblock. Coulson agreed, and shortly after noon, four days into the siege, sixty-four occupants of the CSA camp, including the four wanted members of the Order, walked out of the encampment with their hands on their heads. Agents then entered the CSA where they confiscated evidence leading to a nineteen-part indictment against Ellison and five accomplices. The Order fugitives would be tried separately.

The next day, the *Baxter Bulletin* carried a photograph of the backside of an ATF agent with a blond-haired girl laying her head on his shoulder.[47] The photo was picked up by wire services and carried nationwide. It later became a symbol on plaques awarded by the ATF to agents for outstanding service. The plaque—called "In the Arms of the Law"—symbolized everything federal law enforcement stood for: the need to rescue innocents from evil. It would endure as a symbol of federal law enforcement until it was replaced by another iconic photograph, this one taken on April 19, 1995. This photo showed a fireman turning from the hellish jumble of glass, steel, and concrete of the demolished Federal Building in Oklahoma City. In his arms is the body of a dead baby.

4

Charisma, Conflict, and Style

The Order

Edwin Sutherland argued that all criminal behavior is learned, and that it is learned in interaction with other persons in a process of interpersonal communication. According to Sutherland, this learning process involves two characteristics: techniques of committing the crime—skill, or criminal trade craft—which can sometimes be very complicated; and ideology, or the specific motives for the offense.[1] Because terrorism is a special form of criminality (arguably, it is the most serious form of criminality within any society), it requires a third element in a person who is willing to use it as a tactic: fanatical dedication to a cause. The confluence of skill, ideology, and fanatical dedication has been the engine driving most terrorist groups throughout history. Yet in the rarest of cases—reserved only for the followers of Carlos the Jackal, Osama bin Laden, and a few others—there has been a fourth dimension of terrorism. And that is charisma, or the power of the gifted.

Sociologist Max Weber viewed charisma as an inherent gift that evoked the loyalty of people afflicted by a crisis so great as to defy resolution by constituted authorities or institutions. A charismatic person is seen as capable of alleviating the crisis and restoring equilibrium to the community. This person's capabilities are a function of his or her unique talents; indeed, the charismatic leader's authority derives solely from these talents. Psychologist William Fried points out that the characteristics of a leader's talents will always be a function of the nature of the crisis facing the community.[2] Therefore, if the crisis involves spiritual decay, the leader's gifts will be in the area of religion. If the crisis involves disease or famine, the gifts tend to be organizational. If the critical problem involves political conflict, the gifts will be in the realm of oratory. And if that conflict leads to violence, the leader is likely to be gifted in military tactics.

In practice, most charismatic leaders are endowed with not one, but with combinations of these gifts in varying measures. Fidel Castro, one of the most charismatic leaders of modern times, has proven to be an exceptional administrator, an electrifying orator, a fabled paramilitary commander, and a deified social reformer. Castro is not a terrorist in the classic definition of the term, but some of his personal gifts *have* been ascribed to the man who led the near-mythical American neo-Nazi terrorist cell known as the Order. "It was the way he carried himself," remembered a confederate, "sinuously, as though at any moment he were poised to leap—a graceful leap to some strange place."[3]

BACKGROUND

On December 30, 1985, ten members of the Order were convicted of racketeering charges following a four-month federal court case in Seattle. Founded in 1983 by Robert Mathews, the Order (also known as the Silent Brotherhood), drew its members from James Ellison's CSA, Aryan Nations, and various Klan splinter groups. As a blueprint for their "revolution," the Order relied on William Pierce's novel, *The Turner Diaries*, and many of the crimes for which Order members were convicted resembled terrorist acts described in the book.

The Revolutionary

Robert Jay Mathews was born into a hard-working, middle-class family in the small, desolate town of Marfa, Texas, on January 16, 1953.[4] His father, Johnny, ran an appliance store in Marfa, and his mother, Una, stayed home to raise "Robbie" and his two older brothers. Research suggests that the formative years of a charismatic leader may be marked by such experiences as profound loss, injustice, repeated episodes of failure and/or humiliation, and early exposure to rigid belief systems. It was this last experience that would shape Mathews's eventual leadership style.

The world began to change for the Mathews family in 1957. Hard times had fallen on Marfa, and business at Mathews Appliance was in trouble. After selling the store, Johnny went into the import-export business, but that failed, too. When he next took a job as an insurance agent, that also proved to be fruitless. By late 1958 he was broke. Una sold enough of their personal property to stake a road trip, and before Christmas the Mathews family left Texas. Johnny Mathews and his wife had worked hard, raised themselves to prominent stature in the community, and then were summarily beaten into rank poverty.

They settled in Phoenix where Johnny found work as an accountant. Una went to work in a bank and the boys continued their schooling. Robbie excelled at history and, with his mother's encouragement, became an avid reader of the daily newspaper. In 1964, the biggest news story in Phoenix was the presidential race between Lyndon Johnson and Barry Goldwater, the hard-line conservative who represented Arizona in the U.S. Senate. At the time, Goldwater advocated using small nuclear bombs to defoliate the jungles of South Vietnam. Against this perilous backdrop, Mathews experienced the most significant change of his early life.

On Sunday, October 25, 1964, the *Arizona Republic* ran a sixteen-page special feature on the John Birch Society. The Birch Society was then waging a media assault against the communist influence—something that resonated deeply among Goldwater supporters. Mathews locked himself in his bedroom and studied the article fully. The thought of Russian communists taking over America seemed to have frightened him severely. Mathews clipped a coupon for more information and sent it into regional headquarters in Santa Monica, California. Shortly thereafter, Mathews became a card-carrying member of the John Birch Society. He was twelve years old.

Thus began his journey into political extremism. As Mathews entered his teenage years, he rebelled against the fad and fashion of sixties youth subculture by adopting a hard, iconoclastic masculinity. At a time when millions of youth were letting their freak flags fly, Mathews kept his hair short and stayed away from marijuana and LSD. Nor did he date. Instead he took up wrestling and weight-lifting, trimming off his body fat and leaving him as fit as a Marine. In his Birch Society meetings, Mathews learned the skill of public speaking and began to express his feelings about patriotism and what he took to be the communist menace.

His involvement with the Birch Society coincided with two other pivotal events that contributed to his emerging extremism. First, in 1969 the Mathews family moved to Tempe where Robbie enrolled in a high school dominated by Mormons. Mathews viewed these students as quintessential Americans. Like him, they were clean cut, diligent, and proudly conservative. And second, through contacts made upon joining the Mormon Church in 1970, Mathews began attending tax resistance seminars. Here he was taught that paying income taxes was not only illegal, but that doing so actually aided the communists. His enthusiasm for the subject was contagious, and Mathews was rewarded by an appointment to the post of Sergeant-at-arms for the seminars. At this point, according to Flynn and Gerhardt, "Una and Johnny began to worry that their youngest son was turning into a revolutionary."[5] What began as a hatred of the Soviets was now turning into a hatred of the United States. This would affect Mathews's educational career and everything that followed.

Robbie began his senior year of high school in 1970. Soon he got into an argument with his economics teacher over the efficacy of the Keynesian theory of government intervention in the free market. Through the tax resistance seminars, Mathews had been taught that President Franklin D. Roosevelt's endorsement of Keynesian theory was responsible for leading America into the first stages of socialism. In protest against his teacher's approval of Keynesian theory, Robbie stopped going to class altogether. When informed that this would affect his chances of getting into college, Mathews told his parents that he wasn't going to college because universities were nothing more than "hotbeds of communism."

By the end of 1971, Mathews was adrift. Because he failed to complete his economics course, he was not allowed to graduate from high school. Unemployed, unskilled, and romantically unattached, he drifted further onto the fringes of the extreme right where he came under the influence of an organization called the Minutemen. Founded by Robert Boliver DePugh in Independence, Missouri, in the early 1960s, the Minutemen ultimately became one of the most formidable right-wing groups in America. DePugh's followers carried military-style weapons, were organized into secret cells, and were dedicated to eradicating communist infiltrators whom they believed to be working for the U.S. government.

In 1972, nineteen-year-old Robert Mathews assembled a ragtag guerrilla army of his own. He drew his followers from the tax resister's group, from the Mormon Church, and from local gun and motorcycle shops. In all, Mathews recruited some thirty men into a group he christened the Sons of Liberty. And it was here that Mathews began to show the first signs of charismatic leadership.

That summer, Mathews anonymously phoned a Phoenix television reporter and told him that the Sons of Liberty were training for guerrilla war in the desert. Knowing a good story when he heard one, the reporter showed up with a camera crew at night at a prearranged location where he was met by a band of camouflage-masked men with assault rifles and bandoliers of ammunition and grenades strapped to their chests. As the film rolled, one of them stepped forth and proudly said: "We are the Sons of Liberty." The film showed a young white man speaking with confidence and passion. He said that the Sons were made up of army vets who believed that the United States was doomed to collapse under communist infiltration. Twenty-four hour later, after the reporter contacted the FBI and turned over his tapes, a federal investigation was launched to find out the identity of the articulate young man behind the camouflage mask.

By day, Mathews was now working at a Carnation plant making ice cream. By night, he split his time between the Sons of Liberty, the Birch Society, the tax resisters, and the Young Republicans. Through this ambitious political activity, Mathews honed his orator's gift, impressing the older activists with his hatred for communists and tax collectors.

In the fall of 1972, the FBI found a snitch inside the Sons of Liberty who could identify the individual on the news tape. It was a young Mormon tax protestor named Robbie Mathews. Agents then visited Johnny Mathews at his home in Tempe. Robbie had left town, Johnny told the feds, whereabouts unknown.

The Good Lieutenant

Charismatic leaders are only as good as the loyalty they inspire in their followers. For Robert Mathews, no one would prove as loyal as Bruce Pierce.

Bruce Carroll Pierce was born in Frankfort, Kentucky, on May 14, 1954.[6] His father, Eugene, was a successful carpenter, specializing in wood furniture. Lucilla, Pierce's mother, was a housewife who gave birth to Bruce late in life; she had borne four children some twenty years earlier, and now they were raised and living on their own. For all practical purposes, Bruce Pierce was an only child.

Pierce's childhood was marked by intense isolation. With no siblings around and few neighbors to play with, he spent most of his time alone, exploring the hills around Devil's Hollow Road, several miles from the desolate grave of Daniel Boone. The boy dreamed of working with his father in the carpentry shop, as had his older brothers before him, but that dream vanished in1967 when an arsonist burned the shop down and Eugene retired from the business. Two years later, Pierce underwent another trial when his parents divorced after years of marital problems.

Bruce was an average student at Frankfort High School, yet at a strapping six-foot-two he easily made the varsity basketball team. He also had no trouble with the opposite sex, and during his senior year Bruce's girlfriend, Elizabeth Scott, became pregnant. After secretly marrying on April 1, 1972, Pierce exhibited the first signs of a character flaw that would dog him for years to come. Smarting from an argument with Lucilla over Elizabeth's pregnancy, Bruce impetuously dropped out of school before graduation and headed to Atlanta with his young bride.

A year later the couple returned to Frankfort where Pierce landed a job as a circulation manager for the *Lexington Herald Leader*. Over the next five years Pierce made friends, drove a sports car, wore fashionable clothing, smoked marijuana, and enjoyed listening to then-popular country rock bands like the Eagles. By 1979, though, he had grown tired of his job, and he impulsively resigned without employment prospects elsewhere. Having also grown tired of his wife, Pierce began a series of extramarital affairs.

His impetuous nature arose again later that year when Pierce confessed to Elizabeth that he was consumed with a dream of living in the wide-open expanses of the American West. Elizabeth would have no part of it, however, and in August she filed for divorce, leaving Pierce free to move to Missoula, Montana, with his brother Greg.

Bruce found work at a Western Wear store and moved with Greg into a house near the University of Montana. In late 1979, Pierce met a divorcee named Julie Wilson and by early 1980, they were living together with her infant daughter and his son, who had come for a visit with his father and stayed. A year later, the couple married. But things were not so rosy on the employment front.

Pierce left Western Wear and began to bounce from one menial job to the next. By 1981 he realized that the "romantic West" was not all it was cracked up to be. Pierce was a playboy at heart, and he missed his sports car, weed, friends, and the affairs he had left behind in Kentucky. Now, however, he was trapped in a house trailer with little money, a new wife, and two screaming kids. Things only got worse. In the fall of

1981 Pierce moved his family into a broken down house trailer on a mountainside near Plains, Montana. On November 22, 1982, Julie gave birth to the couple's third child, and Pierce was reduced to drawing food stamps. It was at this juncture that Pierce found solace in Christian Identity.

It all happened fortuitously. One day in the fall of 1982, while lifting weights at a Plains gymnasium, Pierce overheard a group of boys quarreling about the Holocaust. One boy maintained that the Holocaust was a hoax, and four others began to berate him. Pierce jumped to the lone boy's defense, and when the argument was over, the boy thanked Pierce. A week later, the boy brought his father to the gym and introduced him to Pierce. The man's name was Jefferson Butler, and over the next several months he introduced Pierce to the Identity philosophy.

In March 1983, another Identity convert invited Pierce to join him on a trip to the Church of Jesus Christ Christian at the Aryan Nations compound at Hayden Lake, Idaho. Pierce was introduced to Aryan Nations founder Pastor Richard Butler (no relation to Jefferson Butler) and a number of his followers. In these people, Pierce seemed to have found not only spiritual succor, but an escape from the loneliness that had afflicted him since moving west. Pierce returned to Aryan Nations with Julie and the kids several times, and soon he began to wear the blue uniform of an Aryan Nations security guard. The defining event of his life took place that summer.

On June 26, 1983, Butler led an Aryan Nations rally at the Riverfront Park in Spokane, Washington. Because the rally had attracted wide publicity and plans for counter-demonstrations, Butler arranged to have his security detail on hand. Pierce was among them, taking his place with a half dozen men at the base of the speaker's platform. In the crowd stood some three hundred Aryan Nations supporters and an equal number of counter-demonstrators, police, bystanders, and media people.

As Butler took the stage, protestors, including one with a bullhorn, began shouting, "Racists!" and "Nazis!" Near the stage a small group of protestors held signs reading "Smash Racism. Build Multiracial Unity." Some of them started pushing and shoving. Then a woman protestor stepped up to the security detail and kicked one of Butler's men in the groin.

At this point, a muscular guard moved toward the protestors with his arms outspread. He looked about thirty and was dressed simply in blue jeans and a T-shirt. His eyes showed fierce determination. When he reached the protestors, he pointed at them and unleashed a torrent of angry words. Shocked by the sheer force of the man's words, the protestors grew silent. Pierce felt himself drawn to the man's side, and together with the other guards, they linked arms to form a human wall and began forcing the protestors back.

It was an extraordinary moment for Pierce. He had never before engaged in political activism, let alone experienced a small victory like this one; but then again, Pierce had never witnessed such intensity as he saw in that man's eyes. For Pierce and the other guards at the rally that day, something about this man made a lasting impression. He was someone who clearly put action behind his words. This man was, of course, the charismatic Robert Mathews.

THE PLOT

Mathews had been in the Pacific Northwest for nearly a decade. He moved there in 1974, in his words, with "only twenty-five dollars to my name . . . and the dream of someday acquiring my own farmland."[7] Mathews found work first in a zinc mine and then at the Lehi Cement Company in Metaline Falls, Washington (population 850). After buying a fifty-three-acre plot of forested land and building a home, Mathews put a personal ad in *Mother Earth News* and thereby met Debbie McGarrity from Jackson, Wyoming. The couple married in 1976 and had a child four years later. Johnny, Una, and his two brothers moved onto the property in 1977.

During this period, Mathews continued his voracious reading of history. One book, *Which Way Western Man?* by the racist William Gayley Simpson, introduced Mathews to the idea that white Christians were in danger of losing their racial identity because of affirmative action and interracial marriage. The book's publisher, William Pierce (no relation to Bruce Pierce) of the Virginia-based National Alliance, also had a decisive influence on Mathews's thinking. In fact, Mathews worshiped William Pierce. Not only was he the author of *The Turner Diaries*, but Pierce was also responsible for introducing Mathews to Aryan Nations in 1982. A month after his show of leadership at the 1983 Spokane rally, Mathews attended the Aryan World Congress where he met James Ellison and the white supremacists who were about to begin their conspiracy to topple the federal government.

Bob Mathews and Bruce Pierce formed the Order, also known as *Bruders Schweigen*, or the Silent Brotherhood, at Mathews's home in September 1983.[8] They were accompanied by two Aryan Nations activists: Randy Duey, a thirty-two-year-old air force veteran and history student at Eastern Washington University, and a twenty-nine-year-old former marine and ex-convict from Arizona named Gary Lee Yarbrough. "The unifying thread binding them together," write Flynn and Gerhardt, "was their own brand of super-patriotism, based on their vision of America's meaning."[9] This vision formed the cultural myth of the Order and created a social space that allowed Mathews's charisma to flourish.

Organization

It was from here that Robert Mathews embarked upon one of the most profitable crime sprees in American history. More than anything, this required the creation of an effective criminal enterprise, something traditional racists had never been particularly good at. Most scholars assert that the Order achieved its criminal syndicate by integrating neo-Nazism with Christian Identity and the fantastic possibilities of *The Turner Diaries*.[10] As one member told undercover journalist Peter Lake at the dawning of the Order, "Read *The Turner Diaries*. It's all there." Beneath the surface, though, was a more precise criminal sensibility.

The Order was comprised of men who had come of age in the crucible of Vietnam, yet none of its inner circle had made a personal appearance on the battlefield. As adults, they came to view America as a land beset with dark forces of chaos in the forms of immigration, drugs, crime, and Ronald Reagan's "trickle down" economy. Since these hot-button issues were seeded with race and gender considerations, it became morally imperative for some powerless white men to transform their personal rage into a political cause. Masculinity and whiteness became entwined as never before—to be a "real" white man was to be hyper-masculine. In this way, paramilitary mythology became the path to redemption.[11]

This obsession was displayed in many ways. It was demonstrated in the behavior of men like Duey, Yarbrough, and Randall Rader, all of whom liked to play war but wanted no part of the real thing. It was also displayed in the Order's cultural orientation to everyday life. One of Mathews's favorite films was Charles Bronson's *Death Wish II*, the story of a vigilante who avenges his wife's death in a post-apocalyptic New York by killing a gang of street thugs. "That is what is wrong with society today," Mathews said of the fictional murders. "We have to do that because the government won't. Our police state doesn't do that. We have to cleanse the land ourselves."[12] Hence, the men of the Order fashioned themselves into Aryan warriors.

As he had done a decade earlier with the Sons of Liberty, Mathews recruited his followers from different sources—Aryan Nations, National Alliance, CSA, and the Klan. Because these were national organizations, Mathews was able to assemble some of the most dangerous white militants in America. "We were all a bunch of lost souls," said Order operative Tom Martinez. "Our parents were all fucked up."[13] While the Order would eventually include some fifty members, its "action group" was made up of nine men. In addition to Mathews, Pierce, Duey, and Yarbrough, they included:

- Andrew Barnhill, a twenty-seven-year-old former seminarian from Plantation, Florida, who was introduced to Ellison's CSA through his involvement in the American Pistol and Rifle Association. After Ellison anointed himself King of the Ozarks, Barnhill left the CSA and moved to Missoula where he became a poker dealer. He was recruited into the Order in 1983 by Bruce Pierce during a visit to Aryan Nations.
- Richard Kemp, a twenty-year-old former high-school basketball star from Salinas, California. Kemp met Mathews at a 1981 National Alliance convention in Virginia.
- David Lane, a forty-three-year-old champion amateur golfer from Aurora, Colorado. During the late 1970s, Lane was an organizer for David Duke's Knights of the Ku Klux Klan; in 1981 he became the Colorado organizer for Aryan Nations. A year later, Lane moved to Hayden Lake where he met Mathews, who later appointed him minister of propaganda for the Order.
- Denver Parmenter, a thirty-one-year-old former soldier with a drinking problem from Brownwood, Texas. After his honorable discharge from the Army, Parmenter became an administrator at Eastern Washington University. There he met Randy Duey who introduced him to Mathews. Parmenter would later say that he was an "unstable person" before joining the Order, but that Mathews had given him a purpose in life. "I thought we were

fighting the second American Revolution," said Parmenter. "Our goal was to take the government down."[14]

- Richard Scutari, a thirty-six-year-old former navy officer, deep sea diver, and martial arts expert from Port Salerno, Florida. In 1979, Scutari met Minutemen founder Robert DePugh at a conference in Fort Lauderdale, and later joined the American Pistol and Rifle Association. Through APRA, Scutari met Virgil Barnhill, Andrew's father. Andrew Barnhill then introduced Scutari to James Ellison, who, according to Flynn and Gerhardt, dispatched Scutari to South America to provide security at a CSA-owned gold mine. In early 1984, Andrew Barnhill invited Scutari to Metaline Falls where he was introduced to Mathews. Scutari would eventually become Mathews's closest confidant. But more importantly, Scutari's criminal skills would play a major role in the Order's reign of terrorism.

Most members of the Order were adherents of Christian Identity, though Mathews himself was an Odinist (a theological reconstruction of Viking-era Norse mythology). And like the fictitious guerrilla army in *The Diaries* (known as "The Order" or simply "The Organization"), the real-life Order began by drawing up a list of Jewish assassination targets. These included former Secretary of State Henry Kissinger and Baron Elie de Rothschild of the international Jewish banking family. The Order would finance its cause through armed robbery, thereby creating a "war chest" to support a campaign of violence against what propagandist David Lane termed "a coalition of blacks, browns, yellows, liberals, Communists, queers, race mixing religious zealots, race traitors, preachers, teachers and judges."

At the suggestion of Denver Parmenter, Mathews created cells for each operation and implemented security procedures to guard against informants—beginning with the requirement that each member take a loyalty oath in a ceremony where inductees held hands in a circle around a white infant that symbolized the future of the Aryan race. In his *Politics of Righteousness*, sociologist James Aho describes this oath, quoted below, as a "ritual ordination into the cult."[15]

I, as a free Aryan man, hereby swear an unrelenting oath there upon the green graves of our sires, upon the children in the wombs of our wives, upon the throne of God Almighty, sacred be his name, to join together in holy union with those brothers in this circle and to declare forthright from this moment on I have no fear of death, no fear of foe, that I have a sacred duty to do whatever is necessary to deliver our people from the Jew and bring total victory to the Aryan race.

The Order wrote the book on living in the white underground. For starters, each member was trained in the acquisition of false identity documents. This involved visiting cemeteries and locating tombstones showing the birth and death of an infant. Members would then use that information to apply for a death certificate. From the death certificate they would apply for a birth certificate. Once they had that in hand, they would apply for drivers' licenses and motor vehicle registrations. They also used code names. Pierce, for instance, was known as "Brigham" or "Logan" (good Mormon names). Yarbrough was called "Yosemite Sam" or "Reds" because of his long red beard. Scutari was known as "Mr. Black." And Mathews went by "Carlos"—in honor of the Jackal (more on this in the next chapter). Operating on a need-to-know basis, most Order members knew each other only by these code names, thus making the identification of accomplices impossible in the event of arrest by law enforcement.

Mathews eventually set up safe houses around the country—in Philadelphia, Boise, Idaho, and other small towns in the Northwest— and required his men to move frequently from location to location. The houses were rented under assumed names and paid for in cash, thus leaving no paper trail. Each member was also instructed in the use of disguises. They wore wigs, fake beards, and mustaches; some dyed their hair, and others dressed as women. They bought cars in cash using false names and were armed at all times. And, perhaps most important of all, in an effort to control informers, each Order member was required to periodically submit himself to one of Mr. Black's lie detector tests performed on a sophisticated voice stress analyzer. "The Order," said an FBI agent familiar with the case, "was the most organized group of terrorist-type people ever to have operated in the United States."[16]

THE ATTACKS

In her controversial work on the American neo-Nazi movement, *A Hundred Little Hitlers*, Elinor Langer correctly observes that "the Order is undoubtedly the best-known chapter in the history of the American racist movement in the 1980s."[17] This is due, in no small measure, to the outstanding research of journalists Kevin Flynn and Gary Gerhardt. Within the literature on right-wing American terrorism, Flynn and Gerhardt's *The Silent Brotherhood* is a book without peer. That said, it should be noted that Flynn and Gerhardt did not systematically examine the Order's crimes committed in support of a terrorist agenda. That was not their purpose; but it is mine.

These crimes began with a haphazard plan to rob drug dealers and pimps in Spokane. Around mid-October 1983, Mathews and two associates combed the downtown area for cocaine dealers and hookers. For the Order, these people stood for everything that was wrong with America. After several hours, they found a dealer and accosted him in an alley. Yet the dealer proved too tough, and the three Aryan warriors backed down.

So Mathews turned his attention to robbing a pornography store. On October 28, Mathews, Pierce, and Duey entered Spokane's World Wide Video Store disguised as Mexicans and armed with pistols and knives. They bound and gagged two clerks with duct tape and rifled the till, making off with a mere $369. The "revolution" was off to a poor start; in fact, it nearly imploded on take off.

Ten days later, Mathews, Pierce, Duey, Kemp, Parmenter, and two others loaded their cars with firearms and drove to Seattle where they conducted surveillance on armored vehicles which they intended to rob for the money they carried. They scouted these trucks for several days, taking note of security arrangements and timing getaway routes. During this time, two key events transpired

First, Pierce saw a newspaper story about an upcoming lecture at a Seattle synagogue by Baron Elie de Rothschild—one of the Order's assassination targets. This led to a split in the Order (which at this point was only weeks old). Contrary to the lore that has grown up around the Silent Brotherhood, Mathews's gang was not an authoritarian organization but a democratic one. Reflecting those roots, Pierce led one faction that wanted to jettison the armored truck heist in favor of a spontaneous plot to assassinate de Rothschild. In their discussions, Pierce's group talked about the possibility of conducting a suicide mission in which one of them would strap on a bomb and detonate it inside the Olympic Hotel, killing the Baron and anyone who got in the way. Equally important, and also a "first-ever" in the white underground, while conducting research on explosives at the University of Washington, Denver Parmenter attempted to forge a coalition with UW's Arab American Student Association. This marked the beginning of the Order's attempts to create an Aryan-Islamic alliance capable of fomenting violent revolution. Mathews led the faction opposing Pierce, arguing that assassinations would come later, once the group had built up its war chest. Unable to reach a consensus, the Order abandoned both plans and returned to Metaline Falls on November 12.

Meanwhile, Yarbrough and Lane were involved in criminal activities that were also unique for their time. Today, there is mounting evidence of terrorists' involvement in the lucrative underworld of counterfeiting. In 1996, for example, the FBI confiscated 100,000 T-shirts bearing fake Nike "swoosh" and Olympic logos which were intended to be sold at the 1996 summer Olympic Games. The operation reportedly generated millions of dollars and was run by the followers of Sheik Omar Abel-Rahman—who was later sentenced to prison for his role in plotting to bomb New York City landmarks.[18] But in 1983, counterfeiting among terrorist groups in the United States was unheard of.

Yarbrough and Lane set up their racket at Aryan Nations, using the church's printing press. But their foray into counterfeiting was an abject failure. Most counterfeiters press $20 bills and pass them with small purchases. Yarbrough and Lane began by printing $200,000 worth of phony $50 bills which were then dried and treated with coffee grounds to make them look older.

On December 23, Pierce and Lane spent the day passing the poorly made bills at stores in Union Gap, Washington. A clerk became suspicious of one of the bills and called the police, who arrested Pierce. He was turned over to the Secret Service (the agency responsible for investigating counterfeiting in the United States) and charged with passing counterfeit money and carrying a concealed weapon. Pierce was held on $25,000 bail, a sum which neither he nor Mathews had.

While under arrest, Pierce posed several security threats. During his interrogation he voluntarily revealed his affiliation with Aryan Nations, thus bringing the heat down on Pastor Butler. Pierce also began calling other Order members from jail, thus linking them to a known counterfeiter. In response, several men contemplated leaving the group, and even Mathews considered pulling the plug. The entire operation, he told a confidant, was "going down the toilet." It was then that Mathews decided to "stand up like a man and fight."

On December 20, Mathews armed himself with a handgun and entered the Innis Arden Branch of the City Bank in Seattle. He told a female clerk to stuff his bag full of cash and ordered several other women employees into the vault. Just then, a snowstorm hit Puget Sound; remarkably, it was Seattle's only snowstorm of the year. As Mathews left the bank, a security device exploded a dye pack inside the bag. The explosion stained the money, showered Mathews in red dye, and knocked him to the ground. Stunned, Mathews slowly drove away in the snowstorm carrying $25,900 in tainted money. The work of a rank amateur, the robbery was distinguished only by its lack of criminal sophistication.

The purpose of the robbery was to raise bail for Pierce. And on that score it was a failure. Before Mathews could clean the money—using Zip Strip that discolored the bills creating what is called "blue backs"—Julie Pierce persuaded the judge to lower her husband's bail to $2,500. Pierce's brother posted a $250 surety bond, and on December 23 Bruce Pierce walked out of jail. Three weeks later, on January 30, 1984, Pierce and Yarbrough robbed the Washington Mutual Savings Bank in Spokane, making off with $3,600. Prior to the robbery, they placed a fake bomb in nearby store as a diversionary tactic.

By February, the Order was in dire straits. After three insignificant armed robberies and a bungled counterfeiting operation—crimes that undermined both the morale and security of the group—the Order had stolen less than $30,000, much of it consisting of useless blue backs. With no other visible means of support (Mathews and the others had given up their day jobs by now), the core members of the group began to pawn their belongings.

Around this time David Lane distributed a *Bruders Schweigen* manual designed to improve the Order's criminal effectiveness. Those tactics began with covert operations. "Sometimes you are a sheep," wrote Lane, "and then you change to a wolf. Until you can sit at a table or in a bar with a beautiful white woman and her nigger boy friend or husband and convince them you are overflowing with brotherly love and affection, you are not yet a completed agent of the white underground." Lane's manual also gave instructions on bank robbery, communications, disguises, and diversionary tactics. The Order was instructed to use police scanners to monitor locations; to wear gloves during all operations (to avoid leaving fingerprints); to always carry at least $500 cash; and to use factory-produced ammunition rather than homemade bullets.

With these new procedures in place, the Order went back to work. Returning to Seattle on March 16, Mathews, Pierce, Yarbrough, and Duey set their sights on a Continental Armored Transport truck—identified in their surveillance the previous November—making pickups at a Fred Meyer department store in a shopping mall. Shortly before the Continental truck arrived at its target location, the Order once again placed a fake bomb in a nearby store as a diversionary tactic.

When a security guard walked out of Fred Meyer pushing a shopping cart loaded with bags of money, Duey blocked the aisle leading to the door. Pierce then drew his gun and stopped the guard as Mathews came up from behind and took the guard's weapon away. At this point Yarbrough pulled a battered old Dodge Dart to the curb—a car so decrepit that its reverse no longer worked. The others grabbed the money bags and loaded them into the car. In less than two minutes, the gang made off with $43,345 in untainted bills. After fits and starts, the Order was finally off and running.

Mathews's organizational skills then began to coalesce. He rebooted the counterfeiting operation, put each member of his action group on salary, and bought them life insurance polices so that their families would be covered in the event of death. Yet his greatest achievements was in the execution of armored truck robberies and the increased authority those robberies gave him within the organization. As one Order member recalled, "Money gave Mathews power."[19]

On April 19, the Order returned to Seattle for another heist. After checking his men into a Motel 6, Mathews split them into three teams. Mathews led the first one, responsible for conducting surveillance on a Continental Armored Transport truck at the Northgate Mall. Pierce's team was responsible for buying two cars for the robbery (a Ford van and a Chrysler sedan). And Yarbrough's group was responsible for bombing a porno theater as a diversionary tactic. Though successful, the robbery was not executed with the military precision that would mark later operations.

On April 22, after building a small explosive device in his motel room, Yarbrough led his crew to the Embassy Theater, a pornographic movie house located in a seedy part of the city. They placed the bomb under a seat in a vacant section of the theater and set the timer. The powerful blast occurred around 5:00 p.m., blowing shards of debris and smoke through the lobby and causing panic but no serious injuries.

Around noon the next day, April 23, as the gang approached the Northgate Mall, Richard Kemp unloaded several boxes of roofing nails in a highway tunnel, hoping to create a massive traffic jam caused by flat tires. An hour earlier, a phone call had been made to the Embassy Theater, warning that another bomb was about to go off. This call was intended to further divert police from the Mall and add to the confusion. Yet these tactics had no impact at all. Despite the nails, tunnel traffic proceeded as usual; the Embassy staff ignored the bomb threat and started showing movies as usual. And the threat, as it turns out, was made hours too early.

At about 3:00 p.m. (four hours after the bomb threat) the armored truck arrived at the Northgate Mall. Pierce and Duey, armed with semi-automatic pistols, posed as window washers at a Mall store. When the armored vehicle pulled to a stop, a courier got out and walked to the rear compartment. Pierce calmly walked up and pressed the barrel of his gun to the courier's head. (Coincidentally, it was the same Continental guard he had robbed five weeks earlier.) Yarbrough then drove up in the Ford van, and Mathews jumped out holding a sign up to the armored truck driver reading: "Get Out or You Die." Parmenter and Barnhill, wearing masks and brandishing shotguns, pulled up in the Chrysler. The Continental driver and courier were forced into the back of the truck while Pierce began throwing money bags into the van. Moments later, the bandits left the scene with more than half a million dollars. Again, the entire robbery had taken less than two minutes.

Strategy

The Northgate robbery was a turning point for the Order. Even though Mathews had to burn some $300,000 in checks, the gang still made off with more than $200,000 in unmarked bills. Mathews put $85,000 into reserve for future operations and gave Yarbrough $40,000 for a donation to Aryan Nations (Butler would turn it down, however). The rest of the money went into stipends for the action group ($24,000 a piece), incentives for new recruits, a printing press for the counterfeiting scam, computers to access the newly established Aryan Nations Liberty Net bulletin board, and firearms. One of these purchases—the April 26 acquisition of a Smith & Wesson 9mm semi-automatic pistol from a Missoula gun shop by Andrew Barnhill (who had failed to acquire fake Ids)—would ultimately have severe repercussions.

The Order's terrorism also began in the wake of the Northgate job. On April 26, three days after the robbery, a bench warrant was issued for Bruce Pierce after he failed to appear for sentencing on the counterfeiting charges. Now a federal fugitive, Pierce moved his family into a school bus converted into a camper and prepared for a major attack on the Boundary Dam (a huge power plant) in northwest Washington. Following directions in a terrorist manual, Pierce built a small bomb made out of dynamite, electrical blasting caps, a battery, and timer. On April 29, Pierce and Kemp tested the device on the Congregation Ahavath Israel Synagogue in Boise. This "act of war," as Pierce would later describe it, was intended to serve "a greater good."[20] The blast did little damage. It did, however, have other consequences. Condemned by Mathews as an "unauthorized" action, the bombing contributed to an unfolding rift between Mathews and his top lieutenant.

Internal conflict wasn't the Order's only problem at this point. Despite the instructions in Lane's *Bruders Schweigen* manual, the group was still saddled with a fair share of criminal incompetence. After Pierce failed to appear for sentencing, sheriffs' deputies visited Mathews's home looking for him. Failing to find Pierce, the sheriff issued a press release asking the public to be on the lookout for the "Aryan counterfeiter." Mathews reacted with an angry reply in the local newspaper, vowing that he and Pierce would stand strong for the white race "even if it costs us our lives." Rarely do terrorists go public with their intentions. When they do, it is almost certain that ideology has trumped criminal skill.

This became even more apparent in May when deputies received a tip on a vehicle matching Pierce's parked at Randy Duey's safe house in Newport, Washington. Inside, officers found Duey, Lane, and a professional counterfeiter named Robert Merki standing at a printing press (which, unknown to the deputies, was being used to produce counterfeit $10 bills) and a phone bill listing the number of Bob Mathews in Metaline Falls. Duey panicked and moved the operation to Merki's home in Boise on May 15, thereby eluding law enforcement for the time being. There, Merki eventually manufactured thousands of bills which were transported by Lane to Philadelphia for passing by other operatives.

After these slip-ups, Mathews hired Richard Scutari to provide internal security. "Bob wasn't street smart," recalled Tom Martinez. "He was very impatient. He took tips from Scutari, Mr. Black. He was the brains behind the whole thing."[21] With that move, the Order became more effective in both its criminal operations and its terrorist actions.

Around this time, Mathews learned that there was a problem at Aryan Nations. Walter West, an unemployed recovering alcoholic, was hanging out in bars around Hayden Lake and saying things about Yarbrough's involvement in armed robberies. To quiet West, and to send a message to other potential informants, Mathews asked Randy Duey to murder Walter West. On May 27, Duey and Kemp, along with two young Aryan Nations activists—Randy Evans and David Tate— lured forty-two-year-old West into a national forest near Hayden Lake. As they walked through the woods, Kemp came up behind West and smashed his skull with a sledge hammer. After a second blow failed to bring him down, West looked at Duey and cried, "What's going on Randy?" Duey then blew the top of his head off with a mini-14 semi-automatic rifle, scattering his brains on the ground. West and his brains were buried in an unmarked grave that has never been found by police. Kemp later bragged to a friend: "I put him so far back in the woods that only God knows where he is."[22] After that, Kemp was given the code name "Hammer" and was often greeted by other Order members with the sing-along refrain to the Beatles' "Maxwell's Silver Hammer" (*"Bang, bang Maxwell's silver hammer/Came down on his head"*). Walter West's murder would go unnoticed, but the Order's next action would make a statement to the world.

That summer, Mathews added three names to the hit list. The first was Morris Dees of the Southern Poverty Law Center. Dees was a well-known civil rights attorney who in 1981 had won a historic $7 million verdict against the United Klans of America over their involvement in the ritualistic killing of a black teenager in Mobile, Alabama. (The Order incorrectly assumed that Dees was Jewish.) The second was television producer Norman Lear, creator of such popular programs as *All in the Family* and *The Jeffersons,* both of which portrayed African Americans in a positive light. The third target was Alan Berg, a controversial Jewish radio talk show host from Denver.

Berg had recently castigated the publisher of Colorado's *Primrose and Cattlemen's Gazette* for making anti-Semitic remarks in his newspaper. The publisher filed an $8 million defamation suit against Berg, but the case was dismissed. Plagued by debts incurred in the lawsuit, the publisher closed the newspaper and laid off his employees. One of those employees was David Lane. Then in June 1983, Lane debated

Berg on Berg's radio show, and Berg humiliated the Klansman by calling him "a sick and pathetic human being." It was an experience that Lane would never forget.

The Order's assassination of Alan Berg has received wide attention. It has been the subject of several books, a news documentary, and two Hollywood movies. Yet typically overlooked in this coverage is the degree to which Mathews was able to use his charisma to build people's sense of outrage over perceived injustices until they felt they had no choice but to act violently. "Mathews had a baby face," an Order member once said to a reporter for the news program *Turning Point*, "so what came out of his mouth seemed acceptable."[23] This seems to have been especially true for the women in Mathews's life. No one demonstrated this better than Jean Craig—mother of Mathews's mistress, twenty-year-old Zillah Craig—of Laramie, Wyoming. In 1984, Jean Craig was a fifty-one-year-old overweight grandmother with health problems. Although she had never committed a crime in her life, Mathews seduced her into his assassination plot.

In early June, Mathews asked Craig to create an "intelligence folder" on Berg by visiting Denver and monitoring his movements. Posing as a "writing student" from the University of Wyoming, Craig walked into the offices of KOA radio and asked for background information on Berg. After being handed a promotional package on Berg, Craig photographed the exterior of the building, including its surveillance cameras. By mid-June, she had tracked Berg's every move. Based on her intelligence, Mathews and Scutari were able to learn what Berg looked like, the model of car he drove, where he lived, when he left for work and departed the station, and what restaurants he ate in.

On the balmy afternoon of June 18, Mathews, Pierce, Lane, and Scutari checked into a Motel 6 in east Denver into a room which had been reserved by Pierce under the name Joseph Shelby. They went over Scutari's plan. It was not complicated: the hit squad would simply follow Berg from the radio station to his condominium where they would kill him.

Around nine o'clock that evening, Lane wheeled a dark blue Plymouth sedan to the curb near Berg's home and turned on his police scanner. Lane was wearing a shoulder-length wig, a fake mustache, and plastic framed glasses. Mathews sat in the passenger seat, Pierce was in the back, and Scutari was waiting in a backup car several blocks away. In his hands, Pierce held a case carrying an Ingram MAC-10 automatic machine pistol—purchased by the Order's Andrew Barnhill from CSA's Randall Rader several months earlier. Unloading the weapon from its case, Pierce slipped a silencer over the barrel and jammed a thirty-round magazine into the clip.

At about 9:15, Berg pulled his shiny black Volkswagen into the driveway. Lane started the Plymouth, drove up behind Berg's car, and parked sideways across the driveway. As Berg opened the door and swiveled to get out, Mathews jumped from the Plymouth and opened the rear door for Pierce, who ran up the short driveway and trained his gun on Berg's torso. Then he opened up, sending a dozen .45-caliber slugs into Berg's chest and face. Bruce Carroll Pierce, the impetuous criminal novice from the Kentucky hollers, had now crossed a moral divide.

The Great Heist

While the Northgate robbery had advanced the Order's agenda, funds were now running low, and there were more projects on the horizon. These included Pierce's plan to bomb the Boundary Dam, and then sabotage shipping lanes in Puget Sound. The need for additional capital led to one of the most electrifying crimes in the annals of American crime and justice. The story begins with a man named Charles Ostrout.[24]

Back in 1982, Mathews had placed an ad in the ultra-right magazine, *The Spotlight,* calling for the establishment of a "White American Bastion." His intent was to promote the Pacific Northwest as a natural territory for white families. The ad offered an invitation to visit the Northwest and meet Mathews who would act as a local guide. Among those who replied was Charles Ostrout, a money room supervisor at the Brinks Security agency in San Francisco. During his visit, Ostrout lamented the fact that he had been passed over for promotion in favor of blacks because of the company's affirmative action policies. Mathews commiserated by welcoming Ostrout into his home and giving him $50. Two years later, Mathews began to pump Ostrout for inside information about Brinks security arrangements.

In late June 1984, Mathews and Parmenter met with Ostrout in San Leandro, California. Ostrout talked about a Brinks armored truck run on California Highway 20 between Eureka and Sacramento, about a hundred miles north of San Francisco. He gave Mathews a map of the run and pointed out a location near the small town of Ukiah where the truck had to climb a steep and winding hill. At that point, where the highway rises 350 feet in less than a mile, the six-cylinder Brinks truck would be traveling at less than twenty miles an hour. With this information, Mathews had the ideal location for the Order's next robbery.

By July 4, Pierce and Duey had joined Mathews and Parmenter at a Motel 6 in Santa Rosa, fifty miles south of Ukiah, where they began planning the robbery. Pierce and Duey bought three vehicles for the operation: two Ford pickups and a Fleetside sedan. They also visited the incline on the scheduled day that the armored truck made its run from Eureka; to time the operation, Mathews followed the truck up the hill, clocking its speed. After a week of planning, Mathews sent a message to the rest of the action group: they should come to California at once.

Seven new arrivals, including Richard Scutari, checked into various motels in Ukiah and Santa Rosa on the weekend of July 14. After Mathews went over the plot, Scutari pointed out that they had failed to design an escape plan, the most important part of a successful robbery. After deflecting several hair-brained schemes offered by Pierce, Scutari convinced the others that they should make a fast getaway, switch cars in a secluded area, and then separately go into hiding. This would require no less than three sets of vehicles: one for the robbery, one for the money switch, and another for the getaway. By mid-week, Duey had purchased two more vehicles—a 1971 white Ford van and a 1973 Buick Rivera. Scutari located a spot in the Palmo Recreational area, near Lake Medocino, to make the switch. After clearing a swatch of land in a heavily wooded area down a steep hillside, Scutari brought in food, water, and other supplies in case the gang had to make their getaway on foot. Not only had Scutari designed a comprehensive getaway plan, but he had built in a contingency as well.

Once everything was in place, Mathews called a meeting to lay out the mission's primary rule: "We come for the money," he said. "No one is to get hurt." It is a testament to the Order's discipline, and Mathews's leadership, that this would come to pass. It would also do so by dint of a force multiplier: each man would be armed, and several of them would carry heavy-fire power. This overwhelming show of force would compel the security guards to give up without a fight, thus expediting the robbery so that the gang could make its getaway.

On the morning of July 19, after more than two weeks of meticulous preparation, the counterfeiter Robert Merki drove to the small town of Willits, California, where he pulled into a McDonald's parking lot to wait for the Brinks truck to pass on its way to Ukiah. Merki's Cutlass was outfitted with a CB radio to relay messages to Scutari. Armed with a Ruger .357 Magnum revolver, Merki himself was disguised as an old woman—complete with a grey wig, skirt, blouse, panty hose, and bra and falsies. The rest of the gang was waiting in Mathews's hotel room in Santa Rosa. All eleven men were dressed plainly in ball caps, blue jeans, and T-shirts with bandanas tied around their necks. After applying Krazy Glue to their fingertips, they slipped on surgical gloves to conceal fingerprints. Their final act of preparation was spiritual. As the room fell silent, Scutari recited the 91st Psalm, which ends with the words: "Thou shalt not be afraid for the terror by night, nor the arrow that flieth by day."

Around 9:00 a.m., they climbed into the two Ford pickups and made their way to a staging area along Highway 101. Scutari, armed with an assault rifle, drove a green pickup equipped with a CB radio and a police scanner tuned to the local sheriff's office. Beside him was Mathews, carrying the 9mm Smith & Wesson purchased by Barnhill in Missoula after the Northgate raid. Pierce was in the truck bed, armed with a Heckler & Koch .308-caliber semi-automatic rifle loaded with armor piercing bullets. Next to him was Parmenter, holding a fake bazooka and manning a box of roofing nails. Yarbrough drove a blue pickup and carried the MAC-10 used to kill Alan Berg. Duey sat beside him with an Israeli 9mm Uzi. Barnhill, armed with an H&K .308, was in the bed along with Randy Evans and Richard Kemp, both armed with shotguns.

Shortly after noon, Merki radioed Scutari with a coded message indicating that the Brinks truck was on its way. Moments later, the truck rumbled past the staging area and into the history books of routine activity theory.

Scutari pulled out followed by Yarbrough. They caught up with the armored truck just as it turned onto Highway 20 and began lumbering up the steep incline. Scutari moved his pickup into the left lane and passed the Brinks truck, followed by Yarbrough who stayed alongside the Brinks. Then Scutari jammed on the brakes, forcing the heavy Brinks truck to a stop.

The men in the pickups stood up and trained their weapons on the guards. All had bandannas over their faces expect for the ever-erratic Pierce who brazenly showed his face. One of them held up a sign reading: "Get Out or Die."

Mathews ran to the passenger side, yelling "Get out, now!" Yet the guards didn't move. As they sat there in stunned silence, Parmenter pointed what appeared to be a rocket launcher at them, and after ten seconds without a reply, Pierce jumped onto the hood of the Brinks truck and blistered the top of the bullet-proof windshield with four shots, showering the guards with glass. They jumped out with their hands in the air, shouting, "We'll give you anything you want!"

"Shut up," Pierce snarled.

At this point, the Brinks truck started rolling backward; in his haste to get out, the driver had failed to set the emergency brake. Evans and Kemp turned their shotguns on the rear tandem and blew the tires flat, bringing the truck to a cockeyed stop. Mathews ordered the guards to lie face down on the shoulder of the road; then he tried to open the doors of the cab so he could trip a switch unlocking the rear compartment. But the doors were locked. Mathews tried to enter the truck from the backdoor but it was locked, too. Still sitting in back was a third guard, a young African American woman. When she stood up, Evans fired his shotgun through a side window. Badly shaken, she opened the side door, locking it behind her, and surrendered. Now the truck was locked with no one inside. The only way to enter the rear compartment was by tripping the unlock switch in the cab.

Scutari was manning the police scanner and calling out the timing of the robbery every thirty seconds as Duey directed traffic on Highway 20 with his rife. By now, the Order had been on the road for ten long minutes, and Scutari expected to hear the robbery called out over his scanner at any moment. Mathews got in the woman's face and screamed, "Open that door! Get that door open now!" Then Pierce aimed his weapon at her head. The force multiplier worked. She pulled the keys from her pocket and opened the cab, allowing Mathews to trip the unlock switch.

After Scutari backed up to the rear of the Brinks truck, Mathews jumped in the back of the Brinks and took his place at the front of a bucket-brigade, passing one bag of money after another to the other men who stacked them in Scutari's bed. After passing a few bags, Mathews felt his pistol digging into his waist. To relieve the pressure, he shoved the gun down his pant leg. After Mathews passed several more bags, the gun fell on the floor and was covered by debris.

Once the bed was filled, Scutari pulled away following Yarbrough. The roofing nails were then tossed onto the road behind the fleeing vehicles. When the pickups were several hundred feet away, the female guard got off the ground; Pierce fired off a round over her head, forcing the woman to hit the ground again.

Within minutes, the pickups arrived at the Palmo Recreational area where the gang quickly transferred everything into the white van—the money, guns, gloves, CB radio, and scanner. Then each man put on a different shirt and piled into the van and the Riviera. The switch cars pulled onto the highway where they easily blended into the routine traffic flow. Several minutes later, the switch cars pulled into two other areas where the money, guns, and equipment were transferred to several getaway cars. The robbers left those areas just as police cars, responding to the robbery, screamed by in the opposite direction.

In less than twenty minutes, the Order had stolen $3.6 million, and, on Mathews's explicit instructions, no one had been hurt in the process. It was, at the time, the most successful overland robbery ever committed on American soil.

AFTERMATH

The gang met up in Reno, Nevada, where they cleaned the inside of the van and ditched it. From there the Order headed to Merki's home in Boise, arriving on July 21, where they counted out the robbery money and discussed plans for the future. Despite their success, this discussion deepened the inter-group conflict, which again centered on Pierce's simmering feud with Mathews.

When Mathews said that he wanted to divide the money among other white power groups, Pierce began bitching that he wanted more say in the Order's structure and direction. The Identity Christians sided with Pierce. Tempers flared, and a shoving match ensued between the Yarbrough and Mathews. Once civility was restored, Mathews agreed to a reorganization plan. From now on, Pierce would lead a break-away cell responsible for "procurements," or future robberies. Mathews would remain the overall coordinator, concentrating on strategy and the recruitment of new soldiers. Duey would take responsibility for indoctrination; Yarbrough would handle assassinations; and Scutari would continue as head of security.

So that's the way it was. Pierce organized his own cell, and Bob Mathews became a roving ambassador for the American radical Right, spreading his largesse far and wide. After a brief visit with Zillah Craig in Laramie—where he dramatically changed his appearance by dying his dark brown hair blond—Mathews loaded hundreds of thousands of dollars in the trunk of a used Pontiac and began donating money to Identity preachers, Ku Klux Klan members, and neo-Nazis. Most of it was earmarked for recruiting youth into the movement. In Columbus, Ohio, Mathews gave a racist college professor an undetermined amount of cash to start a white power rock band that would appeal to America's emerging skinhead movement. He donated $300,000 to Tom Metzger of the White Aryan Resistance in Fallbrook, California; Metzger used these proceeds to support his communications system of racist teen magazines, telephone hotlines, computer bulletin boards, a cable access television program, and rock concerts. In Arlington, Virginia, Mathews gave William Pierce $50,000; Pierce bought a 364-acre farm and began writing *Hunter*, his sequel to *The Turner Diaries*. In Angier, North Carolina, Mathews donated $200,000 to the Grand Dragon of the Confederate Knights of the Ku Klux Klan, which he used to open an all-white Christian school for Klan children. And in perhaps his most audacious attempt to secure the future of the Aryan race, Mathews established a surrogate mother program in Portland. Here, the robbery money was used to support a sperm bank for the "siring" of future Aryan warriors.

Mathews also used the Ukiah windfall to secure the loyalty of his inner circle. Each robbery participant received $40,000. Duey was also given nearly $500,000 to start his indoctrination center in Bluecreek, Washington. His Aryan Academy was soon outfitted with a television, video disc player, loud speakers, and cassette decks. Scutari received more than $100,000 and began spending money like a drunken sailor, buying police scanners, wiretap detectors, telephone scramblers, walkie talkies, and a radio frequency detector—a device that could pick up radio signals and detect FBI informants wearing a wire. Lane was given $310,000 for his propaganda program, and Pierce was handed $642,000 to support his splinter group. He immediately went to work identifying robbery targets in San Francisco. Totally obsessed with his role as an Aryan warrior, Pierce envisioned a scheme to hit a Brinks cash vault and then rob an incoming air shipment of Brinks money at the San Francisco Airport. The expected take: $20 million. But the Order's most ambitious plans were for terrorist training. This included a plan to forge an alliance between the Order and an official of the Syrian government. Any enemy of the Jews, Mathews reasoned, was a friend of the Order.

At the center of this new initiative was the ever-skillful Randall Rader. Less than a week after the Ukiah robbery, Scutari traveled to Gentry, Arkansas, where he met Rader and offered him $145,000 to set up two paramilitary training bases. Unemployed and adrift from the CSA, Rader jumped at the chance. He began by amassing supplies ranging from combat boots, backpacks, and paramilitary uniforms to flares, tents, and camping gear. In September, Rader left his wife and re-located to the Northwest with a nominally talented cook named Nash. After scouting the area, Rader paid $88,000 for 110 acres of rural property near Priest River, Idaho—a place of breathtaking beauty—and began converting the land to a training compound. (A 160-acre parcel in Shannon County Missouri was later purchased for a second camp.) With this, according to Flynn and Gerhardt, "Rader became the Rommel of the Radical Right by running Mathews's guerrilla camp."[25] Rader's crew cleared the land, dug foxholes, set up a mess tent, and sur-rounded the area with machine gun nests. As a cover, Rader formed the Mountain Man Supply Company for the purpose of buying equipment for the camp. On shopping sprees to Las Vegas and Reno, Rader spent more than $40,000 on radio towers, a base station, chainsaws, all-terrain vehicles, snowmobiles, generators, a trailer, and surveillance cameras, along with dozens of firearms and tons of ammunition. It is worth re-membering that all of this took place years before Osama bin Laden es-tablished his first terrorist training camp in the mountains of Afghanistan.

Yet the training and re-organization created more heat than light. As the Order set out to develop more sophisticated skills for the future, the FBI was taking advantage of the gang's mistakes of the past.

EVIDENCE AS TOTEM

Once again, the primary goal of this research is to identify the distin-guishing features of terrorist-oriented criminality. The FBI's investiga-tion of the Brink truck robbery revealed such a distinction. And as in all cases of terrorism, this distinction was located in the varieties of crimi-nality associated with deviant subcultures.

When the CSA's Richard Snell was found with a .22-caliber pistol following his killing of an Arkansas state trooper—the same gun Snell previously used to murder a pawnshop owner—he was not simply showing a lack of judgment. Nor was he exhibiting the sort of criminal stupidity we've so far witnessed with the jihadists. This was something entirely different. Instead Snell was demonstrating a fundamental characteristic of the American radical Right. Rather than concealing incriminating evidence, American terrorists actually hold onto this evidence, thereby recasting it as a symbol of their struggle. The terrorist's ends (bombing targets, assassination victims, etc.) are always symbolic. And so are the means to those ends. For Snell, the .22-caliber pistol was far more than physical evidence worthy of capital punishment. For him, it was proof of a noble performance.

This facet of domestic terrorism is all about individual reputation, or the prospect of generating stories that cast the terrorist as brave, loyal to confederates, and fearless to a fault. In these stories, the terrorist assumes a heroic identity that becomes a permanent part of his biography. Terrorists use evidence gained in battle, then, to create stories that reveal themselves as admirable to present and future audiences. "Why do terrorists consider evidence to be venerated emblems of their crimes?" I asked the FBI's Danny Coulson. "Beats me," he said. "It's kind of like the Sioux when they slaughtered Custer's troops at Little Big Horn. They cut off fingers of dead soldiers and wore them as necklaces. To them, it was totem."[26]

Manhunt

Within days of the Ukiah robbery, FBI agents from San Francisco traced the 9mm Smith & Wesson pistol found in the Brinks truck to Andrew Barnhill of Laclede, Idaho. This information was passed on to the special agent in charge of the investigation, Wayne Manis of the FBI office in Coeur d'Alene, Idaho. When Manis and two agents kicked in Barnhill's door several days later, they discovered evidence indicating that the Ukiah heist was anything but a conventional armed robbery. Along with racist material tying Barnhill to Aryan Nations, the agents discovered totem in the form of a newspaper article about the Continental armored truck robbery at the Northgate Mall in Seattle. "The article was neatly folded," said Manis. "It was in a stack of personal items, including Barnhill's baby teeth. It was being preserved, and we knew that it was very personal to him."[27] All of the precautions and security procedures previously implemented by Lane and Scutari therefore came to naught. For the Order, the value of acquiring criminal skills would be undermined by the temptations of acquiring totem.

The article was just the beginning of evidence linking Barnhill to a broader conspiracy. A background check revealed that on June 19, 1984, Andrew Barnhill (again using his own name) had been arrested in Madras, Oregon, on weapons charges. Arrested with him was Randy Evans, who also gave his real name to police. When officers asked Evans for his car registration, he handed over a title and registration issued to Denver Parmenter. That caused the FBI to take another look at Randy Duey, Parmenter's former roommate in Newport, Washington, who—along with David Lane and Robert Merki—had been questioned in May by deputies looking for Bruce Pierce.

Barnhill's failure to use a fake ID when purchasing the Smith & Wesson in Missoula was the thread that unraveled the conspiracy, yet Barnhill was not the only one who exhibited a slipshod criminality. The Order's greatest failing was in the area of communications.

Back in January 1984, Mathews instructed Robert Merki's wife, Sharon, to set up a communications system in the basement of the couple's home in Boise. Known as the "Bear Trap," a separate telephone line served as a message center, and all contact between Mathews and the others was to be made through this center using code names only. This way, operatives would never have to phone Mathews directly. Instead, they would phone the Bear Trap, and Sharon Merki would log in the call and relay the message to Carlos. Yet this system was not used for ordinary calls to family members, and that was straw that finally broke the Order's back.

Following the Brinks robbery, agents in Santa Rosa interviewed several people who sold cars to the robbery suspects (agents located these people by tracing license numbers from the vehicles after they'd been abandoned by the Order near the robbery site). The seller of the Buick Riviera told agents that the car was sold to a Caucasian man who said he was staying at the Motel 6 on Cleveland Street. Agents then began checking toll call records from pay phones in the Cleveland Street area made prior to the robbery. Knowing that a man from Idaho (Barnhill) had purchased the abandoned gun in the Brinks truck, investigators narrowed the vast volume of toll records to ten telephone calls from pay phones around Cleveland Street to various locations in the Montana-Idaho-Washington area.

Among these was a call to a number belonging to "Gary Olbu" in Sandpoint, Idaho. Several months earlier, Wayne Manis had quietly begun investigating allegations of an armed robbery committed by an Aryan Nations security guard named . . . Gary Lee Yarbrough. On September 5, 1984, following the leads provided by the check of phone records in Santa Rosa, Manis set up a stakeout in a strip mall near the address for Gary Olbu. To his amazement, Manis saw Gary Yarbrough leave that house, get on his motorcycle, and drive to a pay phone. "I knew this was unusual," Manis recalled, "because I'd just phoned his house sixty seconds earlier, and the phone was working fine. So, why was he going to a pay phone?"[28] A search of that pay phone record showed that Yarbrough had called a number belonging to Sharon Merki's daughter, Suzanne Stewart, in Boise.

There were also calls made from the Santa Rosa pay phones to the homes of Denver Parmenter's wife in Cheney, Washington; Zillah Craig in Laramie; Charles Ostrout in San Leandro; and Bob Mathews in Metaline Falls. But perhaps the most important call was made to the home of Sandra Glee in Troy, Montana. For "Sandra Glee," as it turns out, was an alias used by Bruce Pierce's wife, Julie.

On September 8, Manis left his surveillance of Yarbrough's house to supervise the execution of a search warrant on Pierce's home in Troy. Finding the house empty, Manis and his colleagues searched the grounds, where they came across a plywood silhouette target of a police officer shot full of holes. Buried in some nearby trees, the agents discovered numerous slugs from a .45-caliber weapon. Ballistics tests showed that they came from the Ingram MAC-10 automatic machine pistol used to kill Alan Berg.

Essentially, the FBI now had the Order dead to rights, primarily because of their inattention to the security of communications. "Most of them were not seasoned criminals," said Manis. "They thought they were dealing with a toothless dog [in the FBI] at the time. They thought the phones would be safe, but, of course, they weren't. The records gave us leads to discover the whole organization."[29] Had the Silent Brotherhood lived in the age of cell phones, the investigation may never have gone beyond the leads associated with Barnhill's purchase of the gun found in the Brinks truck. But the fact of the matter was that Mathews's gang was burdened not just by one loose cannon; rather, the Order was comprised of nothing but loose cannons. Their incompetence was about to play itself out in the Berg investigation as well.

In many ways, selecting David Lane as the wheel man for the Berg assassination was the most dimwitted decision ever made by Mathews and Scutari. Back in 1981, when Lane was pulled over on a routine traffic stop in Denver, police had discovered a batch of Aryan Nations material in his trunk. The media were called in, and the next day Lane's picture was splashed across the front pages of the newspapers. Also, Lane had debated Berg on the radio in June 1983, so there were publicly available tapes of that program. Not surprisingly, then, following the Berg assassination, Denver police announced that Lane was wanted for questioning, and again his picture appeared in the newspapers. In response, Lane wrote an open letter to the Denver media denying his involvement in the Berg murder. Investigators got another break in the case when they checked registrations at Denver hotels. Near the Motel 6 in east Denver, where "Joseph Shelby" and three other men stayed prior to Berg's murder, records showed that calls were made from pay phones to Mathews' home in Metaline Falls, as well as to a number in a home in Fort Lupton, Colorado, that was situated around the corner from an occasional residence used by David Lane.

It would take months for the FBI to make the arrests, however. Because bureau officials believed that the evidence was not yet strong enough, Manis and his investigators were instructed to remain in "intelligence-gathering mode" by placing the suspects under surveillance. By the end of September 1984, some forty FBI agents had joined the surveillance. They staked out Mathews's home in Metaline Falls, Craig's house in Laramie, Parmenter's apartment in Seattle, the Merki's bungalow in Boise, and, of course, Yarbrough's home in Sandpoint. This final stakeout set in motion a series of events that would bring the case to a close.

On the morning of October 18, three FBI agents, dressed in blue jeans and with no identifying insignias, drove a U.S. Forest Service vehicle down a dirt road leading to Yarbrough's rented house, passing a "no trespassing" sign he had posted at the edge of his property. As the truck neared the house, Yarbrough pulled on a military fatigue jacket, grabbed his .45-caliber pistol, and ran toward the moving vehicle. Then, from about one hundred feet away, Yarbrough opened fire. The bullet cracked over the vehicle and then Yarbrough fired again. The shooting, he would later claim, was a "stupid thing" on his part, intended only to scare the agents away. That, of course, made little difference to the agents on the morning of October 18.

As Yarbrough escaped into the dense woods, the agents made their way back to town where they summoned the FBI's Hostage Rescue Team. Nine hours later, the agents obtained a search warrant and returned to Yarbrough's house. Meanwhile, other agents were dispatched to nearby Samuels, Idaho, where Yarbrough's brother, Stephen, lived. By this time, Gary Yarbrough had made his way to Stephen's house, and he saw the agents coming in the dead of night. Rather than making a break for it, though, Yarbrough rolled into a ditch, pointed his gun at the house, and pretended to be an undercover agent himself. Remarkably, no one questioned him. After awhile, Yarbrough saw his chance to escape and, for the second time that day, disappeared into the tree line.

As this was going on, Manis led the search of Yarbrough's home in Sandpoint. In the bedroom, agents found a copy of Kenneth Goddard's *Balefire,* a book about a terrorist strike on the Los Angeles Olympic Games, with key sections outlined in red. Firearms and ordinance were spread throughout the residence; they included pistols, shotguns, and assault rifles, along with thousands of rounds of ammunition; wigs and ski masks; brass knuckles, switch blades, and a commando crossbow, plastic explosives, dynamite, and tear gas grenades. Next to a mantle piece was a large portrait of Adolf Hitler, surrounded by black crepe paper and candles, and nearby was a picture of Jesus Christ. On the floor was a brown case, and inside was an Ingram MAC-10 automatic machine pistol.

Agents also came across a document labeled *Bruders Schweigen,* which set forth a national command structure headed by someone named "Carlos," along with a roster of dozens of operatives responsible to him. Further hinting at the gang's sophistication, the document contained information on local law enforcement officers, including computer printouts with their names, home addresses and phone numbers, and vehicle license plates, along with photographs of these officers and other pertinent information. But even that paled in comparison to the totem that was discovered.

Among Yarbrough's papers, Manis found receipts for equipment delivered to the Mountain Man Supply Company at Priest River. "I assigned two agents to go to the camp," Manis recalled with a tone of regret, "but I was told [by higher-ups] that there was a shortage of manpower. Had we gone to Priest River, we could have got them all, right then. Everything else could have been avoided."[30]

Last Call

By the time agents were searching Yarbrough's home, he had made his way to a pay phone where he contacted Carlos via the Bear Trap, indicating that he had been shot during the raid (which turned out to be a lie in order to gain sympathy). Mathews, in turn, put out a message saying that "Gary has been shot by the FBI." This call led to a gathering of the Order at the Priest River camp two days later.

At 8:00 p.m. on the cold night of October 21, Mathews stood inside the mess tent before twenty members of his Silent Brotherhood—the largest gathering of the organization ever—and attempted to regroup after the Sandpoint raid. First and foremost, Mathews instructed Duey to travel to Washington, D.C., and meet with his Syrian contacts. Mathews's goal was to form an Aryan-Islamic alliance capable of mounting a campaign of urban terrorism, focusing on the assassination of FBI agents. The campaign would begin with a strike against the FBI office in Sandpoint to retrieve the documents taken from Yarbrough. The plan to establish a confederacy of American neo-Nazis and Middle Eastern jihadists was, and remains to this day, a unique development in the history of global terrorism—one that goes far beyond the revolutionary screed of *The Turner Diaries* or any other anti-government tract of the era.

Cooler heads would prevail, however. After delivering his battle cry, Mathews was taken aside by Scutari and Rader who persuaded him that the others were not up to a commando war against the Federal Bureau of Investigation. This was especially so for Rader's crew, which included Barnhill, Parmenter, Kemp, and half a dozen others. Rader's training camp may have preceded bin Laden's, but the Order was no al-Qaeda. Having grown tired of the camp's primitive living conditions, Nash's poor cooking, and the driving Idaho snow storms, Rader's cell had fractured within a matter of weeks. Three of his men were drinking heavily, one had a drug problem, and another was being held in disciplinary custody for spending too much money, gossiping, and running home to his mother. There was talk of mutiny. Their leader, Randall Rader—the maniacal neo-Nazi munitions expert who once ate his own dog—had become lost in a netherworld of delusion and paranoia.

Rader had come to believe that his camp was being monitored by a coven of witches living down the road, so he was conducting surveillance on the place. He also became more ruthless than ever by cracking down on his men with reminders of Walter West's brutal murder. As a defense attorney would later say in court, at this point the Order's likelihood of mounting a war against the FBI was akin to "the Three Stooges trying to conduct brain surgery."

Mathews, it seems, had lost his charisma. One man at the Priest River summit later recalled that Mathews had aged ten years since the Berg assassination. Rader testified that Mathews had "flipped out at this point, he was really losing it." Another said that Carlos had gone "cuckoo." Others (including Barnhill, Kemp, and even Rader himself) left the Order shortly after Mathews's call to arms. Though Mathews was ready for battle, only a handful of his cohorts were still willing to follow him. So Carlos closed down the Priest River camp and divvied up roughly $1.5 million in remaining loot, and his warriors went their separate ways. Mathews and his closest remaining allies—Scutari, Yarbrough, and a new recruit from California named Frank Silva— would head to Portland.

THE MARTYRDOM OF ROBERT JAY MATHEWS

Tom Martinez was an Order operative responsible for passing counterfeit bills in Philadelphia. He was arrested on June 29, 1984, after passing some phony tens at a liquor store near his home. After his release on bail, Martinez called Mathews to discuss his legal problems, and Mathews convinced him to skip bail and go underground. Shortly thereafter, however, Mathews came up with a plan to murder the liquor store merchant who was the primary witness in the Martinez case. To avoid that murder, Martinez made the decision to cooperate with the FBI in its investigation of Mathews's secret army. By this point, the FBI had identified the Order as the most serious terrorist threat in the nation.

Martinez's ability to become an informant said less about the FBI's capacity to flip an operative than it did about Martinez's special relationship with Carlos. "Bob had surrounded himself with a bunch of country bumpkins," said Martinez. "I was a city kid, and I guess he thought I was more [criminally] sophisticated."[31] That may explain why, in early August 1984, Mathews had allowed Martinez to decline a test on Scutari's voice stress analyzer. "You drop that guy like a hot potato, Bob," Scutari had allegedly said to Mathews. "If he won't come across this voice box, he's no good."[32] Mathews ignored that warning at his own peril.

On November 23 Martinez flew to Portland where he was met at the airport by Mathews and Yarbrough. "I liked Mathews a whole lot," said Martinez. "But he'd become a weird bird by then. And Yarbrough: he had two grenades in the back seat and talked about nothing but finding some prostitutes to fuck up."[33] Through Martinez's cooperation, the FBI tracked the three men to the Capri Motel—Martinez to Room 14 on the ground level and Mathews and Yarbrough to Room 42, on the second floor. After Yarbrough checked the walls (and Martinez) for hidden microphones, they met in Room 42 where Mathews explained Martinez's new role in the gang. "I was supposed to meet with David Lane in Mobile, Alabama," he said, "and then assassinate Morris Dees." (By now, Jean Craig had already been in Montgomery, Alabama, where she'd conducted surveillance on Dees's home and office.) "Mathews was crazy," Martinez recalled. "I could see it in his eyes."[34]

By 4:00 a.m., on November 24, the Capri was surrounded by twenty FBI agents, including a SWAT team. Their primary target was Gary Yarbrough—not only because he had shot at one of their own back in Sandpoint, but also because agents had discovered a perfect match between the firing pin of the MAC-10 found at Yarbrough's house and the shell casings taken from the Berg murder scene in Denver. Yarbrough, the only career criminal in the Order, had apparently learned little in his criminal career. Investigators never expected to find the murder weapon, assuming instead that it was corroding at the bottom of a lake somewhere. "Incredibly," writes Danny Coulson, "Yarbrough had preserved the best possible evidence short of a confession."[35] But that is a rather polite accounting of events. When asked about Yarbrough's possession of the gun, Wayne Manis replied: "It was one of the stupidest things I've ever seen."[36] Coulson was even more adamant in a later interview: "What an idiot! Yarbrough wasn't even at the Berg murder. He had nothing to do with it."[37] That's one way of looking at it. Another is that Yarbrough could not avoid the temptation of gathering totem.

When the sun came up, Manis evacuated all of the guests from the Capri, except for those in Rooms 14 and 42. Around 8:40 a.m., Mathews appeared on the catwalk outside his room. He was carrying a clipboard in his hands, a wad of robbery money his pockets, and a 9mm pistol in his belt. As he began walking down the stairs on his way to Martinez's room, Mathews caught a glimpse of someone hiding in the bushes near the parking lot.

As he bolted down the stairs, an agent fired at him. The bullet missed and ricocheted into the motel office, injuring the manager. Mathews ran across the parking lot, down the street, and around a corner. Agents followed shouting, "Stop Mathews!" "Halt, FBI!" and "Freeze, you bastard!" Outrunning them, Mathews found cover behind a concrete wall, drew his gun, and waited. Hearing the commotion, Yarbrough jumped from the bathroom window of his room into some bushes where he was instantly surrounded by Uzi-toting agents and taken into custody.

When one of the agents reached the wall, Mathews squeezed off two rounds, hitting him in the foot and leg. Another agent fired back with a shotgun, blasting the pistol out of Mathews's right hand and tearing a chunk of flesh from it. In searing pain, Mathews bolted down the street, jumped a fence, and disappeared down an alley.

Several blocks away, he met two workers installing a burglar alarm on a house and persuaded them to take him to the emergency room of a nearby hospital. Yet this was simply a ruse. On the way, Mathews spotted a car with skis mounted on top sitting at a Union 76 gas station. Presuming the car was headed to the ski resort on Mount Hood, Mathews told his driver to stop, and then he ran up to the car, hiding his bloody hand, and asked for a ride. A half hour later, Mathews was let out in the small community of Brightwood where, coincidentally, Silva and Scutari had recently rented a safe house. Through nothing but his own sheer determination, Mathews had eluded the dragnet.

Scutari tended to Mathews's wound by cutting the torn flesh off his hand with a hunting knife—sans painkiller. After Mathews explained what had happened at the Capri, Scutari made the case for leaving for Arizona at once. Mathews, though, favored a move north—to safe houses Duey and Merki had rented on Whidbey Island, a vacation resort located in the middle of Puget Sound near Everett, Washington, north of Seattle.

Mathews and Silva left immediately for Whidbey Island. They were joined there a day later by Scutari, Duey, and Robert and Sharon Merki, who helped Mathews settle into a two-story cedar home on a cliff overlooking the sound. Based largely on articles published in William Pierce's *National Vanguard*, Mathews then began writing a "Declaration of War on ZOG," awkwardly scrawling out thoughts with his left hand. On November 25, after hearing about the shootout in Portland, Bruce Pierce—who had been living with his cell in a trailer park in Pahrump, Nevada—arrived on the island along with Randy Evans.

Pierce and Mathews buried the hatchet and embraced one another. Pierce congratulated Mathews for showing his mettle in Portland and then filled his comrade in on what he'd been up to during the past few months. Before hitting the Brinks vault in San Francisco, Pierce said his cell had plans to re-rob the armored truck in Ukiah. (Plans to bomb the Boundary Dam had been abandoned.) With that money, they would fund the bombing of three major power lines in Los Angeles (Pierce had already gathered ammonium nitrate fertilizer for the bomb and had stored it in a Texas rental locker). Amid the ensuing bedlam, they would unload a barrel of cyanide into the L.A. water supply.[38] As in *The Turner Diaries,* this would trigger an urban race war. "The niggers'll be in the streets in an hour," Pierce predicted, "and the cops'll be shooting."

Mathews handed Pierce a typed copy of his eight-page "Declaration," indicating that the Order was "in a full and unrelenting state of war with those forces seeking and consciously promoting the destruction of our faith and our race." The document was then signed by Mathews, Pierce, Duey, Scutari, Evans, Silva, and Robert Merki. Pierce left with Evans the following day to rejoin his group in Nevada. On December 1, Duey ferried to the mainland and had a thousand copies of the "Declaration" made for distribution to the nation's biggest newspapers.

An uneventful week passed. Then, on December 7, one of Mathews's confidants went to a payphone on Whidbey Island and called the FBI office in Seattle. This confidential informant—whose identity has never been revealed—told the FBI that Mathews was staying in one of three houses the Order was renting on the island and went on to identify those addresses.

The previous day, December 6, Scutari and Silva had left the island to locate safe houses in the Southwest. They tried to persuade Mathews to come along, but he declined, preferring, in his words, to "go out in a blaze of glory." Shortly after receiving their December 7 tip, FBI agents took the Merkis into custody without incident. Duey was also arrested, as he ran from the backdoor of his house with a fully loaded submachine gun in one hand and a loaded 9mm pistol in the other. Inside agents found two copies of the "Declaration of War" along with eleven copies of *The Diaries*, ten thousand dollars in cash, and a letter to an unnamed Syrian authority stipulating terms of financial assistance to the Order.

Mathews was now in his safe house along with Merki's son, Ian Stewart. Mathews had one good hand, a 9mm Uzi machine gun, a gas mask, and several thousand rounds of ammunition.

On the afternoon of December 7, approximately one hundred FBI agents surrounded the safe house, causing Stewart to surrender. Danny Coulson telephoned Mathews and attempted to coax him out, but that came to no avail. After several attempts, Mathews quit answering the phone. Then, shortly after sundown, a gunshot rang out from the house, followed by a mournful wail.

The next morning, SWAT teams began pumping CS gas into the house in order to drive out any living person. Mathews, they assumed, was dead. At midday—after pumping more than 250 rounds of tear gas into the second floor—agents threw flash bang grenades into the ground floor and stormed inside. Suddenly, through the ceiling above them came a torrent of machine gun fire. The agents retreated and took cover behind some trees. Then Mathews opened up again, causing the agents to fire back in a thunderous clank of firepower that went on for fifteen minutes.

At sundown, an FBI gun ship flew in and cast a huge searchlight on the house. Hovering three feet from the roof, the helicopter immediately took on gun fire as Mathews ran across the upper floor shooting round after round through the ceiling. As the chopper pulled away, a SWAT team sent a volley of shots into the second floor. Again, Mathews retaliated with a ferocious barrage of machine gun fire, driving the agents back. Then he opened fire on a second SWAT team and drove them off the perimeter as well.

At this point, a command decision was made to burn the house to the ground. Sometime on the evening of August 8, agents fired a round of phosphorescent flares through a ground floor window. Within seconds, an intense fire erupted that was aggravated by the explosion of ammunition inside the house. As the flames raged upwards two hundred feet into the blackened sky, Mathews still rained down automatic gunfire from his second floor perch. Then, finally, the shooting stopped.

The next morning, after the debris had cooled enough to start the search for evidence, investigators found a scorched bathtub that had fallen from the second floor. Lying beside it were the burned remains of

Mathews's body. Buried in his chest cavity was a piece of molten gold. Still legible was a diagram of a shield with a Roman cross and two German words printed across the center: *Bruders Schweigen*—the Silent Brotherhood.

Approximately one year after Mathews's death, the U.S. Justice Department completed its successful prosecution of the Order. The trial, which cost over $1 million and featured the presentation of 1,538 pieces of evidence and the appearance of 280 witnesses, brought to light sixty-five crimes ranging from robberies, arson, bombings, counterfeiting, and murder, to conspiracy to rob affecting interstate commerce and transporting stolen property across state lines. Together, these crimes constituted 176 overt acts fitting the definition of "racketeering activity" specified in the federal RICO statue (Racketeer Influenced and Corrupt Organization Act), which was originally designed to prosecute organized crime figures. The inner circle received the harshest punishments. Bruce Pierce (captured in Rossville, Georgia, on March 26, 1985) was sentenced to 250 years in prison. Randy Duey received a one-hundred year sentence. Gary Yarbrough was sentenced to eighty years. Andrew Barnhill drew forty-years. Richard Kemp and Richard Scutari were both sentenced to sixty years. David Lane received a life sentence. Randall Rader turned state's evidence and became a key witness against both the Oder and the CSA. He entered the Witness Protection Program in 1986, as did Tom Martinez.

Robert Jay Mathews became a revolutionary role model for the white supremacy movement. He had an especially deep affect on racist skinheads throughout the world. Mathews became their martyr, a fallen hero immortalized in countless underground publications and white power rock anthems. The date of his killing at the hands of ZOG became, in fact, an international memorial day for the white power world, a day to commemorate not only Mathews but all "white warriors who have fallen in battle." Thus, December 8—known in the movement as the Day of Martyrs—ultimately took its place alongside April 19 (the "Date of Doom" commemorating the FBI's deadly 1993 raid on the Branch Davidians at Waco, Texas) and April 20 (Hitler's birthday) in the pantheon of Aryan mythology. Wherever white supremacists would gather in the years after Mathews's death, the Order was held up as the supreme example of racial integrity. That others would seek to emulate their terrorism was inevitable.

PART III

THE CURRENT STATE AND FUTURE OF THE TERRORISM-CRIME CONNECTION

5

The Seduction of Terrorist Mythology

The Aryan Republican Army

One of the most perplexing aspects of terrorism is the question of why certain people become enamored by terrorists and then sacrifice their lives to emulate them. Some scholars explain this process through the social construction of terrorism, or in terms of what media scholar Philip Jenkins describes as "the interests that groups have in presenting a particular image, and the rhetorical means by which they establish this picture."[1] Since the globally televised Munich massacre of 1972, thousands of men and women from around the world have fallen victim to a specific image of the terrorist. In this image, the terrorist is seen as a "freedom fighter"—a revolutionary who uses violence against implacable authorities of the state who are responsible for perpetrating human suffering across the planet. Through this romanticized image, terrorists make meaning for themselves—meaning about their role in a community that has embraced grass-roots theorizing about complicated realities, along with ideas for effecting substantive change for the better, even if that means destroying the world to save it.

Once the image is communicated in literature, music, art, videos, and cyberspace, it travels from place to place, transcending national and generational boundaries. The image then acquires a collective effect: for more and more people (and they are typically young people), the image alters conceptions about local and immediate problems, making it possible for them to experience emotional kinship with cultures from far away. This is how young Middle Eastern Arabs wound up fighting U.S. Marines in Somalia during the early 1990s. It is how members of the Irish Republican Army wound up teaching bomb-building techniques to terrorists in Colombia a decade later. And it explains how nineteen young Muslims from Egypt, Bahrain, and Saudi Arabia were attracted to Osama bin Laden's training camps in remote outposts of

Afghanistan and then to sleeper cells in Florida and New Jersey where they made final preparations for the 9/11 attacks. This dangerous phenomenon draws our attention to how people from different places, at different historical crossroads, create cultures of violence in similar ways. For them, laments for lost places, the suffering of exile, and the promise of redemptive justice all inform, inspire, and incite terrorism.

When it comes to the mythopoeia of modern terrorism, no one has been more influential than Carlos the Jackal. The first terrorist to achieve worldwide media fame, Carlos helped to shape the representation of the terrorist as an incandescent celebrity. Without the Jackal, Osama bin Laden would have never become a living myth of international terrorism. Carlos's story therefore deserves a brief discussion.

CARLOS THE JACKAL

Illich Ramirez Sanchez was destined to become a revolutionary.[2] Born in Caracas, Venezuela, on October 12, 1949, he was named Illich by his father, a wealthy yet militant marxist lawyer, after the founder of Bolshevism (Ilyich was Lenin's middle name). When Illich was nineteen years old, his father enrolled him in Moscow's Patrice Lumumba University, training grounds for the Soviet KGB, where he was taught the arts of espionage and guerrilla warfare. Yet Ramirez Sanchez was expelled in 1970 "for anti-Soviet provocation and leading a dissipated life." He then traveled to a guerrilla training camp run by the Popular Front for the Liberation of Palestine (PFLP) in Amman, Jordan. There he achieved the status of a highly trained guerrilla and was given the pseudonym "Carlos" by Bassam Abu-Sharif, the PFLP's spokesman. After fighting with the PFLP against the Jordanian government in the Black September of 1970, Carlos relocated to Britain and became a student at the London School of Economics.

Carlos performed his first terrorist act for the PFLP on December 30, 1973, when he attempted to assassinate an influential Jewish businessman in London. In 1974 he participated in a bomb attack on a London bank, car bombed three French newspapers which supported the Israelis, and bombed a crowded Parisian restaurant, killing two and injuring thirty. In January 1975 he took part in two failed rocket-propelled grenade attacks on El Al airliners at Orly Airport near Paris. That summer in Paris he murdered two unarmed policemen and an informant and then fled to Algeria. The brazen shooting gained widespread attention, and, following a raid on Carlos's arms cache in London, a reporter for the *Guardian* gave him a new name—"The Jackal"—after police discovered a copy of Frederick Forsyth's 1971 novel *The Day of the Jackal*. With this, the myth of Carlos the Jackal was born.

The peak of his career came just before Christmas 1975, when he led the six-person team that assaulted the conference of OPEC leaders in Vienna. Three of his accomplices were Arabs and three were Germans from the Baader-Meinhoff gang, including Hans-Joachim Klien (the former chauffeur for Jean-Paul Sartre) and the notoriously violent Gabrielle Krocher-Tiedemann. Carlos was tricked out as one of Hollywood's Mexican outlaws with a brown leather jacket, black beret, long hair, a thin beard, and sideburns, and he wielded an Italian-made Beretta machine pistol. Upon entering the conference, Krocher-Tiedemann shot and killed two policemen. Carlos killed a Libyan economist by shooting him in the neck with his Beretta before rounding up the eleven OPEC oil ministers, along with fifty-one other OPEC staff. After negotiating with the Austrians for a DC9 jet liner and crew, he pirated the eleven ministers to Tripoli via Algiers—handing out Cuban cigars and autographs like a rock star—and then walked away with $50 million in ransom money paid by the Crown Prince of Saudi Arabia and the Shah of Iran, as well as a $1 million bonus from President Muammar al-Gaddafi of Libya, who supported the OPEC attack 100 percent.

The OPEC raid spawned worldwide media coverage, which gave Carlos a reputation as the "terrorist's terrorist." In 1976, Carlos selected operatives for the hijacking of Air France Flight 193 to Entebbe and set free Arab prisoners held in a French prison. He was treated like a prince at training camps in Libya, Iraq, and Syria. One writer claimed that Carlos's humiliation of the hostages in Vienna had done more to moderate OPEC oil prices than Henry Kissinger. The jet-set terrorist traveled on diplomatic passports and maintained safe houses in Bucharest, Belgrade, Damascus, and Khartoum. Because of tight internal security, Carlos's organization was as impenetrable as his missions were unpredictable. He was a master of disguise who lived under assumed identities surrounded by a cosmopolitan group of Syrian, Lebanese, West German, and Swiss radicals who boasted a variety of criminal skills. Carlos reportedly had possession of a nuclear bomb and freelanced for such high-profile clients as Saddam Hussein, Marshal Tito, the Italian

Red Brigade, the Spanish Basque ETA, and the secret services of several Soviet bloc countries.

Carlos therefore provided the West with a perfect Cold War enemy and became the target of assassination attempts by the world's most powerful intelligence agencies. Carlos and his group killed twenty-four people and maimed another 257, yet he evaded capture thanks to powerful backers and the blunders of western intelligence. Also nicknamed "Il Gordo" ("The Fat One"), he had millions in Hungarian and Czechoslovakian bank accounts, drove a red Ferrari, maintained a stable of high-class prostitutes, and drank far too much. But more than anything, Carlos was a walking paradox. The Jackal was a millionaire playboy who murdered in the name of Third World revolutionary causes. Individual terrorists must avoid publicity or exposure, yet Carlos thrived on international attention.

By the early 1980s Carlos was considered the most feared international terrorist of the twentieth century. As the "most wanted man in the world," he generated even more media attention, much of it bestowing Carlos with superhuman qualities. And ultimately, "Carlos the Jackal" entered the realm of folklore. Robert Ludlum wrote a series of novels in which Carlos was portrayed as an invincible criminal mastermind (*The Bourne Identity*, *The Bourne Supremacy*, and *The Bourne Ultimatum*). America's most successful novelist, Tom Clancy, devoted his *Rainbow Six* to a band of terrorists who attempt to free "Carlos" from prison.

The most lustrous projection of the American psyche—the movies—portrayed him as a romantic revolutionary of the champagne Left. The Jackal's murderous reign was glorified in *True Lies* (starring Arnold Schwarzenegger as a secret service agent who pursues a terrorist called "Carlos"), *The Jackal* (with Bruce Willis in the role of an assassin), *The Assignment* (in which "Carlos" is played by actor Aidan Quinn), and the erotic *Death Has a Bad Reputation* (where Elizabeth Hurley plays a reporter seduced by "Carlos"). Half a dozen biographies were written about Carlos, and the myth eventually overcame reality.

Dozens of hijackings, car-bombings, and assassinations were linked to Carlos for lack of anyone else to claim the credit. He was believed to be responsible for the massacre of Israeli athletes at the 1972 Munich Olympics. In 1980 it was assumed that Carlos had assassinated the ousted Nicaraguan dictator, Anastasia Somoza. The same year he was credited with masterminding the hostage-taking at the United

States embassy in Tehran. And in 1986 he supposedly organized a Libyan hit squad bent on assassinating President Reagan. None of it was true.

The Jackal's career came to an end in August 1994 when the government of Sudan "sold" him to France. An early press report claimed that the vainglorious romantic was seized by French intelligence in a Khartoum hospital while under sedation for liposuction surgery; years of extravagant living had left him a bloated and melancholy chunk of a man. In reality, he was having a minor operation on a testicle. In 1997 Carlos was sentenced to life imprisonment for the murder of two French counter-terrorism agents.

By this time, however, the myth of Carlos the Jackal had become synonymous with terrorism. "Myths do exist," Carlos recently told a British reporter; "it is our duty to use the 'Carlos myth' to further the revolution."[3] But the Carlos myth had scattered traditions of terrorism by setting standards no one could follow. Christopher Dobson and Ronald Payne call this pattern the "Carlos complex."[4] The world has seen other wholesale terrorists, but only Carlos the Jackal functioned like a multinational conglomerate.

Yet this description not only obscures the role Carlos has played in cultures obsessed by celebrity; it is also a narrow conceptualization of the complex. In other words, it may be entirely appropriate to consider the "Carlos complex" in both organizational and psychological terms. The Order is a good example. Organizationally, America's most accomplished terrorist leader was Robert Jay Mathews. The Order's string of professionally executed armored truck robberies stands as a testament to that proficiency. Yet for Mathews, symbolism was everything: from the Silent Brotherhood medallion and the use of evidence as totem to code names and to the very name of the group, symbolically defined as the Order. These symbols were not constructed by the media, but rather they were the product of an organic and very ordinary human activity of mythmaking on the part of terrorists themselves. For Matthews and his followers, mythmaking legitimized their own self-identities as Aryan warriors and the role they saw for themselves in the larger scheme of things. Mythmaking is one of the key ways in which a terrorist group forms and perpetuates itself, thereby enabling terrorists to create an emotional connection with other cultures of violence, regardless of the myth's factual basis.

In his *Brotherhood of Murder,* Tom Martinez, who would play the role of Judas in the Order, writes the following about his early discussions with Mathews:

> He's Carlos. He robs banks. For the first time, it occurred to me that the name Carlos was familiar. It should have been. Bob had adopted it in emulation of Carlos Sanchez, the terrorist who had murdered the Israelis at the Munich Olympics.[5]

Martinez later expanded on the subject:

> "Bob told me [how he took the name "Carlos" in emulation of Carlos Sanchez] in my living room in my house. We talked for hours about that kind of stuff. He was always praising Carlos. Carlos Sanchez was an idol to him. All those guys [in the Order] were into that stuff [international terrorism]."[6]

Yet "Carlos Sanchez" was *not* part of the eight-man Arab hit team at Munich; indeed, history records no terrorist with that name. Carlos the Jackal (nee Illich Ramirez Sanchez) played no part in the Munich affair whatsoever. Not only did Mathews confuse the two names, but he mistakenly assumed that Carlos the Jackal carried out the Munich atrocity. Put simply, America's most criminally sophisticated terrorist embraced the Carlos myth without reservation. That Mathews not only ascribed to the myth but also conferred on it a magical aura was evidenced by the fact that he dressed as a Mexican outlaw during the Order's robberies. And in the end, Mathews died for that myth. So in this way, then, the "Carlos complex" may be viewed as representing a powerful set of repressed ideas related to the disjunction between terrorism's facts and legends, a disjunction upon which the image of terrorism is built in the first place.

In the early 1990s, these illusions would guide a new generation of American terrorists. Though better educated, more widely read, and more urban than their predecessors, the new terrorists would also prove to be so in love with their images and legends that they would pay for them with their lives. "Revolution devours its own children," said Carlos; "it is a price which true revolutionaries are ready to pay."[7]

THE FORMATION OF THE ARYAN REPUBLICAN ARMY

In 1996 the FBI broke up one of the most dangerous cells ever assembled by the radical Right—the Aryan Republican Army (ARA). The ARA were a flamboyant gang of gun-and-bomb-toting extremists who crossed the Midwest, robbing banks in Iowa, Wisconsin, Missouri, Kansas, Ohio, Nebraska, and Kentucky. They wore FBI ball caps and masks that impersonated various U.S. presidents. They used FBI agents' names to buy getaway cars and mocked their pursuers in cartoons and letters to local newspapers. They printed their own business cards, produced their own recruitment video, and recorded their own CD of "terrorist rock" music. If terrorism is theater, as Brian Jenkins argues, then the ARA was the Barnum & Bailey of terrorism.[8] Their story begins with two wildly eccentric career criminals.

The Warrior

Peter Kevin McGregor Langan was born on May 18, 1958, on the Marianas island of Saipan, the sixth child of Eugene Langan and the former Mary Ann McGregor.[9] Like the Jackal, Langan had extremism in his blood. Eugene was an agent of the Central Intelligence Agency and a decorated veteran of World War II. Mary Ann was a descendant of the outlaw Rob Roy MacGregor—a giant of Scottish folklore who was the hero of Sir Walter Scott's novel bearing his name.

After the Langans moved to Saigon in 1961, Eugene became involved in a plot by South Vietnamese rebel generals to assassinate South Vietnam's ascetic Catholic president, Ngo Dinh Diem. These were times of great excitement and untold terror for the Langan children. They witnessed violent street riots between Buddhists and the Diem government, as well as the historic self-immolation by the Buddhist monk Quang Duc in May 1963.

Following the Diem assassination later that year, Mary Ann and the kids moved to Wheaton, Maryland, a suburb of Washington, D.C., while Eugene continued his work for the CIA in Vietnam—including a stint in the notorious Phoenix program (known for its systematic torture and mass murder of the Vietcong). When Eugene died in 1967, Peter dropped out of school and slipped into a lifestyle of petty thievery and drug abuse. Despite his lack of formal education, at this young age Peter spoke three languages (French, Vietnamese, and English) and was a voracious consumer of popular culture. S. E. Hinton's *The Outsiders,* a deeply sympathetic portrayal of a gang member's search for identity, Abbie Hoffman's ode to anarchy, *Steal This Book,* the Rolling Stones' *Sticky Fingers,* and David Bowie's *The Rise and Fall of Ziggy Stardust* would all contribute to Langan's evolving identity. Whatever he did, he would do intelligently—especially his crimes.

After progressing to car theft, burglary, and drug dealing, Langan left Maryland in 1974 to avoid arrest warrants for breaking and entry, grand theft auto, and assault against a police officer. He hitchhiked to Florida where he became a homeless teenager. On May 15 of that year, at sixteen years of age, Peter armed himself with a loaded .357 Magnum, kidnapped a department store manager, and robbed the business of $78. When he was spotted by police the next day, Peter fired on the pursuing officer. The officer shot back, ripping a chunk of flesh and bone from Peter's left hand and blowing a hole in his rib cage.

Young Langan was given a twenty-year sentence and remanded to Florida's adult prison system. In 1975, Peter, a small-built seventeen-year-old who had begun to experience confusion about his sexuality, was raped by a white cell mate doing time for child molestation. During the fall of 1976, Peter was raped again, only this time by a gang of black prisoners. After that, Langan was involved in numerous fights and took several serious head shots. For protection, he carried shanks and flammable liquids, which he would throw at the predatory convicts, most of whom were black. "I was a small person you didn't wanna fuck with," he told me. Sometime in early 1978, prior to his twentieth birthday, Langan met a group of prisoners who were involved in the southern white supremacy movement. In short order, he became seduced by what is known as the religion of Christian Identity.

Upon his parole in 1979, Langan returned to Maryland where he found work as a night watchman at the American Foundation's Biomedical Research Institute in Rockville. He also bought a used Harley Davidson, grew his hair long, developed a cocaine habit, and immersed himself in the outlaw biker subculture where the ex-con met a man he would later describe as "a raving psychopath, a cross between Ted Kaczynski and Ted Bundy."

THE JOKERMAN

Richard Lee Guthrie, Jr. was born to Scotch-Irish parents in Washington, D.C., on February 25, 1958.[10] Guthrie's mother died when he was fifteen years old, leaving his father with the difficult task of raising five children on a modest printer's salary. Guthrie attended Wheaton High School where he was an above-average student. Like Langan, Guthrie also developed several traits during his early years that would ultimately define his criminal identity. The first was a considerable aptitude for science and history. The second was an exceptional eccentricity that manifested itself in a dark, racist sense of humor. And the third trait was an unbridled appetite for destructiveness.

By the time he met Langan in 1979, Guthrie had been arrested for destruction of personal property and carrying a concealed weapon and had gotten away with at least one armed robbery. Despite his criminal record, Guthrie joined the U.S. Navy in December 1979. After completing basic training, Guthrie was assigned to the Department of Defense's (DOD) Redstone Arsenal in Huntsville, Alabama, where he received training in nuclear, biological, and chemical weapons. Later he received additional training at DOD's explosive ordinance disposal school in Indian Head, Maryland. He was accepted into the SEALS—the navy's elite sea, land, and air team—but quickly washed out because he couldn't meet its rigid physical demands.

Guthrie was reclassified a "black shoe" navy man—a position he hated—and posted in Europe. After going AWOL, Guthrie served time in the ship's brig where he was introduced to *The Turner Diaries*, the same book that would inspire the creation of the Order. Not surprisingly, his reaction to the book was eccentric and destructive: he crawled out a porthole and painted a swastika on his ship. For that he was court-martialed. Following his dishonorable discharge in March 1983, Guthrie began a one-man vendetta against the U.S. government.

Guthrie returned to Maryland where he devised a sophisticated buy-and-return scam on area Kmart stores. Guthrie would later tell authorities that he raised "hundreds of thousands of dollars" in the scam and that he'd sent the bulk of the money to Richard Butler at Aryan Nations headquarters in Idaho. He supplemented this revenue with several insurance scams and half a dozen more armed robberies. All of these crimes were committed with a finesse that left no trace of

Guthrie's hand. During one of the robberies he assaulted a female employee sexually as well as physically. Twice he pistol-whipped his victims before making off with the cash. Guthrie also shot his own brother in a dispute over money, tried to dynamite the car of an enemy, and may have torched an abortion clinic.

In 1990, Guthrie briefly visited Aryan Nations where, no doubt, these violent tendencies were reinforced. That summer, he was arrested in Rockville on assault charges and served three weeks in jail. He did not return to face charges in court, and a warrant was issued for his arrest.

THE PLOT

Unable to hold down a steady job, Langan moved to Cincinnati in 1991, and Guthrie met him there in December.[11] Six months later, in July 1992, the two drove to Aryan Nations headquarters in Hayden Lake, Idaho, in Guthrie's pickup truck festooned with Nazi symbols and a bumper sticker reading "Just Say No to ZOG," followed by the Aryan Nations telephone number. This was a time of intense emotions at Butler's encampment, as everyone was following the dramatic events unfolding between federal agents and white separatist Randy Weaver and family at nearby Ruby Ridge, Idaho. Langan and Guthrie met with Pastor Butler and a gaggle of racists who had known Bob Mathews and the Order. "They were losers," Langan recalled later. "They were nowhere near ready to start the so-called second American Revolution . . . Aryan Nations had more security leaks than just about anything."

Langan and Guthrie were more serious than that. They had begun to see "the movement," not in terms of living in a public compound surrounded by rednecks celebrating some bygone illusion, but as a clarion call to revolutionary action that demanded anonymity and mobility. By the time he left Aryan Nations in August, Langan had become an "ordained minister" of Christian Identity and an Aryan warrior armed to the teeth.

As Langan's militarized masculinity intensified, so did his sexual identity problems. Privately, following his visit to Aryan Nations headquarters, Langan began spending time dressed as a woman. "I went from one extreme to another," he said. "The radical politics and macho behavior were just overcompensating for when I was ashamed of how I felt."

When Langan and Guthrie returned to Cincinnati in the fall—shortly after the shoot-out at Ruby Ridge—they began meeting with a heavily tattooed Aryan Nations skinhead, whom Langan had befriended in a common law seminar, named Shawn Kenny. Kenny, who would ultimately play a key role in the FBI's investigation of the ARA, already had a felony conviction and a long history of racist activity—to such an extent that the Southern Poverty Law Center had been tracking him since 1988. In the summer of 1993, about a year after Kenny met Langan, Cincinnati police officer Matt Moning would respond to a routine domestic violence call on Montana Avenue. Upon arriving at the scene, Moning saw a drunken teenage skinhead standing naked on top of a car, shouting obscenities at his girlfriend. This was Shawn Kenny. After Moning arrested Kenny for public intoxication and disturbing the peace, Kenny posted bail and was released. In the lead up to Kenny's day in court, two FBI agents from the Cincinnati office visited Moning and instructed him to drop the case; the agents had bigger plans for the young skinhead. In short, they had already met with Kenny and had offered to have his charges dismissed if he was willing to share information on two individuals within the local anti-government/neo-Nazi movement: Richard Lee Guthrie and Peter Kevin Langan.[12] Kenny accepted the deal and flipped.

During meetings held at Langan's sister's house in 1992 and 1993, Langan and Guthrie introduced Kenny to two books that would ultimately serve as the basis for the group that became the Aryan Republican Army. The first, Flynn and Gerhardt's *The Silent Brotherhood*, would serve as the ARA's ideological blueprint. The second, Richard Kelly Hoskins's lesser-known *Vigalantes of Christendom: The History of the Phineas Priesthood*, would become the gang's spiritual guide—replacing the fictitious *Turner Diaries* as a rightist manifesto.

In his book, Hoskins (who had been converted to Identity by Byron de la Beckwith, the Klansman responsible for the 1963 assassination of civil rights worker Medgar Evers) argues that assassination and robbery are biblically and historically justified when employed to restore what is seen to be God's law. To prove his point, Hoskins links the violence of the biblical Phineas (in Numbers 25:6, Phineas slays a couple wedded in an unlawful union with a javelin and appeases God, or Yahweh) to the "distinct priestly military orders" of the Crusaders, who drove the infidels from the Holy Land. From there, the Phineas legacy runs to Robin Hood. And from there, Phineas has common ancestry with John Wilkes Booth, Jesse James, and finally, Robert Mathews. These are the Phineas priests.

Langan and Guthrie saw themselves as part of this racist hagiography and set out to complete what they called the Order's "unfinished business." Kenny would later testify that, "Langan and me were pretty much convinced that what [the Order] had done was right, except as far as the mistakes they made. We were analyzing [Flynn and Gerhardt's *The Silent Brotherhood*] and trying to figure out . . . if they had done things a little different, how they could have been successful." These discussions centered on the criminal skills necessary for robbing banks, bombings, and assassinations, including the assassination of the president of the United States.

The Carlos Complex Revisited

Shortly before the 1992 elections, President George H. W. Bush made an old-fashioned whistle-stop campaign through north Georgia, delivering speeches at small towns along the way. A few days before his planned stop in Atlanta, the Secret Service received a tip that "some individuals" in the area were planning to gun down the president when he arrived in the city. The ringleader of this plot, said the informant, was one Richard Guthrie of Livonia, Georgia. Guthrie had boasted of his plan to kill the president during a recent conversation at his Livonia apartment. The informant also said that Guthrie had acquired a Heckler & Koch .308-caliber semi-automatic rifle for the killing and had loaded it with armor piercing bullets. This he had done in honor of Bruce Pierce, who had used the same type of armament in the Order's famous 1984 Brinks holdup. Furthermore, the informant admitted that he had recently participated in an armed robbery of a Livonia Pizza Hut, at the behest of Guthrie and an associate known as Pedro Gomez. Agents raided Guthrie's apartment and found an assortment of weapons and Aryan Nations literature. The raid was filmed by CNN and shown to audiences around the world. But Guthrie had moved on. The Secret Service then mounted a nation-wide search for Guthrie and his partner, Pedro Gomez.

Meanwhile, the greatest challenge facing Pete Langan was how to attract apprentice terrorists into his underground army. Once that was accomplished, he and Guthrie had the necessary technical skills to train them. Langan hit upon the novel idea of reinventing himself as a romantic urban guerrilla in the Carlos tradition. His first step took the form of symbolic mythmaking. Because Mathews had chosen "Carlos" as his code name, Langan took the similar moniker: "Pedro." Pedro Gomez was therefore fabricated from a myth no more trustworthy than the Jackal's. In creating this identity, Langan simply carried on the process of self-deception by making the Carlos myth contingent on his own Phineas-inspired illusions.

Due to an earlier traffic violation, though, law enforcement also knew about Pedro Gomez, and on November 9 Langan was arrested in Cincinnati in connection with the Livonia Pizza Hut robbery. Ten months later he was extradited to Carnseville, Georgia, to await trial in the Franklin County jail for armed robbery—a crime punishable by life imprisonment. Once again, Langan found himself in a southern hell-hole of the first degree.

The Secret Service was still keenly interested in Guthrie for his threat against Bush, however, and in September Langan agreed to help the Secret Service find Guthrie in exchange for a signature bond and a ticket out of jail. Now an informant for the Secret Service, Langan returned to Cincinnati where he made a half-hearted attempt to find the would-be assassin. Eventually, Langan did find Guthrie; but instead of turning him over to the Secret Service and saving his own hide, Langan decided to double-cross the government and renew the violent political agenda he had begun with Guthrie ten months earlier. First and foremost, that included robbing banks to support the terrorist underground.

Langan emerged from this experience with an invigorated commitment to build his army and a burning hatred of FBI, especially because of their recent actions against the Branch Davidians in Waco. Thus was born the Aryan Republican Army and its audacious leader, Commander Pedro. In the Carlos tradition, Langan began dressing as a Mexican outlaw in cowboy boots, jeans, sunglasses, and black shirts. This outfit—combined with his dark hair cascading below his shoulders, his eyes lined with mascara, and his bullet wounds from previous gun battles—gave him the air of a rock star from the American badlands—a sort of Jim Morrison figure, before he lost his step.

Prosecutors would later describe Langan as a "transsexual white-supremacist bank-robbing terrorist," but that ignores his exceptional criminal skills. To his followers—Guthrie, Kenny, and those who would come later—Langan presented himself as a revolutionary at war with the federal government. Like Carlos the Jackal's leftist intellectuals "with a pistol in the drawer," Pedro could recite lines from Shakespeare's *Merchants of Venice* one minute and quote The Who's "My Generation" the next. He once told Sam Donaldson of ABC's *Primetime Live:* "I'm just another person caught up in the tyrannical legal system. Power to the people. Up with revolution! Now is the time to set free the oppressed people of North America." Such rhetoric would be panned by the media, but it wasn't really intended for the mass media, or even the alternative media. Langan's pomposity was meant to speak to the emotional cracks between media representations of current events— namely, to the neo-Nazi skinhead counter-culture where "in-depth analysis" is worthless. Langan represented a new kind of American terrorist who fed off the urban taste for quick takes: one minute photo-ops, bumper-sticker summations of complex issues, and the coarsening of youth culture. To recruit his army, Pedro would rely on the high-energy blood and thunder of white power heavy-metal music.

Organization

By 1994 Langan and Guthrie (now both fugitives wanted by the Secret Service) had developed extensive contacts in the white underground. They included a forty-four-year-old Identity preacher and Aryan Nations activist named Mark Thomas. Thomas had spent the last several years cultivating his ability to reach out to young people at a confusing point in their lives and then using that confusion strategically, to draw them into the neo-Nazi movement. At his "farm" outside Allentown, Pennsylvania (actually a bleak parcel of land sitting across from a toxic waste dump), Thomas held weekend religious retreats involving sermons, white power rock concerts, and firearms instruction, sometimes drawing as many as three hundred skinheads and members of the Ku Klux Klan, the Posse Comitatus, Aryan Nations, and other disenfranchised whites. Thomas preached a mixture of racist ideas: Christian Identity; Odinism, the religion of pre-Christian Nordics; an interpretation of Carl Jung's social archetype theory, which said that the Norse-Germanic people's archetypes could only be inherited, not culturally transmitted; and the apocalyptic view of Jim Morrison of The Doors. (Thomas claimed to have experienced an epiphany in the late 1960s when he had a chance encounter with Morrison in Greenwich Village.) Often dressed in a Jim Morrison T-shirt and shades, Thomas had recently gained national attention for his activities, first by appearing in a Fox television documentary called *Face of Hate*—a wholly unflattering portrayal of the preacher as a latter-day Hitler (whom Thomas resembled slightly, even wearing a trimmed mustache like the Fuhrer's), and then as a guest on *Geraldo,* as the subject of a *New York Times* article, and other nationally broadcast news shows.

On October 5, 1994, Langan and Guthrie visited Thomas at his farm for the purpose of recruiting others into their bank robbery crew. "We could care less who they were," Guthrie coldly reflected in an unpublished memoir, "as long as they agreed with the same things we did: to conduct [the robberies] the old-fashioned way, the Jesse James way—to plunder with extreme prejudice." And plunder they would. These young men would become the ARA's foot soldiers:

- Scott Stedeford, the dynamic twenty-six-year-old drummer and front man for a Camden, New Jersey, skinhead band called Cyanide. Highly intelligent and with no criminal record, Stedeford also claimed to have had a life-changing experience during his high school years after hearing the music of Jim Morrison and The Doors. He met Thomas in the summer of 1993, whereupon Thomas introduced Stedeford to *The Silent Brotherhood.* Stedeford began distributing Aryan Nations literature at his gigs and changed the band's name to Day of the Sword. After joining the ARA, Stedeford used a portion of the money gained from bank robberies to record an acclaimed white power CD, *Ear to Ear,* which combined the sensuality of The Doors' music with the legacy of Carlos/Mathews to justify a vision of apocalyptic terror. Stedeford's ARA code name became "Tuco," after a character in the classic Hollywood western, *A Fist Full of Dollars.*
- Kevin McCarthy, a seventeen-year-old junior high school dropout from Philadelphia who suffered from brain damage as a result of alcoholism. After several institutional commitments for his drinking problem, McCarthy became a homeless teenager in Atlantic City, New Jersey, where he was indoctrinated into Christian Identity by a recruiter for the Atlantic City Skinheads (the AC Boys). He then embarked upon a crime spree with other AC Boys up and down the Jersey Coast, robbing and beating

homeless men. McCarthy met Scott Stedeford in early 1993 and became his bass player. Soon after that, McCarthy met Mark Thomas and moved into a spare room at the farm. That summer, Thomas drove the sixteen-year-old to Elohim City, Robert Millar's Identity enclave in the Ozarks, where McCarthy participated in firearms training and paramilitary maneuvers with other armed children and adults. McCarthy's ARA code name became "Blondie," after another character in *A Fist Full of Dollars.*

- Michael Brescia, twenty-one. Brescia's father was a Philadelphia-area fire chief and his mother was a socialite. A former Eagle Scout, Brescia enrolled in Philadelphia's La Salle University in 1990. Also an aspiring rock star, he met Stedeford three years later and took up rhythm guitar. Brescia was asked to leave La Salle in the spring of 1993 after failing to heed prior warnings concerning his distribution of Aryan Nations literature. That fall, after meeting Thomas through McCarthy, Brescia relocated to Elohim City. He moved into a house with EC's thirty-three-year-old security director, Andreas Carl Strassmeir, and became engaged to Robert Millar's granddaughter. Brescia's ARA code name was "Tim" in deference to Timothy McVeigh.[13]

Strategy

For terrorists, raising money through bank robbery is not only logistically sensible; it is also politically correct because it can be interpreted as dispossessing the state of its most precious resource (capital), which, in turn, can be portrayed as a proletarian action. This criminal dynamic has been played out for years in the international terrorist underground, most recently in the audacious $26-million bank robbery allegedly committed by the Irish Republican Army in Belfast on December 20, 2004. Led by a Carlos-like IRA sympathizer known as "The Striker," the robbery damaged the peace process between Sinn Fein (the IRA's political arm) and the British government, causing Prime Minister Tony Blair to declare, "There could be absolutely no place, not merely for terrorist activity, but for criminal activity of any sort by people associated with a political party."[14]

Rendering such a heavy political cost to the state, while simultaneously filling the war chest, is the ultimate terrorist dream. The ARA began to chase that dream by making a detailed study of the IRA—its namesake. Through his reading of the *Handbook for Volunteers of the Irish Republican Army*, Langan envisioned what this so-called "Green Book" describes as "dispersed units," each of which "decide[s] its own local targets and carr[ies] out its jobs" by "deceiving the enemy as to [its] methods and intentions." Central to this strategy is the use of decoys. "The guerrilla will use many ruses," says the Green Book. "He can always [find ways] to cover his tracks."

From this study came a pattern to the ARA bank robberies. From January through August 1994, Langan's gang hit seven midwestern banks located in and around shopping malls—for the protection offered by pedestrian foot traffic. Planning was the key. After casing and video-taping their targets, the ARA designed escape routes and monitored law enforcement dispatch channels with radio scanners. They purchased cheap getaway cars (referred to as "drop cars") with fake IDs and "combat-parked" these vehicles outside the targets. (Combat parking involves backing a car into a parking space, thereby concealing the car's license plate and permitting a quick getaway.) Each robbery took no more than sixty seconds, and the ARA took only what was in the cash drawers (known as "teller runs")—never getting greedy by attempting to hit the vault. Posing as construction workers and wearing ski masks, they carried hand-held radios and armed themselves with assault rifles and grenades, but their signature was what they called the "hoax device" that they would leave behind as a threat—a phony but deadly-looking bomb made of road flares, gun powder, black electrical tape, wires, and a small clock.

With each successful robbery, Langan and Guthrie grew more confident in their bank-robbing skills—to the point, in fact, of becoming cocksure and arrogant. By the time they hit the Society National Bank in Springdale, Ohio, on June 8, 1994, a dark sense of humor had been added to their repertoire—humor based not on the pages of *The Silent Brotherhood*, but on the script of the 1991 Hollywood movie *Point Blank*, starring Patrick Swayze as the leader of a California bank robbery gang called the "Ex-Presidents" because they wore masks of Richard Nixon, Jimmy Carter, Ronald Reagan, and Lyndon Johnson. During the Springdale heist, life imitated art as Langan wore a mask of Richard Nixon and Guthrie wore a Jimmy Carter mask.

More low-brow humor would follow, due mainly to the influence of Richard Guthrie (code name: Commander Pavell after an unknown idol). "Guthrie as a person," testified an FBI agent at Langan's trial, "had a remarkable sense of humor." It was Guthrie who came up with the idea to register drop cars in the names of FBI agents; to wear FBI raid jackets and ball caps during the bank robberies; to send letters and cartoons to newspapers; to produce and distribute their recruitment video (*The Aryan Republican Army Presents: The Armed Struggle Underground*), complete with advertisements for such phony products as "Blammo Ammo . . . the choice of Revolutionaries everywhere"; and to print his own business cards reading: ARA IS EVERYWHERE! COMING TO YOUR TOWN SOON! But while Guthrie's inventions could be funny, they were no joke.

Like the robberies, Guthrie's humor was a Phineas deed modeled after the Jesse James legacy. History books are replete with examples of such humor on the part of the James gang. Not only did the gang print their own press releases and taunt law enforcement at every turn in their string of seventeen violent bank robberies, but Jesse James eventually became a commodity—a criminal rock star on perpetual tour. After Jesse's death, his landlord sold bloody splinters from the floorboards for a quarter a piece. When all the splinters sold out, the landlord soaked new floorboards in ox blood and kept the business alive. Upon his release from prison years later, Frank James, Jesse's brother, embarked upon a second career as a successful carnival attraction.[15]

Appreciating this showcasing of imagery and style is one way to distinguish American terrorists from international jihadists. Al-Qaeda operatives, for example, would never dream of using appearances or panache to make ironic statements about their violence. The ARA took this trait to a new level by portraying themselves as entertainers rather than terrorists, thereby making violence a performance. During the robberies, Guthrie would typically run around the bank in his Jimmy Carter mask, yelling Arabic gibberish and waving a fake bomb in the air like a lunatic. Langan would end the heists by shouting: "Up the revolution! Bank you very much!" For the ARA, the whole point of this was to mock their victims. Their cruel sense of humor, intended to parody the misfortune of helpless bank employees and innocent citizens by transforming terrorism into carnival, was exemplified by the December 9 robbery of the Third Federal Savings & Loan Bank in the Cleveland suburb of Middleburg Heights.

In this robbery, Langan approached the bank dressed as Santa Claus, followed by Kevin McCarthy in an elf's hat and a black ski mask. As they entered the bank, Langan chanted "Ho! Ho! Ho! Merry Christmas!" as a group of children cheered him on. Moments later, Scott Stedeford approached the teller window, also dressed in a ski mask and elf's hat. In one hand he carried a Christmas stocking holding a fake bomb and in the other he held a Ruger 10mm revolver. None of the victims was hurt; but, then again, it is likely that none was ever the same.

THE DEFINING ATTACK

By early 1995 the ARA had amassed an unprecedented record of successful robberies. Their spree had netted roughly $300,000, allowing the gang to purchase numerous vehicles, guns, military gear, and video equipment. They also rented a safe house in Pittsburg, Kansas, near the Missouri border. Around this time, *USA Today* ran a lengthy article about the gang—referred to as the "Midwestern Bank Bandits"—explaining how they had eluded authorities for more than a year, stealing hundreds of thousands of dollars, some of which might have been funneled to the terrorist underground. An FBI spokesman called the Bandit investigation "a major case." Much to the delight of Langan and Guthrie, the article ended by saying that the Bandits were on the verge of breaking Jesse James's record for bank robberies carried out along the Kansas-Missouri border between 1866 and 1882. (In fact, the ARA had already broken that record). "The number of banks they robbed [twenty-two] is *not* unique," countered FBI agent Gil Hendrickson, who would later investigate the ARA. "We've seen gangs rob as many as thirty banks before. They are unique because, unlike other robbers, [the ARA] used their money to create a war chest to overthrow the United States government. They did it for a cause."[16]

Yet unlike the Order, who squandered vast sums on personal indulgences and futile paramilitary operations, the ARA lived a simple life. They drove used cars, did their own mechanical work, bought their clothing at army surplus shops, stayed in cheap hotels and campgrounds, and ate at family restaurants. What was truly unique about them, though, and the factor that explains their successes more than anything, were the ways in which the ARA exploited routine activities.

Much like al-Qaeda in the East Africa embassy attacks and later in the 9/11 plot, the ARA devoted considerable attention to reconnaissance. Langan and Guthrie would spend weeks casing banks, taking into account every moment in the taken-for-granted order of daily life in and around their targets. They would fully occupy these urban spaces by entering the banks in disguise, walking the streets and sidewalks, visiting area stores and eateries, and driving escape routes over and over again. These spaces were then videotaped and studied for the small, often unnoticed practices of routine security. In this way, they were able to reconstruct urban space on their own terms. Such attentiveness to urban space is not unusual for society's transgressors. As criminologist Jeff Ferrell notes incisively, all manner of criminals—from burglars and graffiti writers to gang members— "read the everyday functionality and legality of the city in reverse, re-making the urban grid in their own image and animating it with their own illicit desires. In their worlds the most common of urban spaces—freeway on-ramps, stairwells, alleys and alley walls, front stoops and back doors—are re-imagined as illegal staging areas, entry points, [and] escape routes."[17]

The ARA had both the creativity to re-imagine these city spaces and the patience required to abort a mission when the situation required it. Langan called off more than a dozen robberies, after weeks of recon-naissance, due to such things as changes in bank security, shifting po-lice patrol patterns, and the unexpected presence of construction crews near the banks. He once scrapped plans to rob an Indianapolis bank after discovering that the city's financial institutions were connected to a sophisticated security radio system which made monitoring on the ARA's scanner impossible.

But just as Jesse James would be undone by his own almighty self-confidence, so, too, did the first chink in the ARA's armor come as a re-sult of their showcasing of imagery and style. This was played out in Pete Langan's most careless move as a serial bank robber, and it stands as an exemplar of terrorists' hubris in criminal affairs.

Melodrama in Ohio

In early October, 1994, Langan, Guthrie, Stedeford, and Kenny moved into a motel in Columbus, Ohio, and began a three-week surveillance of the Columbus National Bank on Livingston Avenue—studying the bank, running the escape route, selecting disguises, gathering weaponry, and constructing their hoax device. (It must be pointed out that, at this point, half of the bank robbery crew consisted of govern-ment informants.) On October 23, Guthrie purchased a five-hundred-dollar 1979 gray Ford Galaxy for the drop car. Two days later, they were locked and loaded.

Guthrie parked in front of the bank, combat style, at 11:00 a.m. Fifteen minutes later, Langan and Stedeford got out, brandishing semi-automatic pistols. They wore gloves, jungle boots, bulletproof vests, and disguises of hard hats over camouflage ski masks and sunglasses. The masks were functional because they disguised identity. But the hard hats and sunglasses were redundant—they served only to highlight a sort of bad-assed identity through the presentation of imagery and style. The same can be said of Stedeford's decision to tote an automatic assault rifle inside his guitar case as a backup weapon. He also carried a lunch box containing a fake bomb, to which Guthrie had attached a pack of Hostess Twinkies for a touch of humor.

Sprinting to the entrance, Langan and Stedeford bolted through the front door with such fury that they created an air vacuum, jarring the bank lobby and frightening everyone inside. Amid the bedlam, Langan pulled his gun and took a running leap over the counter, smacking his knee hard and causing the hard hat to fall over his eyes. Regaining his composure, Langan yelled, "Everybody get down! Everybody get down on the floor! Lay down!" Then, unable to see and frustrated with the clumsy get-up he was wearing, Langan yanked off the mask, sunglasses, and hard hat, and tossed them on the floor, exposing his face.

Stedeford went to a second entrance, placed the lunch box on the floor, opened it, and returned to the center of the lobby where he began waving his gun around, yelling, *"Andale! Andale!"* (Hurry! Hurry!) Just then two women walked into the lobby and Stedeford pointed his gun in their faces, shouting "Get down on the ground now!" As Langan went down the line of teller stations, scooping money into a bag, the bank's loan officer, Lisa Copley, waited—not face-down on the floor, but crouched at the end of the teller line. Two female tellers lay next to her, one hyperventilating from fear.

When Langan reached Copley's station, he bent over to open the drawer; it hit Copley in the head, knocking her backward and giving her a clear view of Langan's face. He muttered something about not getting enough money and ran to the drive-through window's teller station and tried to open the drawers, but they were locked. *"Andale! Andale!"* Stedeford shouted. "Come on, man, we gotta get out of here, now!" Langan jumped over the counter yelling, "We didn't get shit!" A moment later they ran outside and jumped in the Galaxy.

Guthrie wheeled away and within minutes they pulled into an apartment complex, jumped into a Ford van, and headed down Interstate 70. Guthrie was monitoring the police frequency on his radio when it reported that the Columbus bomb squad and the FBI were called to the bank, where they investigated the hoax device after rendering it safe with a water cannon. As usual, once this broadcast was heard, laughter erupted inside the van. Three hours later the ARA pulled into a truck stop in Wheeling, West Virginia, where Langan counted the money. It was a lousy score—only $3,400. Three weeks of planning had gone into the robbery and each man had earned less than the minimum wage. Not only that, but Lisa Copley had given authorities a description of one of the robbers. An all-points-bulletin then went out for a white male, possibly Hispanic. The bulletin also stated that the explosive device was "very complicated in its making" and that it was a "live" bomb capable of causing injury or death.

Under federal law, the robbery of a financial institution with such a device is a crime punishable by life in prison. That is precisely the sentence Langan would ultimately receive for his part in the Columbus robbery, due entirely to his decision to add the nonessential sunglasses and hard hat to his disguise. This was more than criminal stupidity. Rather, the existential need to assert one's identity through imagery and style had trumped criminal competence in the pursuit of terrorist goals. "Looking back with the benefit of hindsight," Langan would later recall, "I can see a lot of the mistakes I made as far as causes, ideology, methods, and associates. But just because I was wrong does not absolve the system I was fighting of its crimes."[18]

AFTERMATH

For the FBI, the path connecting the fugitive "Pedro Gomez" to the Midwestern Bank Bandits and the Columbus robbery would be circuitous, to say the least. The investigation would ultimately turn on the pathologies of individual ARA members combined with the FBI's intelligence on the far Right and the extraordinary events of April 19, 1995.

On April 19, the so-called Date of Doom, Richard Wayne Snell— originator of the plan to bomb the Alfred P. Murrah Federal Building in Oklahoma City during his days with the Covenant, the Sword, and the Arm of the Lord—was executed by the State of Arkansas for the murder of pawnshop owner William Strumpp. On the same day, Timothy McVeigh ignited a 7,000-pound ammonium nitrate fertilizer bomb in front of the Murrah Building, instantly killing 169 people, including nineteen children. Hundreds more were injured. This act of terrorism was intended to revenge the deaths of some seventy-five adults and children at the hands of the FBI in Waco on April 19, 1993. Some view the relationship between Snell's execution and McVeigh's monstrous crime as purely coincidental, others see it as part of a broader conspiracy, but neither perspective is of interest to us here. Rather, our concern is with six specific facts related to the early stages of the Oklahoma City bombing investigation, all of which provide circumstantial evidence indicating that members of the ARA had, at the very least, provided logistical support for the bombing.

First, on April 21, two days after the bombing, a former ATF informant at Elohim City, Carol Howe, reminded her handlers of a previously filed report indicating that Andreas Strassmeir, the commune's security director, was a terrorist instigator who had frequently talked about targeting federal buildings in Oklahoma City for "destruction through bombings." According to the previous report, Strassmeir had traveled on at least three occasions (November 1994, December 1994, and February 1995) to Oklahoma City where he and others inspected the Murrah Building.[19] Now, on April 21, after seeing photos of McVeigh, Howe recalled to agents that she had seen McVeigh, whom she knew as "Tim Tuttle," at Elohim City in the company of Strassmeier sometime around July 1994. Howe also told agents that "no one in the world looks more like the sketch of [bombing suspect] John Doe 2 than Michael Brescia"—Strassmeir's roommate at Elohim City. Furthermore, the FBI learned that on April 5, 1995—two weeks before the bombing—McVeigh had made a 1-minute-and-56-second phone call to Elohim City, looking for Strassmeir. According to an FBI memorandum, McVeigh "was believed to have been attempting to recruit a second conspirator to assist in the OKBOMB attack."[20] Staying at Strassmier's house that day were three members of the ARA: Michael Brescia, Scott Stedeford, and Kevin McCarthy.[21]

Second, the intelligence that Howe provided to the ATF—later described by a high-ranking ATF official as "reliable information from a reliable informant"—was corroborated by an FBI plant inside Elohim City.[22] That informant was an employee of Morris Dees's Southern Poverty Law Center.[23] Dees would later assert that McVeigh stayed at

Elohim City a dozen times under the name Tim Tuttle.[24] According to an FBI document, the Elohim City informant "could have knowledge and/or conspiratorial input into . . . criminal activities."[25] The FBI was also receiving intelligence from its Cincinnati informant, Shawn Kenny. Since hooking up with the ARA, Kenny had provided weapons training to the Aryan Nations of Ohio and had assisted in the planning of at least one Ohio bank robbery. But more importantly, according to both Richard Guthrie's manuscript and his subsequent confession to the FBI, Kenny had accompanied Guthrie and Langan to Fayetteville, Arkansas, during the second week of October 1993, when they attempted to recruit others into a conspiracy to rob an armored truck. Court records show that Timothy McVeigh (a former armored truck driver) and Terry Nichols—both strapped for cash at the time—registered at a Motel 6 in Fayetteville on October 11, 1993.[26]

Third, on April 21, FBI agents in Pensacola, Florida, began questioning McVeigh's sister, Jennifer, about her brother's alleged involvement in a series of midwestern bank robberies. She told agents that in the fall of 1994 her brother had given her several one-hundred-dollar bills and asked her to exchange them for "clean money" at a Lockport, New York, credit union. These hundred-dollar bills, according to McVeigh's statement to Jennifer, came from a recent bank robbery he had helped to plan. Jennifer also told agents about a December 24, 1993, letter she'd received from her brother, in which he fulminated about powerful Jews and bankers and concluded that, since the banks were "the real thieves," people who rob them were not criminals at all. "It's a sort of Robin Hood thing."[27]

Fourth, an internal FBI memo, heavily redacted, states that McVeigh made several visits to Elohim City and indicates that he was involved with the "Midwest Bank Robbery Gang." Specifically mentioned in that memo is Richard Guthrie, the former would-be navy SEAL with extensive training in explosives. Hence, by April 24, at least some FBI agents knew, through investigation and informants or both, that there was a connection between McVeigh and members of the ARA.[28] These suspicions only intensified in the days ahead. On May 4 the FBI began investigating a link between McVeigh and the ARA's robbery of a bank in Maryland Heights, Missouri. On May 11 the bureau explored a connection between McVeigh and an ARA bank robbery in Springdale, Ohio.[29] And on May 8 an FBI official told *Time* magazine that McVeigh, who had not held a steady job for the past two years, was in possession of some $10,000 in cash and bank accounts at the time of his arrest and concluded that "the bombing was financed by a series of unsolved bank robberies throughout the Midwest."[30]

Fifth, during this period, the FBI identified more than fifty witnesses who saw McVeigh and a man resembling the composite sketch of John Doe 2 in Kansas and Oklahoma in the weeks before the bombing. More than thirty witnesses reported seeing the car McVeigh was later arrested in—a battered yellow Mercury Marquis—being driven in Oklahoma City in the days before the bombing. Several witnesses noticed that the car had a dangling Arizona license plate. At least fifteen witnesses saw McVeigh and another man near the Murrah Building on the morning of April 19. Several witnesses claim they saw a woman directing McVeigh toward the building. (It is undisputed that Terry Nichols was at home in Herington, Kansas, on the morning of April 19.) Also, FBI interviews indicate that there were several sightings of McVeigh and another person in a Ryder truck on the morning of April 19.[31]

Sixth, on April 25 the U.S. Secret Service reported that it had security video footage of the bombing and witness testimony indicating that McVeigh had accomplices at the scene. A log of agents' activities and evidence in the investigation reads: "Security video tapes from the area show the truck detonation 3 minutes and 6 seconds after the *suspects* exited the truck" (emphasis added). According to the Secret Service, the purpose of the video was "to locate *personnel* lost in the bombing and determine if the agency was a specific target of the attack" (emphasis added).[32] Questions as to the identity of the accomplices or why the Secret Service was at the Murrah Building on the morning of April 19 remain a mystery. What is known, of course, is the following: at the time Richard Guthrie was being actively investigated by the Secret Service for threatening to assassinate President Bush, and Pete Langan was a rogue informant (personnel) for the Secret Service.

In the bombing's aftermath, widespread media attention was given to this connection between McVeigh and the midwestern bank robbers. In early May, for example, *Newsweek* screamed that the end was near in the hunt for McVeigh's co-conspirators. Quoting an unnamed source, the magazine reported that "an Aryan Republican Army compound in Elohim City, Oklahoma," was about to be surrounded and taken by the FBI.[33]

None of this was lost on the ARA. "The media blitz about the Midwestern Bank Bandits had deeply concerned us," wrote Guthrie in his memoir. "And during the weeks to follow, everyone in [the ARA] began to notice that the media had become rediculous [sic] with their contemplation." As a result, the ARA became saddled with paranoia.

EVIDENCE FETISH

Suspicion, backbiting, and contentious lying have long characterized the radical Right. These internal problems ultimately brought down the CSA and the Order, and soon they would cripple the ARA as well. Beginning in the summer of 1995, a rift developed between the already troubled Richard Guthrie and the equally neurotic Pete Langan. By this point, Langan was spending most of his time in Kansas City where he was known in the transsexual community as Donna McClure—a red-headed, chain-smoking drag queen. In late June, incapable of dealing with such emotional messiness, Guthrie attempted to kill Langan at the Kansas safe house.

Then Guthrie came to loggerheads with Stedeford. Their conflict reached a breaking point during the August 16 robbery of the Magna Bank in the St. Louis suburb of Bridgeton, Missouri. McCarthy gathered the cash on this job, making off with $17,000 from the drawers, as Stedeford held the lobby with a semi-automatic rifle, a hoax device, and a smoke grenade. Guthrie handled the getaway. When McCarthy and Stedeford exited the bank, however, they were astonished to find that Guthrie was nowhere to be found. Despite the sweltering 95-degree heat, Guthrie had shown up for the robbery drunk on tequila—and was now vomiting in an alley as Stedeford and McCarthy stood foolishly alone on the sidewalk with their assault rifles and stolen money. Guthrie made the pick up and then left behind in the drop car the August 11, 1995 edition of *USA Today*, opened to an article on Timothy McVeigh and the Oklahoma City bombing. The Magma job signaled the beginning of the end for the bank robbers, as Stedeford vowed never to work with Guthrie again. Kevin McCarthy would later testify: "Me and Scott Stedeford and also Peter Langan came to the conclusion that Guthrie was an unstable person." Realizing that Guthrie had just implicated them in the Oklahoma City bombing by leaving behind the newspaper article on McVeigh, Langan and the others began discussing a plan to kill Guthrie.[34]

By November the ARA's revolutionary dreams had blown away. It was then that Guthrie rented a second safe house in a run-down apartment duplex in Columbus, Ohio, where he slipped further into alienation. Now thirty-seven years old, Guthrie had no friends, no lover, and no hope of fitting into conventional society. He was terribly out of shape: too much beer and too many White Castle hamburgers had swollen his belly, leaving him in a constant state of crankiness that was only aggravated by the ceaseless cacophony of car traffic and boom-box thunder outside his door. Guthrie hated this noise with a passion equal to his contempt for the neighborhood's hookers, crack heads, and undercover cops. "They are low-life degenerates," he wrote, "who are worth less than the feces they produce every day." He was also immensely paranoid and delusional—and for good reason. Guthrie was wanted for multiple armed robberies, for plotting to assassinate the president of the United States, and for questioning in connection with the mass murder in Oklahoma City.

And so, he attempted to vicariously relive his glory days through the gang's remembrances. On December 24, Guthrie left Columbus in the Ford van bound for Pittsburg, Kansas, to close down the safe house there. He arrived on Christmas night in a blue funk and pulled slugs from a fifth of tequila until he passed out. On December 28, Langan arrived, and the two patched up their relationship, agreeing to participate in one last bank robbery together, this one in Indiana.

The next day, Langan and Guthrie loaded their vans and drove to Shawnee, Kansas, and Joplin, Missouri, respectively, where they rented storage lockers. And into those lockers they moved totem—everything from the masks of Richard Nixon and Jimmy Carter to three dozen notary public seals and numerous fake ID cards, Semtex explosives, blasting caps, and a military TOW missile, along with FBI ball caps and police uniforms, thousands of rounds of ammunition, shotguns, rifles, pipe bombs, hand grenades, numerous copies of *The Aryan Republican Army Presents: The Armed Struggle Underground* (in which Guthrie talks about an impending "courthouse massacre"), and a video containing footage of banks and an armored car in Columbus. Essentially, these storage lockers now held enough evidence to condemn every member of the ARA to life in prison.

Why did Langan and Guthrie follow the path of other domestic terrorists by saving such incriminating evidence, rather than destroying it as any smart criminal would? In a clever play on Karl Marx's thoughts about the nature of capitalist exchange, cultural critic John Leland refers to the connection between people and objects they live with the condition of commodity fetishism. This process changes the value of objects, endowing them with an aura based on qualities like newness, status or sex appeal, rather than such mundane factors as how well they work. "You could become attached to this aura," Leland argues, "independent of the things themselves."[35] The aura therefore represents a kind of coded information that not everyone can see. Conceived as a sort of *evidence fetish*, the evidentiary base of terrorism—weapons, ammo, explosives, disguises, and manifestos—provides terrorists with a coded reminder of their existential immersion in the physical task of killing and mayhem. An evidence fetish is similar to what criminologist Jack Katz refers to as "the sensual attractions of crime," the magical and creative appeals of transgression.[36] For American terrorists like Langan, Guthrie, Gary Yarbrough, Andrew Barnhill, and Richard Snell, evidence of terrorism offered a means of self-transcendence, a method for overcoming the dreariness associated with such banal routines as casing banks, building bombs, and stalking assassination victims.

It may be no coincidence that these men drew their criminality from the well of Nazism. Criminologist Wayne Morrison reminds us that it was the perpetrators of the Nazi Holocaust who recorded their own voluntary participation in the genocide by memorializing the slaughter of Jews in photographs that they took, passed around, pasted into family albums, and sent home to loved ones.[37] Just as the German Nazis took pride in their genocidal vocation through the photographic record, the American neo-Nazis celebrated their experiences by amassing mementoes of the terrorist moment.

FINAL DAYS

Upon his return to Ohio on January 6, 1996, Guthrie began casing banks in Dayton and then drove to Cincinnati where he sought the assistance of Shawn Kenny to drive the getaway car. By this time Kenny had joined the U.S. Army, despite his Nazi tattoos and his previous arrests on weapons charges in October 1995 and again in 1990, as well as the fact that he had helped plan the ARA's robbery of the Society National

Bank in Springdale, Ohio, in June 1994.[38] Nevertheless, Private Kenny, who was now on military leave from Fort Benning, Georgia, said he'd consider Guthrie's plan and would call with his decision in several days. One of Langan's security procedures was that details of an operation should only be shared with others on a need-to-know basis. But Kenny was no Langan, and during the interval Kenny shared plans about the Dayton heist with his wife, Tabitha. While the ARA had survived FBI manhunts, intense media attention, and numerous threats to internal security, it would not withstand the meddlesome nature of Tabitha Kenny. Guthrie called her the "Dragon Lady." "The Dragon Lady had a mouth the size of the Holland Tunnel," he wrote, "and the face of a bull dog; [she] spent more time talking than she did breathing."

For Tabitha, the feeling was mutual. Having no fondness for Guthrie to begin with, she instantly picked up the phone and called her husband's FBI handler, Special Agent Ed Woods of the Cincinnati office, who met with Shawn Kenny sometime around January 11. Woods instructed Kenny to go along with Guthrie's plan to hit the Dayton bank and notify him of their next meeting. That date was Monday, January 15, Martin Luther King, Jr., Day, and the rendezvous location was an Italian restaurant in the Cincinnati suburb of Chevoit, at 4 p.m.[39]

For Guthrie, the end came not with a bang but a whimper. Around 5 p.m., as he approached the restaurant in his van, Woods put a tail on him in an unmarked Ford Thunderbird. Guthrie drove away at forty miles an hour, turned into a housing development, and pulled into a cul-de-sac where the Thunderbird easily cut him off. Guthrie jumped out and slowly ran toward the woods. Moments later, he fell into a three-foot snowdrift; then he stood up and drew his gun on Woods. Woods and more than a dozen agents then piled onto Guthrie and cuffed him face-down in the snow.

It took Guthrie exactly one hour to roll over on Langan, informing agents that his old friend was scheduled to arrive at the Columbus safe house on January 16 to prepare for an Indiana bank robbery. Guthrie told Woods that Langan was an "Aryan Nations zealot" who was responsible for the 1994 robbery of the Society National Bank in Springdale and added that Langan had vowed "not to be taken alive" should federal agents try to arrest him. Pedro would go out with a bang.

In the early morning hours of January 18, a thirteen-member FBI SWAT team surrounded the safe house, along with ten supporting officers from the U.S. Marshals Service and the Columbus Police Department. They were armed with pistols, batons, chemical spray, shotguns, submachine guns, and assault rifles.

At 9:45 a.m., Langan walked out the back door dressed in several layers of black winter clothing. He wore cowboy boots, had dyed shoulder-length red hair tied back in a ponytail, and carried a black bag in his left hand. Strapped to his leg was a .38-caliber Bersa semi-automatic pistol. He walked to his vehicle, a white 1979 Chevy van with Iowa plates, and slowly entered the driver's seat. Suddenly the agents charged down the alley shouting, "Put your hands up!" "FBI!" "Police!"

Langan froze at the wheel, lifted his hands slightly, and hesitated. Then he whirled out of the driver's seat and dived into the back of the van, out of sight. An agent saw Langan come forward in a two-handed shooting stance, pointing a blue-steel pistol at him.

"He's got a gun," another agent shouted. "Take cover!"

Then seven SWAT team agents fired a total of forty-eight full metal jackets at the cargo bay where Langan was hiding, creating a thunderous clank of firepower. Unlike Robert Mathews, it turned out that Langan never did shoot at the agents, yet they fired more bullets at him than the German police fired at the Palestinian terrorists following the mass murder in Munich.[40]

Langan stood up bleeding from the face and put his hands through the broken glass on the driver's side. He had survived the rain of steel by crawling headfirst into a four-by-four wooden toolbox in the back. Someone opened the door, and Langan tumbled onto the ground where agents spread him out face-down in the dirt and began stomping him.

Records say that the van was still full of smoke from all the firepower when agents entered to begin their search. In the front seat they found the bag Langan had been carrying. It contained a Bible case—which, when opened, held a loaded 9mm Taurus pistol—a hand grenade, and a live pipe bomb. Then they checked the cargo bay: It held a loaded .223-caliber SGW carbine rifle, a loaded Chinese AR-15 assault rifle, and more than three thousand rounds of Chinese-made ammunition packed into military-style bandoliers.

Agents pumped Langan and Guthrie for information about the identity of other cell members, but no matter how hard the agents tried, they couldn't ferret out this information because neither Langan nor Guthrie knew the last names of their accomplices. This was part of the ARA's need-to-know arrangement, and it paid off with Guthrie at a time when he was ready to drop a dime on everybody, especially Stedeford. All he was able to tell Ed Woods was that three skinheads from Philadelphia were also involved in the bank robberies. For what it was worth, their names were Kevin, Scott, and "Tim."

The first major break came by coincidence when the FBI's Gil Henrickson began questioning Philadelphia police about the local skinhead scene. During the third week of February 1996, an officer told Hendrickson that he had a nephew who was involved in the white power movement—a heavily tattooed kid who was living with his grandmother in northeast Philly. His name was Kevin McCarthy. Thus began a three-month, round-the-clock surveillance of McCarthy.[41]

Love of hard-core music had inspired the skinheads to become ARA foot soldiers, and it would now lead to their demise. Around May 1, agents saw McCarthy get into his grandmother's car and head for Terminal Station. There he parked the car and walked into the Sound Under recording studio carrying his guitar case. Agents then recorded all license numbers of the vehicles parked in the vicinity. The computer check showed that one of those license numbers belonged to Scott Stedeford.

Three weeks later, on May 24, teams of armed FBI agents quietly surrounded the home of McCarthy's grandmother and the Sound Under studio. Stedeford and McCarthy were taken into custody without incident. Facing a fifty-year sentence, McCarthy turned state's evidence and began divulging details about the bank robberies. That included information about Michael Brescia's involvement in the June 1995 robbery of Bank One in Madison, Wisconsin. It was later determined that McCarthy, who claimed that he was in Iowa on April 19, lied to the FBI concerning his whereabouts on the day of the Oklahoma City bombing.[42] (For that matter, no one in the ARA, except Mark Thomas, had an alibi for April 19.)

Back in Ohio, Guthrie had pled guilty to nineteen bank robberies in seven states and claimed to have given a large portion of the stolen money to individuals within the terrorist underground. Included in an FBI document related to Guthrie's case is the following statement: "Guthrie both admitted to paying McVeigh money derived from bank robberies and identified McVeigh as an accomplice in certain bank robberies."[43] In a sealed agreement, Guthrie cut a deal with federal prosecutors both to identify those who had benefited from his largesse and to testify against Langan, Stedeford, and Thomas in return for a reduced sentence. Guthrie was scheduled to disclose information related to the terms of his plea agreement under oath before U.S. District Judge John D. Holschuh in Columbus on July 15, 1996. But that never happened. At 6 a.m. on July 12, Guthrie was found hanging from a bed sheet tied to a heating duct in his Covington, Kentucky, jail cell. He had committed suicide.

On January 29, 1997—after more than one million investigative hours that generated more than one billion documents and 43,000 checked tips—the FBI concluded that there was no concrete evidence linking McVeigh to any conspirator beyond Terry Nichols—this, despite Guthrie's confession to the contrary. The Justice Department announced that the infamous John Doe 2 never existed. The next day, Michael Brescia was arrested and indicted on charges of conspiring to commit seven of the midwestern bank robberies.

Three months earlier, in November 1996, Mark Thomas was subpoenaed to testify for the defense in the government's case against Langan. Thomas was prepared to take the stand and reveal that Kevin McCarthy had assisted McVeigh in the Oklahoma City bombing. A week before Thomas was scheduled to testify, however, he was indicted in the Eastern District of Pennsylvania on bank robbery charges, thus canceling his appearance at the Langan trial. FBI agents arrested Thomas at his farm in early 1997. An FBI interview, dated April 4, 1997, indicates that in February 1995 Thomas had said to his girlfriend: "We are going to get them. We are going to hit one of their buildings during the middle of the day. It's going to be a federal building. We will get sympathy if we bomb the building." Agents told Thomas that he'd be going to prison for twenty-five years, unless he cooperated. Forty-seven-year-old Thomas buckled under pressure and became an FBI informant.

Not everyone was willing to close the book on Oklahoma City, however. According to a 1997 *Time/CNN* poll, 77 percent of the American public did not believe that the FBI had identified and captured all those responsible for the bombing. A 1997 Gallup poll found that seven in ten Americans thought someone responsible for the bombing had escaped capture, and still other polls indicate that a considerable percentage of Americans believed that the federal government itself was involved in the bombing.[44] Why this near-universal uncertainty? "I think you have too many coincidences here that raise questions about whether other people are involved," said Danny Coulson, the FBI's veteran scene commander for the Oklahoma City investigation in 1995. "The close associations with Elohim City and the earlier plan to [bomb] the same Murrah building all suggest the complicity of other people."[45] Yet to acknowledge the complicity of the Aryan Republican Army in the attack and to build a case against them would have been a public relations nightmare for the FBI. Knowing that the ARA leader, Pete Langan, was himself a rogue government informant for the Secret Service, it would have served the government's interests if Langan were somehow killed, which the FBI sharpshooters clearly attempted to do in Columbus. Failing that, once Langan was behind bars for the bank robberies, the FBI simply ignored him.

Such skepticism reflects a central premise of this book; namely, that sophisticated acts of terrorism like the Oklahoma City bombing require an equally sophisticated level of criminal skill. Professionals I have spoken with contend that the bomb was likely built by an explosives expert, someone who knew how to perform the complicated task of fusing dozens of rounds of non-electrical blasting caps to boosters (in this case, Tovex sausages) so that the blasting caps would go off with millisecond precision, igniting more than three tons of ammonium nitrate fertilizer, diesel fuel, and nitro methane. Once the bomb was built, transporting it to the Murrah Building, setting it off, and then fleeing required experience in the logistics of urban terrorism—individuals accomplished in the crafts of deception, radio surveillance, and getaway. But perhaps more than anything, the attack required the patience necessary for planning and the ability to learn from dry runs. Such advanced criminal skills are not learned overnight: they are developed over time through repeated practice forged in the fires of chaos. These experiences give certain criminals the presence of mind to anticipate the unexpected in street movement and to act coolly at the time of the big moment.

Timothy McVeigh did not possess those skills. Nothing in his background, education, or training (in the army, at Elohim City, or elsewhere) prepared McVeigh to construct such a bomb or to deliver it to the Murrah Building—unless, of course, he was assisted by professionals. The circumstantial evidence presented in this chapter indicates that McVeigh was in league with the Aryan Republican Army—a gang led by two of the most highly skilled American paramilitary criminals since Robert Mathews and Richard Scutari—despite McVeigh's pronouncement to the contrary. Referring to the bombing prior to his 2001 execution at the Federal Penitentiary in Terre Haute, Indiana, and parroting the government's theory of the case, McVeigh said: "It's hard to believe that only one man could do this. Get over it. That's what happened."[46] Yet results of a polygraph test administered to McVeigh by his defense team in 1995 showed "indications of deception" regarding the involvement of others unknown. And in his memoir of the case, McVeigh attorney Stephen Jones admits that "there was a John Doe #2." The source for that claim: McVeigh himself.[47]

6

Al-Qaeda, the Radical Right, and Beyond

The Current Terroist Threat

Today the United States remains just as vulnerable to terrorism as it was prior to 2001, if not more so. But citizens of the United States are not the only ones who are vulnerable. The terrorist's life also changed after 9/11, and now the terrorist groups that menace America, and the rest of the world, are vulnerable as well. They are vulnerable to travel restrictions, the profiling of airline passengers, having their email and telephone messages intercepted, and many other things, but mostly they are vulnerable to the imperatives documented throughout this book. Terrorists are not "criminal masterminds." Their organizations are full of contradictions, inconsistencies, and weaknesses. When investigators concentrate on common crimes committed by these groups, they may preempt larger, more catastrophic events. Terrorism thrives in places where law enforcement fails to do so.

AL-QAEDA CENTRAL

Despite President George W. Bush's promise to capture Osama bin Laden "dead or alive," reports indicate that bin Laden is still living, hiding somewhere along the Pakistan-Afghan border where he appears in videos for the Arabic satellite television station Aljazeera, exhorting his followers to mount new attacks against the United States and its allies in the Iraq war and thereby expand al-Qaeda into a global ideology. As Daniel Benjamin and Steven Simon point out in their 2005 book, *The Next Attack,* bin Laden and his top lieutenant, Ayman al-Zawahiri, have now eluded capture for a period longer than it took the United States to fight World War II.[1] Although al-Qaeda's organizational capabilities were badly damaged in the U.S.-led coalition's military strikes against

Afghanistan, recent reports show that al-Qaeda, along with a resurgent Taliban have regrouped in the border region where they have grown in numbers, ruthlessness, and criminal sophistication, particularly in the area of heroin trafficking. According to CIA estimates, the cultivation of opium poppies in Afghanistan doubled from 2002 to 2003, then the 2002 amount *tripled* in 2004. Afghanistan now supplies nearly 90 percent of the world's heroin, providing an economic windfall to the Taliban and jihadist warlords who control major smuggling routes out of the country.[2] In October 2005, the major Taliban drug lord Baz Mohammad was extradited to the United States and charged with conspiring to import some $25 million worth of heroin into the United States and other countries.[3]

Pakistan President Pervez Musharraf, one of America's most important allies in the war on terrorism, has admitted that the trail for bin Laden has gone cold, and that the Qaeda leader currently has several thousand fighters at his command, including some of the organization's top figures. Purportedly among them is the former operational commander of the 1998 embassy bombings in East African, Abdullah Ahmed Abdullah (aka "Saleh"), believed to be serving as bin Laden's commander for operations worldwide.[4] A senior Pakistani official recently described the country's rugged South Waziristan province as the hub of al-Qaeda operations. Already an Islamic radical stronghold, the region has taken the brunt of recent U.S. air strikes—strikes that have killed an estimated 9,673 Afghan and Pakistani civilians since the U.S.-led campaign began in 2001.[5] In early 2006, for instance, an unmarked U.S. Predator drone aircraft fired six missiles into a village in the Bajur tribal area, killing at least eighteen people in an attempt to take the life of Ayman al-Zawahiri. Yet the United States acted on bad intelligence, and most of those killed turned out to be women and children; local sympathy for al-Qaeda grew as a result, and the search for bin Laden became even more difficult.[6]

According to officials from Pakistan, Afghanistan, and India, guerrilla training camps have again sprung up in the border tribal regions, offering militants instruction in firearms, rocket-propelled grenades, and remote control bombs.[7] Far from being a secret, al-Qaeda-produced videos of these camps are routinely shown throughout the Muslim world by Aljazeera and Al Arabiya.[8] Referring to the camps, a militant leader told the *New York Times:* "We are better organized [today] and better skilled to fight an enemy that is high-tech and sophisticated."[9]

American intelligence officials have repeatedly warned that al-Qaeda remains determined to transform its training and technological skills into a tightly choreographed operation that will surpass the nearly 3,000 causalities of the September 11 attacks. The next attacks on U.S. soil "are in the planning stages," warned bin Laden in a 2006 video-tape released through Aljazeera, "and you will see them in the heart of your land as soon as the planning is complete."[10] In public testimony given in 2005, CIA director Porter J. Goss declared that it "may only be a matter of time before al-Qaeda or another group attempts to use chemical, biological, radiological and nuclear weapons."[11] There has never been any doubt about bin Laden's intentions in this area. Michael Scheuer (a.k.a., Anonymous, the former CIA agent who created a secret intelligence unit tracking bin Laden) notes that bin Laden has obtained a fatwah justifying a nuclear attack against America on religious grounds. "Muslims argue that the United States is responsible for millions of dead Muslims around the world," says Scheuer, "so reciprocity would mean you could kill millions of Americans."[12] But such an attack would be contingent upon al-Qaeda's criminal skills. As we saw earlier, in 1998 al-Qaeda attempted to buy weapons-grade uranium on the Sudanese black market; yet the Qaeda buyers were not physicists, and the enriched uranium they were offered turned out to be low-grade reactor fuel that was unusable for a weapon.[13]

In *Nuclear Terrorism: The Ultimate Preventable Catastrophe,* Harvard University's Graham Allison argues that al-Qaeda is most likely to steal a small nuclear weapon from Russia's arsenal or construct its own rudimentary nuclear bomb made from highly enriched uranium, and then smuggle the device into the United States inside a ship or truck.[14] Bin Laden has admitted that the *theft* of a nuclear weapon is unnecessary. During his interview with journalist Hamid Mir in November 2001, bin Laden described the ease of obtaining nuclear weapons. "It's not difficult, not if you have contacts in Russia and with other militant groups," bin Laden said. "They are available for $10 million to $20 million."[15] Today that possibility may be more real than ever before. Intelligence research indicates that the primary threat of nuclear terrorism stems from both the availability of materials and the potential willingness of terrorist groups to use them.[16] Afghan heroin is now entering Russia from the south, aided in part by corrupt military officials. From there the heroin smuggling routes run through the country's "nuclear belt"—a series of nuclear research and weapons facilities—thus raising concerns about al-Qaeda's access to the black market in radioactive materials.[17] Twice in 2002, Russian authorities interrupted terrorist plots to conduct surveillance of these weapons storage facilities. Even more troubling, the CIA has conceded that some Russian nuclear stockpiles are believed to be missing, perhaps sold to terrorists. "I can't account for some of the material," confessed Goss in his testimony.[18]

Other experts contend that the ultimate security nightmare facing the United States is an attack in which the key factor is neither training nor technology, but commitment—the essential ingredient for suicide bombing.[19] On September 11, of course, the Qaeda hijackers demonstrated that they were willing to die for their cause. But the 9/11 attacks required much more than commitment. They demanded breaching airline security; hijacking and hostage taking; slitting the throats of those hostages; and flying commercial jetliners into predetermined targets. The tactic of suicide bombing—as it has been practiced in places like Jerusalem, Beirut, and Baghdad—requires little more than boarding a subway train or a bus and pulling the switch on a detonating device. A 2005 government security assessment warned that in addition to attacks against mass transit targets, al-Qaeda might use suicide bombers to derail trains or crash a truck carrying flammable material into trains. Still other targets considered vulnerable are shopping malls, high-rise apartment buildings, and, still, the aviation industry.[20]

While hundreds upon hundreds of innocent civilians have died in suicide bombings over the years, three-fourths of all suicide bombings since 1968 have occurred between September 11, 2001, and the middle of 2005.[21] The research of Robert Pape indicates that al-Qaeda has been involved in at least seventeen bombings since 2002, most of them suicide missions, which killed approximately 700 people—more attacks and victims for al-Qaeda than in all the years before 9/11 combined.[22] Moreover, intelligence estimates indicate that al-Qaeda remains intent on attacking large targets in the United States and that suicide bombings are clearly "a preferred method of attack."[23]

Most experts focus primarily on the method of the next attack and speak in generalities about potential targets. But Scheuer reminds us that the symbolism of *place* matters a great deal to bin Laden. "Bin Laden and his allies have demonstrated that they will attack in countries where their organizations have been hurt," Scheuer writes, "and against *the organizations* they hold responsible for inflicting the damage. Al Qaeda operates very much on an eye-for-eye basis."[24] According to

Scheuer, bin Laden once said that his attack in Nairobi was made in part because the U.S. embassy "housed the largest CIA center in the African Continent" and because it "had supervised the killing of at least 13,000 Somali civilians in the treacherous aggression against Muslims in that country."[25] When bin Laden's Afghan camp was bombed by U.S. cruise missiles two months after the Nairobi bombing, intelligence sources told *Time* they had evidence that bin Laden was planning his boldest move yet—a strike on Washington or possibly New York City in an eye-for-eye retaliation; this assessment presaged the 9/11 attacks by nearly three years.[26]

If the past is a prologue for al-Qaeda, then the place of its next attack is not hard to figure out. In a letter written from hiding in the summer of 2005 and intended for the eyes of the Jordanian Abu Mussab al-Zarqawi, head of al-Qaeda in Iraq, bin Laden's top lieutenant, Ayman al-Zawahiri, talked about watching his wife and young daughter die after being crushed by the concrete of a collapsed ceiling in an American bombing of a school in Afghanistan.[27] The U.S. Department of Defense, the government unit responsible for al-Zawahiri's loss, is located, of course, in Washington—as are the agencies that have sponsored illegal detentions, torture, and secret CIA prisons. By the logic of retaliation, the government agencies that allowed the raping of Muslim men with broom handles at Abu Ghraib prison would be directly in bin Laden's crosshairs.

How serious is al-Qaeda's current threat against the United States? Official statements provide little help in answering that question. In his 2003 Congressional testimony, then-Attorney General John Ashcroft declared that "more than 3,000 foot soldiers of terror have been incapacitated . . . and hundreds of suspected terrorists have been identified and tracked throughout the U.S."[28] Two years later President Bush announced that "federal terrorism investigations have resulted in charges against more than 400 suspects, and more than half of those charged have been convicted."[29]

Independent investigations reveal, however, that only fourteen federal terrorism cases can be linked to al-Qaeda, and most of them involved either the 9/11 conspiracy or plots that occurred around the same time, some of which are highly questionable (such as the cases against the "Lackawanna Six," Yemeni Americans from Buffalo, New York, convicted of attending an al-Qaeda training camp in Afghanistan, and the mentally impaired Iyman Faris, who allegedly planned to take down the Brooklyn Bridge with a blowtorch).[30] Yet investigators generally agree that there is at least one bona fide case of an al-Qaeda plot against the United States since 9/11. This case, which serves as an example of the kind of attack that may be in the works, revolves around the criminality of a naïve young Pakistani named Uzair Paracha.

Al-Qaeda in America: Post–9/11

Uzair Paracha's story begins with his father, Saifullah Paracha, a wealthy Pakistani real estate developer who had ties to the Taliban regime during the late 1990s.[31] Through those contacts, Saifullah Paracha met Osama bin Laden while on a charity mission to Afghanistan in 1999. At the time, Paracha also maintained a home in New York City where he ran a garment import business. Sometime in 2002, bin Laden's associates began asking favors of Paracha, first asking him to launder some $200,000 in cash. Paracha honored the request, thus establishing his bona fides with al-Qaeda and leading to a series of meetings between Paracha and three key figures of the organization.

The first was with none other than Khalid Sheikh Mohammad (KSM), mastermind of the 9/11 attacks. The second was with KSM's nephew, Ammar al-Baluchi, the paymaster who delivered funds to the 9/11 hijackers. And the third was with a man named Majid Khan, a member of al-Qaeda who needed documents to travel to the United States. While Khan had earlier been given political asylum in the United States and had lived in Baltimore, after 9/11, he returned to Pakistan where he joined al-Qaeda. Because he had left the United States without giving the authorities the notice required of political refugees, Khan needed help to return after leaving the country improperly. And this is where Paracha's twenty-one-year-old son, Uzair, entered the picture.

Uzair Paracha lived in New York where he ran a business out of his father's office in mid-town Manhattan, selling shares in his father's Karachi apartment complex to Pakistanis who were increasingly moving back to Pakistan following 9/11. Uzair Paracha came to the United States on a travel visa in January 2003, after receiving a graduate degree from the Institute of Business Administration in Karachi. Before leaving Pakistan, he had met twice with his father's al-Qaeda contacts.

In one of those meetings, held over dinner, al-Baluchi and Khan asked Uzair Paracha to complete a number of tasks when he arrived in the United States; namely, he was asked to retrieve Khan's passport from a Maryland post office box, deposit money in Khan's bank account, and use Khan's credit cards to make it appear as if Khan had never left the United States illegally. Khan also gave Paracha a list of instructions on how to deceive immigration officials into thinking that Khan was still living at his Baltimore home. According to the plan, this pretext would remove the cause for an immigration violation, thus allowing Khan to re-enter the United States where he would conduct surveillance for al-Qaeda and procure chemical weapons for a terrorist attack. In return for Paracha's cooperation, al-Qaeda promised to invest $200,000 in his New York business venture.

Between January and March 2003, Uzair Paracha fulfilled his part of the bargain. He retrieved Khan's passport, along with his driver's license and social security card, and ran up charges on Khan's Bank of America ATM card. Paracha also opened a mailbox in Maryland, in Khan's name, and periodically checked to see if Khan's immigration documents had arrived, which, upon arrival, he would forward to Khan in Pakistan. To further create the impression that Khan was Stateside, Paracha called the New York INS office from a pay phone near Madison Square Garden, claiming to be Khan.

At this point, the Bush administration experienced its most triumphant moment in the war on terrorism. On March 1, an unkempt Khalid Sheikh Mohammad (KSM) appeared on television screens and front pages around the world following his predawn arrest in Rawalpindi, Pakistan. During his interrogation, conducted at a military "black site" using the technique of water-boarding (later described by the CIA Inspector General as constituting "cruel, and degrading treatment under the [Geneva] convention"), KSM told his handlers about the scheme to bring Majid Khan to the United States, thus effectively aborting the plot. KSM's confession led the FBI to Uzair Paracha's office where he was arrested on March 28.

Uzair Paracha was ultimately found guilty of conspiring to provide material support to a foreign terrorist organization and locked up in the Metropolitan Detention Center in Manhattan. In May 2003, the FBI learned that al-Qaeda had made a $277,000 deposit into Saifullah Paracha's bank account. The elder Paracha was arrested on July 5 at Karachi airport while embarking on a trip to Thailand. Paracha was taken by U.S. forces to Afghanistan and then to Guantanamo Bay where he was tried by a military tribunal in November 2005. Based on information provided by KSM, Khan and Ammar al-Baluchi were also arrested, and today they are in U.S. custody at undisclosed locations. As it turned out, Uzair Paracha was a dupe recruited by KSM solely for his community connections—much as KK Mohamed had been recruited into the Tanzania embassy bombing plot because he lived in Dar es Salaam and knew the local culture and spoke Swahili. To be sure, al-Baluchi later told authorities that Uzair Paracha was "totally unwitting" of his ties to terrorism. But what, exactly, did that involve?

There is little doubt that Khan was planning attacks in the United States. He was eventually accused of plotting to bomb underground storage tanks at several Baltimore gas stations. But given KSM's involvement in the conspiracy, that plan seems unlikely. After all, this was the man who, together with his other nephew, Ramzi Yousef, engineered the first World Trade Center bombing in 1993. Then, in 1995, KSM and Yousef conspired together on the Bojinka plot to blow up a dozen 747s over the Pacific. Moreover, KSM also played a key role in coordinating the 1998 embassy bombings in East Africa and the USS *Cole* bombing in 2000. A year later, he directed the 9/11 attacks. And in 2002, KSM assisted in the beheading of *Wall Street Journal* reporter Daniel Pearl. Each act of terrorism was more spectacular than the previous one. Why, then, would KSM settle for something as unspectacular as blowing up some gas stations in Baltimore? A more likely scenario is hinted at in Saifullah Paracha's testimony before the tribunal that reviewed his case at Guantanamo. The tribunal said that Paracha had been involved in a plan to smuggle explosives, had received nearly half a million dollars from al-Qaeda, and had once suggested to an unidentified al-Qaeda agent (perhaps KSM himself) that he knew how to build nuclear weapons.

HOMEGROWN AL-QAEDA AFFILIATES: THE SELF-STARTERS

Surely the most enduring lesson of September 11 is that the global rise of Islamic extremism threatens Americans at home. Yet the evolving face of terrorism can strike anywhere. Since 9/11, the jihadists have bombed their way from Tunisia to Indonesia, hitting synagogues, embassies, oil tankers, nightclubs, hotels, and airports. Amid the numerous attacks of the period since 2001, a new phenomenon began to appear. This is the trend toward nameless, homegrown terrorist cells whose members tend to seek al-Qaeda's blessing for a specific attack, or what Benjamin and Simon call "self-starting terrorists." The jihadist self-starter groups pose a special challenge for intelligence and law enforcement agencies, argue Benjamin and Simon, because "[t]hey are likely to be smaller, comparatively self-contained and, if well run, more difficult to penetrate than the larger terrorist groups."[32] An analysis of three examples of the self-starter phenomenon may provide further insights into its potential threat.

Casablanca, 2003

On May 16, 2003, five bombs exploded within thirty minutes of each other in Casablanca, Morocco, killing forty-five people and wounding more than a hundred others in the deadliest terrorist attack in the nation's history. Police later learned that these were suicide missions carried out by a group known as Salafiya Jihadiya (SA), or the Jihad of the Righteous Ancestors.

Inspired by the radical preaching of an imam named Mohamed Fizazi, who belonged to the Qaeda-affiliated Moroccan Islamic Combat Group, the SA was made up of impoverished young men from the Casablanca slums and led by two Sunni extremists named Zakaria Miloudi and Youssef Fikri. Neither was trained by al-Qaeda, yet the Casablanca attack bore all the trademarks of a Qaeda operation (multiple, simultaneous strikes carried out by homicide assailants against lightly defended targets). While the SA drew its ideology from a hardline interpretation of Islamic law, it operated more like a street gang than a jihadist group. Much like a cult leader, Miloudi controlled every aspect of the gang's life, even providing SA members with employment as street venders. Miloudi himself was also a hashish dealer, whose trade provided funds for the Casablanca attacks.[33] Fikri was the gang's henchman. A former prisoner, Fikri and his crew terrorized local neighborhoods, meting out punishment to those who were considered "depraved." Fikri allegedly committed a number of "Islamic" executions, including the murder of his uncle.[34] Such straight-out thuggery was allowed to go unchecked by city police, and the SA morphed into something far more serious than a street gang.

The Casablanca attacks were intended to kill Jews, hundreds of them, and on that score the bombings were a failure. As Benjamin and Simon write, "This time . . . the terrorists' lack of training showed."[35] Even so, the attacks are significant if for no other reason than the sheer number of jihadists who had volunteered for a martyrdom mission at the same time. Although they were not present themselves, Miloudi and Fikri had assembled a small army of suicide bombers. Shortly after 9:00 p.m., Friday, May 16, fourteen assailants (ages eighteen to twenty-four) strapped on explosive-filled backpacks and approached their targets in and around the city's bustling tourist district: a Jewish-owned restaurant, a Jewish community center, and a Jewish cemetery, along with a Spanish social club and a five-star Kuwaiti-owned hotel. The bombers planned to simultaneously detonate their explosive devices.

At the restaurant, though, two bombers failed to get past the doorman, so, instead of perpetrating a mass murder, one of the attackers blew himself up, killing one bystander, while the other attacker walked down the street and blew himself up in front of the Belgian consulate, killing two police officers. Since it was Friday evening (the beginning of the Jewish Sabbath), the community center was empty; when the bombers pulled their plungers, they killed only themselves. The cemetery was empty, too (it hadn't been used in years), so when one of the bombers blew himself up 150 yards away from the graveyard, he killed three Muslim teenagers sitting on a fountain smoking cigarettes. Most of the casualties occurred at the bar and hotel, whe.e the bombers first slit the doorman's throat to gain entry, then ignited the charges. Inside the social club, two bombers blew themselves up, killing twenty people who were eating and playing bingo. In all, the SA killed thirty-three people, mostly Moroccans; no Jews were among the victims. Twelve of the bombers perished.[36]

After the arrest and interrogation of Mioudi, Fikri, Mohamed Fiżazi, and two of the would-be martyrs, a Spanish investigator told reporters that the Casablanca attack appeared to have been "99 percent local."[37] The motive behind the bombing was said to have been the United States invasion of Iraq.[38]

Madrid, 2004

Ten months later, on March 11, 2004, another group emerged from the ground up, rather than through an international network, this time waging a series of coordinated bombings against the commuter train system in Madrid, Spain. These killed 201 people and wounded more than a thousand, making this the deadliest assault by a terrorist organization against civilians in Europe since the Lockerbie bombing in 1988 and the worst terrorist assault in modern Spanish history. Although vastly different from the Casablanca attacks, the Madrid bombings involved an important parallel: they, too, were the work of Moroccan criminals. According to the Spanish interior minister, the "brains behind the attack" was a thirty-three-year-old career criminal named Jamal Ahmidan.[39] Among the terrorists to emerge from the nascent self-starter movement of the post-9/11 era, Ahmidan was one of the most sophisticated.

Jamal Ahmidan—nicknamed "El Chino" (or "The Chinese")—because of his narrow eyes—came from the northern Morocco city of Tetuan. In 1990, El Chino and his brother began smuggling large quantities of hashish, eventually establishing themselves as major drug traffickers with a network stretching from Morocco through Spain to Belgium and the Netherlands. Over the next several years, Ahmidan was arrested on drug charges by Spanish authorities and jailed on at least one occasion. In 2000, Ahmidan returned to Tetuan where he allegedly killed a man over a drug deal. El Chino was sentenced to prison where he subsequently converted to radical Islam. Upon his release in 2002, Ahmidan used a fake Belgian passport to enter Spain. He moved to Madrid and resumed his drug-dealing, this time selling hashish and Ecstasy to non-Muslims, and he continued to shuttle between Madrid and Morocco using fake passports.[40]

In late 2002, Ahmidan met a thirty-seven-year-old Tunisian named Sarhane Fakhet. Fakhet aspired to be a fashion model before becoming a doctoral student in economics but wound up as a successful real estate agent instead. Steeped in extremist ideology, Fakhet was a follower of Imad Yarkas, the Syrian-Spanish leader of a Madrid Qaeda cell dismantled in 2001. After Yarkas was jailed on suspicion that he helped plan the 9/11 attacks, an enraged Fakhet made it his mission to take care of Yarkas's wife and six children. In 2003, Fakhet and El Chino began meeting at a small barbershop, named Paparazzi, situated in the heart of Madrid, only a ten-minute walk from Atocha station, the major hub of the city's rail system. The Paparazzi was also an after-hours prayer hall for disciples of Takfir wal Hijra, a secretive Islamic sect active in the criminal underworld of North Africa. One of these disciples was a thirty-year-old Moroccan named Jamal Zougam, who owned a cell phone shop. He, too, was a confederate of Imad Yarkas. So it was here, at the Paparazzi barbershop, that the real estate agent, the drug dealer, and the shop owner became blood brothers bound by the Takfir belief that crime can be committed in the name of jihad.[41]

They also had another thing in common: by 2004, Ahmidan, Fakhet, and Zougam were all known to Spanish security forces. Because of his links to the former Madrid Qaeda cell, Fakhet was under surveillance by an anti-terrorist unit. While his phone calls were being recorded, they were not understood because Spanish authorities did not have Arabic translators to interpret the information being gathered.[42] Spanish law enforcement had been aware of Zougam's links to Yarkas since at least 2001, whey they searched his apartment.[43] In a phone call monitored by authorities in August 2001, Zougam told Yarkas that he had been in contact with Mohamed Fizazi, who was connected to the terrorist cell that would launch the Casablanca bombings in 2003.[44] Ahmidan was an informant for an anti-drug unit of the Civil Guard.[45] Ironically, Ahmidan's active involvement in drug trafficking concealed his extremism. That became sweepingly apparent in late 2003 when another police informant failed to tell his superiors that El Chino had stated to the informant that he (El Chino) wanted to blow up the famous Santiago Bernabeu soccer stadium because of Spain's support for the United States invasion of Iraq.[46] The threat was not taken seriously; rather it was chalked up to little more than loose talk between El Chino and his fellow drug informant. These local law enforcement lapses would eventually lead to an international crisis.

On October 19, 2003, bin Laden released an audiotape, broadcast over Aljazeera television, calling for attacks against "all the countries that participate in this unjust war [in Iraq]—especially Britain, Spain, Australia, Poland, Japan, and Italy."[47] The next day, Ahmidan and Fakhet went to work planning the Madrid bombings. El Chino enlisted the help of some two dozen Moroccan drug smugglers who took charge of supplying the cell with money, weapons, explosives, cars, and safe houses.[48] None of them had known ties to al-Qaeda. Ahmidan rented a cottage in the countryside near Madrid on January 28, 2004, turning it into a joint operations center and bomb factory. Then, in late February, he joined up with a former jailhouse contact, named Rafa Zuher, to arrange the exchange of 66 pounds of Moroccan hashish for 220 pounds of industrial dynamite and detonators stolen from a quarry in northern Spain.[49] (Like Ahmidan, Rafa Zuher was a drug informant for the Civil Guard.)[50] Upon transferring the ordinances to the bomb factory, Ahmidan was pulled over for speeding. The officer did not check inside the car, however, nor did he notice that Ahmidan's identity documents were forged.[51]

After that, the fifteen-member Madrid cell came together with remarkable speed. The Moroccan drug dealers joined international Muslim students, laborers, and a few teenagers in Takfir rituals at the Paparazzi. Bomb building began on the morning of March 10. Consisting of a blue cloth sports bag, twenty-two pounds of compressed dynamite, and nails attached to a cell phone, provided by Zougam, each device was designed to detonate by use of the phone's alarm function. The entire operation—explosives, phones, prepaid calling cards, vehicles, and rent on the bomb factory—was funded by the drug smugglers at a cost of roughly $50,000.[52]

Shortly after 7:00 a.m. on Thursday, March 11, thirteen terrorists, dressed in wool caps and scarves, boarded four separate trains. All of the bombs were carefully timed to go off at the exact moment each of the trains pulled into Atocha station; one by one they would be triggered by cell phones. The terrorists exited their trains at about 7:20, leaving the sports bags under their seats.

Four bombs (planted at the front, middle, and rear of a single train) exploded at 7:39, just as it pulled into Atocha station. Three bombs planted on another train went off simultaneously a block away. At 7:41 two more bombs exploded on yet another train at a nearby station, while one last bomb went off on a train at Santa Eugenia station at 7:42.[53] No terrorist organization had ever set off ten bombs at once. A total of 177 people died at the scene, and 24 more died while under medical care; 1,600 people were wounded and 100 of them required extensive hospital treatment. Most of the victims were students and blue-collar workers who could not afford to live in the city and so commuted from outlying neighborhoods.

Sixteen hours after the bombing, a rookie police officer combing through the debris heard a cell phone ringing from inside a blue sports bag. Opening it, he found an unexploded bomb. Through the cell phone memory, investigators were able to connect those involved in the attacks. On April 3, seven of the suspects, including Ahmidan and Fakhet, died in an apparent suicide explosion in a Madrid suburb. When police raided the home of one of the conspirators, they found 125,800 tabs of Ecstasy—one of the largest drug seizures in Spanish history. In all, police recovered nearly $2 million in drugs and cash left over from the criminal activities coordinated by Ahmidan.[54]

Three days after the bombings, Socialist candidate Jose Luis Rodriguez Zapatero was elected Spain's new prime minister in a surprise victory. The next day, after criticizing Spain's police agencies for failing to act on available intelligence concerning the bombers, Zapatero announced that he would withdraw Spain's troops from Iraq, saying that the U.S.-led occupation was "turning into a fiasco."[55] Not only did the bombs wreck trains and kill innocent Spaniards, but as Benjamin and Simon conclude, "they also helped trigger the fall of a Western democratic government."[56] More than that, like Carlos the Jackal, Jamal "El Chino" Ahmidan became something of a criminal legend among young Spanish jihadists; that others would imitate his terrorism was to be expected. Later that year, Spanish authorities arrested more than forty suspects for plotting a sequel to the Madrid bombings—an attack with a half-ton of explosives on Spain's criminal court. Nearly half the group had arrest records for charges ranging from drug trafficking to fraud and forgery.[57]

London, 2005

On July 7, 2005, four coordinated rush-hour bombs exploded in central London, killing 56 bus and subway riders, and wounding 700 more, marking the bloodiest day in England since World War II. Two weeks later, on July 21, a second attack was launched against the London Underground; this time, however, the bombs failed to explode, and no one was hurt. Nevertheless, the dual attacks were viewed by police as a piece of the same cloth.

The conspiracy centered on thirty-year-old Mohammad Siddique Khan, a British-born Pakistani from Leeds, an old mill town in northern England. A graduate of Leeds University and a natural born leader, Khan was a teaching assistant for disabled elementary school students and a community activist who worked with young immigrants, refugees, and asylum seekers. In 1999, Khan came under the influence of a Jamaican-born jihadist cleric known as Abdullah el-Faisal.[58] With the outbreak of the war in Iraq in 2003, Khan began to distance himself from his old friends. He also started socializing with two youths of Pakistani descent with whom he had been working: an eighteen-year-old high-school dropout and delinquent named Hasib Hussain, and a twenty-two-year-old vocational-school graduate named Shahzad Tanweer, who was known as the neighborhood "rich kid" because his father owned a successful fish and chips shop.[59]

In late March 2004, British counter-terrorism authorities rooted out a seven-man sleeper cell of ethnic Pakistanis in southern England, seizing 1,300 pounds of ammonium nitrate fertilizer that the Pakistanis intended to use in a plot to blow up London pubs, nightclubs, or trains in an act of revenge against Britain's support for the United States' invasion of Iraq. All seven men had known contacts with al-Qaeda and had spent time in Pakistan acquiring expertise in explosives. One of the men had allegedly made inquiries about buying an atomic bomb from Russian mafia figures in Belgium.[60] Operation Crevice, as the investigation was known, led to the discovery of a British-born Pakistani who had been in telephone contact with one of the cell members. His name was Mohammad Siddique Khan.[61]

Authorities decided that Khan did not constitute a terrorist threat, however, and that November, he and Tanweer traveled to Lahore, Pakistan, where they spent time studying religion at a madrassa. (Hasib Hussain made a similar trip to Pakistan in July 2004.)[62] When they returned, Khan quit his teaching job and left his wife and infant child, while Tanweer and Hussain began to demonstrate a blatant disdain for all things western. A friend of Tanweer's would later recall that Tanweer "was sick of it all, all the injustice [especially] all the Iraqi kids who die."[63] Around this time a fourth jihadist joined the cell: Germaine Lindsey (a.k.a., Abdullah Jamal), a nineteen-year-old Jamaican-born Brit and Muslim convert from the Leeds suburbs, who reportedly befriended Khan and Tanweer in Pakistan. Like Khan, Lindsey was also on a list of names collected in connection with Operation Crevice, though he, too, was never listed as a major terrorism suspect.[64] Investigators believed that Khan and the others met with hardened extremists while in Pakistan and that those meetings were crucial in turning the four young men into suicide bombers.

In late 2004, Khan and his confederates—two of whom were still teenagers—began meeting at a Leeds bookstore called Iqra the Learning Centre. "Iqra not only sold hatemongering Islamist literature," opined Thomas Friedman in the *New York Times*, "but . . . was the sole distributor of Islamgames, a U.S.-based company that makes video games . . . [featuring] apocalyptic battles between defenders of Islam and opponents. . . . Guess what: Video games matter."[65] Through a series of meetings held at the bookstore over the next several months,

Khan's crew stockpiled explosives and planned their bombings to coincide with the opening of the G8 Summit. The plans also included notifying authorities that their passports had been lost, possibly to cover evidence of trips to Pakistan.

Around this time, the second cell was congregating at a Fitness First gym in North London.[66] Then, working out of a North London housing project, Muktar Ibrahim, a twenty-seven-year-old British citizen born in Eritrea, and Yasin Omar, a twenty-four-year-old Ethiopian who posed as a Somali refugee to gain legal residency in Britain, along with a British resident born in Somalia and another man from East Africa, began constructing explosives inside Tupperware-like containers. These bombs would be used in "follow on" assaults against the London Underground. Ibrahim was the undisputed leader of the operation. A former gang member, he was convicted of a string of muggings and street crimes in 1995 and sentenced to five years in prison. During his incarceration, Ibrahim became a devout and radicalized Muslim.[67] Either in prison or later through the North London Central Mosque in Finsbury Park, Ibrahim became acquainted with Richard Reid, the so-called "shoe bomber" who attempted to blow up a commercial airliner over the Atlantic in late 2001.[68]

Sometime in early to mid-June, Khan's cell moved to the final phase of preparation at a bomb factory at Alexander Grove in Leeds.[69] Four crude devices were constructed, each containing less than ten pounds of military-grade C-4 plastic explosives, Czech-made Semtex explosives, and TATP—a highly unstable explosive composed of common chemicals available from hardware stores (acetone, sulfuric acid, and hydrogen peroxide), which is known among Palestinian bomb-makers as the "Mother of Satan."[70] Once built, the bombs were stored in coolers to stabilize the explosives. Like the devices used in the Madrid bombing, these devices would not be detonated by the bombers themselves, but by some kind of timing device set to go off within 50 seconds of each other.[71] (The source of the explosives and timers remain unknown to the public.) Also like the Madrid bombers, Khan's group would not strap the bomb-laden backpacks to themselves (a technique favored by a legendary Palestinian known as the "Tailor of Death," after his made-to-measure vests and belts for suicide bombers); rather, they would place the backpacks beneath them on the train floors.[72] But whereas the Madrid terrorists would exit the train before the bombs were detonated,

Khan's crew would remain seated and die in the explosions. On June 27, three of the four bombers traveled to London and conducted a dry run on the route they would take ten days later.[73]

They arrived at King's Cross station in London carrying backpacks at 8:30 a.m. on Thursday, July 7 ("7/7"). Minutes after the 311 train left King's Cross, a blast tore through the lead car, killing twenty-one. A second bomb went off a few minutes later on train 204 near Liverpool Street, killing seven. The next one exploded at 8:50 aboard train 216 as it left Edgewood station, blowing a crater in the floor, tearing through a wall and into a train passing in the opposite direction, and killing seven. At 9:47, the final bomb went off on a bus in Tavistock Square, killing thirteen. In all forty-eight people died at the scene, including the four terrorists, whose bodies were later identified when investigators found personal documents close to the seats where they had been sitting when the blasts occurred.

Subsequently, on July 21, Ibrihim's cell made its move. Four assailants boarded four different trains and tried to set off explosives carried in sports bags, and then fled on foot when the bombs failed to detonate. All four men were caught on closed-circuit security televisions, and subsequently apprehended. Investigators later told reporters that the failed bombs were made of the same material used by both Richard Reid and the 7/7 cell—TATP; they also added that one goal of the second set of attackers may have been to divert resources away from the primary 7/7 investigation.[74]

After authorities traced Yasin Omar's travels by monitoring cell phone activity from England to France to Italy, he was arrested in Rome, whereupon he claimed that the July 21 group was not working for al-Qaeda and that the London bombs were "copy-cat" attacks intended to draw attention to anger over the war in Iraq.[75] Then, eight weeks after 7/7, al-Qaeda released a statement from Ayman al-Zawahiri, carried on Aljazeera, praising the bombings as a retaliation for the "inferno in Iraq" and adding that Prime Minister Tony Blair was conducting a "crusader war against Islam." The video also featured a statement from Mohammad Siddique Khan, shot months before 7/7, justifying his actions. Khan praised "our beloved sheik, Osama bin Laden," and referred obliquely to Iraq. "Until you stop the bombing, gassing, imprisonment and torture of my people," he said, "we will not stop this fight. We are at war and I am a soldier. Now you will taste the reality of this situation."[76] Investigators concluded that Khan was not directed by al-Qaeda but that the group had somehow managed to acquire his video and then released it so as to bolster its reputation.

Policing the Self-Starter Problem

For law enforcement, the jihadist self-starter phenomenon carries a number of unanticipated implications. First, it transcends ethnic and national causes by blending ideological fervor with common criminality rooted inside the target country. Self-starters are well integrated inside their home countries, but inscribe their actions in a global perspective: increasingly, the inspiration for terrorism is the United States' involvement in Iraq, which is seen as part of a global trend toward cultural domination. As Richard Clarke notes, there have been twice as many terrorist attacks outside Iraq in the three years after 9/11 than in the three years before.[77] Simply put, self-starters think globally but act locally. Because this violates assumptions about traditional terrorist threats, the self-starter phenomenon complicates law enforcement strategies to combat it.

Second, because self-starter groups represent a mutating form of terrorism, the phenomenon indicates that the centrally controlled al-Qaeda of 9/11 has undergone a significant change. Although self-starters are driven by a reverence for Osama bin Laden, most of them are too young to have been battle-hardened by the wars in Afghanistan, Bosnia, Somalia, and Chechnya. Likewise, they are too young to have trained in the Qaeda camps of Afghanistan. Instead, investigators believe they learn their terrorist strategies over the Internet; thus, there is no need for terrorist training camps.[78] The result, as we have seen, can be a mastery of criminal method and organization designed to exploit technologies and everyday activities of local communities. Self-starter groups are also more heterogeneous than traditional terrorist outfits. They are comprised of individuals from varying socioeconomic backgrounds. Poor, undereducated slum dwellers join university students and young professionals, the former bringing street smarts and criminal sensibilities to the group, the latter bringing the capacity for sophisticated recruitment and proselytizing activities, along with technical skills for complex operational functions. The two factions are bound by a common sense of alienation—of not fitting into the folds of modernity—and by the allure of fundamentalism. Coming from various nations, some self-starters may hold dual nationalities, making it easier for them to travel legitimately—that is, without having to create fake passports, bribe border police, or falsify claims about fleeing political persecution.

Third, self-starter networks are more decentralized and less structured than al-Qaeda. Instead of being organized through top-down command structures, self-starter groups rely on friendship and kinship arrangements in motivating members to carry out their attacks. Thus, if one leader is taken off the streets, another comes along to take his place. This makes law-enforcement's search for outside "masterminds" pointless. As Marc Sageman's research shows, the willingness to carry out suicide bombings depends heavily on a dynamic within a cell in which members are pressured to meet one another's expectations. Central to this dynamic is the fact that these cells often form from pre-existing social groups—what Sageman calls "just a bunch of guys."[79] Criminologist James Q. Wilson defines this dynamic as simply "the instinct to be part of a team."[80] Self-starters are less likely to be drawn together and indoctrinated by a radical imam at the local mosque than they are to congregate secretly, in a bookstore, barbershop, gymnasium, or a prison cell, where they hold intense discussions that lead to the decision to mount an attack and to commit the crimes that support it.[81] In this respect they are much like the European left-wing terrorists of the 1970s, who joined their groups less out of ideological commitment than some type of common experience, such as living in the same neighborhood or hanging out at the same bar.[82] This is a trait that self-starters also share with elements of the American radical Right of the 1990s. The neo-Nazi skinheads who became foot soldiers for the Aryan Republican Army, for example, initially met through the Philadelphia white power rock scene—an experience that set the stage for their recruitment into the American terrorist underground.[83] The decentralized nature of jihadist self-starter cells means that in the future a greater number of terrorists and terrorist plots may escape the notice of intelligence services altogether.

But at the end of the day, self-starters are still Islamic terrorists, and they share some important commonalities with the archetypical cases of terrorist-oriented criminality explored in this research. Most notably—and in marked similarity to the way precursor crimes were ignored by law enforcement in the lead-up to the first World Trade Center bombing—aggressive law enforcement may have halted some of the self-starter conspiracies before they mutated into terrorist cells.

When Casablanca police failed to crack down on the Salafiya Jihadiya gang for victimizing local communities, they opened up opportunities for more strident forms of violence to come. Youssef Fikri in particular, if we are to believe the international press reports, was known in his neighborhood as a human predator, committing executions of people who were guilty of nothing more than failing to conform to Fikri's idiosyncratic world view. Fikri was allowed to continue his violent rampage and, together with Zakaria Miloudi, went on to orchestrate the Casablanca bombings.

A similar law enforcement failure is found in the case of Jamal Ahmidan. Before meeting Sarhane Fakhet and undergoing a conversion to the secretive Islamic sect Takfir wal Hijra, El Chino had killed another man (a crime for which he did precisely two years in prison), committed passport fraud, and peddled drugs for more than fifteen years. Yet he remained free to plan and coordinate the train bombings in Madrid. Like Mohammed Salemeh in the lead-up to the World Trade Center bombing, Ahmidan was actually in police custody for a routine traffic violation while in possession of the explosives that would be used in the attack, but was allowed to go free despite the fact that he was traveling with forged identity papers.

And then there is the case of Muktar Ibrahim. Ibrahim was twelve years old when he arrived in Britain from Eritrea in 1992. Three years later, when he was fifteen, Ibrahim was sentenced to five years in youth detention for using a knife during a street robbery. Upon his release, however, Ibrahim was granted British citizenship, even though he had a serious criminal record.[84] Taking advantage of this lapse of judgment, Ibrahim went on to execute the London attacks of July 21.

Once again, the implication for law enforcement is that when authorities concentrate on the everyday enforcement of law, they may preempt more disastrous events.

There is, however, a further difficulty that resonates throughout the years: namely, the problems associated with the gathering and disseminating of information on terrorist conspiracies. The 1993 World Trade Center bombing; the 1998 East African embassy bombings; the Covenant, the Sword and the Arm of the Lord; the Order; and the Aryan Republican Army—every one of these conspiracies was shot through with informants who supplied their handlers with leads and links related to terrorist planning and operations. And in nearly every case (the CSA being the rare exception), intelligence officials failed to act on the information available to them. Intelligence is the result of information that has been subjected to analysis and synthesis. Here is where the historical record can help us understand the threat posed by jihadist self-starter groups of the twenty-first century. If law enforcement agencies are to avoid mistakes of the past, they must do a better job of transforming information into actionable intelligence. So far, at least in Europe and North Africa, law enforcement's record is dismal.

The three leaders of the Madrid bombings were all under government surveillance while they were planning the attacks in 2004. Information collected from one of them—the Moroccan cell phone expert Jamal Zougam—from as far back as 2001 would connect to Mohamed Fizazi, who would go on to play a role in the Casablanca attacks of 2003, yet that information was not acted upon. Information from another—Fakhet—would set off the Qaeda alarm bell, but it was ignored as well. And information from the undercover drug agent El Chino could have given agents early warning about a bombing plot intended to retaliate against Spain's support for the U.S. invasion of Iraq. But nobody bothered to connect the dots; nobody subjected the information to analysis and synthesis. The FBI and CIA made a similar mistake prior to 9/11 when they failed to place two of the hijackers, Khalid al-Mihdhar and Nawaf al-Hazmi, on U.S. government watch lists.[85] Immigration made an analogous error when, after flying from Miami to Madrid in January 2001, Mohamed Atta was allowed by INS agents to re-enter the United States despite the fact that he had overstayed his previous visa.[86] British counter-terrorism officials also went to sleep in the run-up to the London bombings. During his 2004 trip to Pakistan, 7/7 bomber Shehzad Tanweer visited a guerrilla training camp north of Islamabad where he expressed a desire to assassinate President Musharraf.[87] Intelligence services had previously monitored both the leader of the July 7 attacks, Mohammed Siddique Khan, and co-conspirator Germaine Lindsey, as part of the anti-terror inquiry Operation Crevice, but failed to follow up on their activities.

Self-Starters in America

As of this writing, the jihadist self-starter trend has made only a blip on the intelligence radar screen in America. Nevertheless, on at least one occasion, the response has been a model of intelligent anti-terrorist policing.

During a routine investigation of a string of armed robberies of gas stations in Torrance, California, in July 2005, police uncovered a larger conspiracy being directed from behind the walls of the state prison at Sacramento. In 2003, Kevin James, then a twenty-seven-year-old American citizen also known as Shakyh Shahaab Murshid, used a radical interpretation of Islam to recruit followers while doing time at Folsom Prison. Three fellow prisoners—two American citizens, including a former Los Angeles gang member, and a legal resident from Pakistan—joined James's conspiracy to "kill infidels or non-believers" in a guerrilla war against the United States. Upon their release in 2004, the three recruited jihadists began robbing gas stations, using the proceeds to buy weapons and a computer which they used to conduct surveillance on possible targets, including several synagogues, the Los Angeles International Airport branch of the Israeli airline El Al, and a National Guard recruiting office. James, now incarcerated in Sacramento, directed the plan from his prison cell. James was not connected to al-Qaeda; however, the attacks were scheduled to take place on September 11, 2005. The break in the case came not by an elite federal counter-terrorism unit working under authority of the USA Patriot Act, but by local police who found a cell phone one of the robbers had lost during a gas station stick-up. The subsequent arrests gained national attention, leading FBI director Robert Mueller III to proclaim that the attacks "were well on the way" to being carried out and thereby underscoring the threat of "homegrown extremists" in American prisons and elsewhere.[88]

America faces an emerging threat from its own self-starter jihad groups and a long-standing threat from al-Qaeda central, but neither threat compares to the potential danger now dominating policy discussions in Washington.

BLOWBACK: AL-QAEDA IN IRAQ

From the start, America's war in Iraq never achieved the popular support its neoconservative architects expected. After U.S. forces failed to discover either weapons of mass destruction or a connection between al-Qaeda and Saddam Hussein—the Bush administration's stated purposes for going to war, both of which were based on faulty and willfully distorted intelligence—pessimism about the war reached a dangerous level, calling into question whether the invasion was necessary in the first place. By 2005, more than half of the American public believed that the war had not made the United States safer. The following year a global poll found that 60 percent of respondents from 35 countries believed that the war had increased the likelihood of terrorist attacks around the world. The war in Iraq was officially condemned by the governments of Russia, China, France, Germany, Canada, Pakistan, Spain, and others. It was also denounced by the Vatican, Nelson Mandela, William F. Buckley, and half a dozen Nobel Prize laureates. Protests against the war drew millions of people from across the globe; the February 15, 2003, protest alone attracted more than six million people from more than 600 cities, prompting the 2004 Guinness Book of Records to declare it the largest mass protest in history.[89]

A central concern of the worldwide protest movement has been the number of Iraqi civilians who have died as a consequence of the American invasion. While there is no mathematics of certainty in tallying war-related fatalities, a widely reported estimate is that of the Iraq Body Count (IBC) project, a London-based group of academics and human-rights and anti-war activists. Extracting data from an analysis of over 10,000 press reports, the IBC estimated that 24,865 civilian non-combatants were killed in Iraq during the first two years of the war (between March 2003 and March 2005, though the number would increase to 650,000 by September 2006). Of this number, IBC found that 37 percent (or 9,200 Iraqis) were killed by U.S.-led forces, mostly in air strikes. Another 36 percent (8,951 Iraqis) were killed by post-invasion criminal gangs, while 9 percent of the civilian victims (2,237 Iraqis) were killed by anti-occupation insurgents. (Killers of the remaining 18 percent could not be identified.)[90] When the estimated 9,673 civilians killed by U.S.-led forces in Afghanistan are added to the 9,200 civilians killed by U.S.-led forces in Iraq, the number of casualties totals 18,873. In other words, between 2001 and 2005 the United States military was involved in killing *three times* as many civilians as were killed by terrorists in 9/11, Casablanca, Madrid, London, and Iraq put together. Figures like these, combined with headlines about Iraq's persistent slide toward civil war, have led such influential neoconservative scholars as Francis Fukuyama, an early supporter of the war, to conclude that the United States has overreacted to 9/11 and failed to use its dominant military power prudently.[91] As such, the war on terrorism and the resulting bloodshed in Iraq and Afghanistan have contributed to the pervasive idea that Islam is under siege—feeding the fury that helps radical Islamists win adherents throughout the Middle East and Europe.

No volume better summarizes the terrorist threat emanating from Iraq than the National Intelligence Council's 2005 report titled "Mapping the Global Future." (The National Intelligence Council is the CIA director's think tank.) The report, which took a year to produce and includes the analysis of 1,000 U.S. and foreign experts, concludes that Iraq not only has replaced Afghanistan as the training ground for the next generation of "professionalized" terrorists, but also has provided terrorist groups with increased recruitment and fundraising capabilities and real-life opportunities to develop technical skills. The American-led invasion has turned Iraq into a magnet for international terrorist activity. Hundreds of foreign jihadists have crossed into Iraq, where they have found tons of unprotected weapons caches that have been used against U.S. troops. These foreign fighters, who are believed to make up a large portion of today's suicide bombers, are forming alliances with former Baathist fighters and other insurgents—including the late Abu Musab al-Zarqawi's arm of al-Qaeda in Iraq. The NIC's greatest concern is the possibility that al-Qaeda in Iraq may acquire biological or nuclear weapons.[92] These assessments led CIA Director Goss to warn the U.S. Senate in 2005: "These jihadists who survive will leave Iraq experienced in, and focused on, acts of urban terrorism. They represent a potential pool of contacts to build transnational terrorist cells, groups and networks in Saudi Arabia, Jordan and other countries."[93]

Jihadists trained in Iraq have already established "transnational terrorist cells" in Saudi Arabia and Jordan, where they have begun to carry out attacks. Among them was a plot against some of Saudi Arabia's key oil and gas fields, timed to coincide with the U.S. energy shortages brought on by Hurricane Katrina in September 2005.[94] A month earlier, al-Zarqawi's organization reached across the Iraqi border into Jordan to carry out a rocket attack that narrowly missed a United States warship in the Red Sea port of Aqaba. Then, on November 9, the group bombed three hotels in Amman, killing fifty-seven people, most of them Muslims, in Jordan's deadliest terrorist attack ever. To execute the strikes, al-Zarqawi's organization recruited four Iraqi suicide bombers, including a husband and wife team whose children had been killed by American troops in Baghdad.

If we use those attacks as background for understanding al-Qaeda in Iraq, we find that the threat to U.S. security turns on three issues.

First, al-Zarqawi once pledged his allegiance to bin Laden; bin Laden then urged al-Zarqawi to attack the United States; and, even though al-Zarqawi is no longer alive, the FBI continues to believe that al-Qaeda in Iraq may be planning to broaden it campaign to include strikes in the United States.[95] Second, al-Qaeda in Iraq reportedly has sufficient resources to mount these attacks. The organization is said to bankroll its operations through extortion, kidnapping, and graft. It may also have benefited from the wholesale theft of a portion of Iraq's gasoline supply, perhaps earning millions of dollars on the black market.[96] Last, al-Qaeda in Iraq has developed a loose arrangement of sympathizers in Europe who officials believe to have provided support to various terrorist operations in a number of countries. Sympathizers in Belgium, in particular, have offered jihadists safe haven, false documents, and financing. Some of these jihadists have made their way to Iraq where they trained and fought with al-Zarqawi's forces.[97] One of the Madrid bombers, for example, stopped in Belgium en route to Iraq where he blew himself up in a suicide bombing. Belgium sympathizers also provide a support network for jihadists returning from Iraq and seeking travel elsewhere.[98] Not only do these sympathizers hold European Union passports, but they also look like northern Europeans, thus allowing them to gain easy access to soft targets in western countries.[99] In fact, French intelligence has learned that Islamic terrorist networks in Europe are increasingly trying to recruit Caucasian women to handle terrorist logistics because they would be less likely to raise suspicion.[100]

Therefore, our questions are twofold. If and when they arrive on American soil, what criminal skills will these jihadists bring with them? And, what routine activities are they likely to exploit?

The first question is easily answered: they will bring highly sophisticated skill sets that could have never been achieved at al-Qaeda's camps in Taliban-run Afghanistan. These include surveillance techniques; methods of evading U.S. electronic signals and human intelligence; methods of penetrating police and intelligence services; methods of evading and attacking cyber security; methods of extortion, kidnapping, and beheading; the use of improvised explosive devices (or IEDs), some of which are triggered by encrypted radio signals or laser beams; sniper skills; and a host of techniques for carrying out suicide bombings, including the use of European women on bicycles.

The second question is not so easily answered, but any discussion of the threat must begin with potential methods used by members of al-

Qaeda in Iraq to enter the United States. Due to increased security screening at U.S. airports, terrorists must consider alternative means of entry. One scenario involves the porous 1,400-mile border between the United States and Mexico, which hundreds of thousands of people cross illegally every year. This has raised concerns that members of al-Qaeda in Iraq may exploit the current crossing procedures to make their way into the United States. One way to do this is by paying smuggling networks, especially those operated by organized gangs.[101]

Another method is to exploit a loophole in the system that separates the large number of illegal Mexican entrants, who are automatically refused entry, from citizens of other countries who are allowed in, pending immigration hearings. The Department of Homeland Security refers to these people by the acronym OTM (for "Other Than Mexicans"). Although most OTMs come from other Latin American countries, some come from countries outside the hemisphere. Either way, their numbers are staggering. In 2004, some 44,000 OTMs were admitted to the U.S., while the number of illegal OTMs who were apprehended totaled 65,814.[102] The concern, then, is that terrorists can either legally enter as OTMs, or blend into the human flood of illegal immigrants coming across the border. Either way, the concern is justified. In a 2005 hearing before a House Appropriations Committee, FBI Director Mueller testified:

> "The FBI has received reports that individuals with known al-Qaeda connections have attempted to enter the U.S. illegally using alien smuggling rings and assuming Hispanic appearances. An FBI investigation into these reports continues."[103]

It is not clear how many of these al-Qaeda operatives tried to enter the United States. Nor is it clear if they attempted to enter as OTMs with fake passports. Moreover, Mueller did not identify the *countries* from which they came. A week after Mueller's testimony, though, an FBI official told reporters that Abu Musab al-Zarqawi was planning to strike in America, adding that it "would be easy" to infiltrate the United States through the southern border.[104] According to information obtained by the CIA during the interrogation of a member of al-Qaeda in Iraq, who was taken into custody in 2004 (there is of course no way to determine the conditions under which the information was obtained), the terrorists' plan involved obtaining a "visa to Honduras" and then traveling across Mexico. An operative could then "bribe his way into the U.S." at the border. From there, the plan involved hitting soft targets in the United States, including "movie theaters, restaurants and schools."[105]

THE RADICAL RIGHT

In the wake of 9/11, it is easy to forget that racist, anti-government, and anti-abortion groups have been responsible for nearly all of the terrorist attacks in the United States over the past two decades—the 1993 World Trade Center bombing and the 9/11 attacks are the exceptions. The American radical Right was responsible for both the Oklahoma City bombing and the bombing at the 1996 Olympics in Atlanta, as well as bombings of abortion clinics, the assassination of abortion providers, multiple cases of individual rampages, mass shootings at U.S. high schools, and bogus anthrax mailings. These attacks killed and injured scores of Americans. By no means has this threat diminished, even though it receives little media attention. In the ten-year period since the bombing in Oklahoma City, the radical Right has been the source of some sixty terrorist plots. These have included plans to bomb federal buildings, refineries, banks, bridges, synagogues, and mosques. The radical Right has also assassinated police officers, minorities, and informants and attempted to assassinate politicians, judges, and civil rights activists. And it has amassed machine guns, explosives, missiles, and biological and chemical weapons.[106]

Like their predecessors, the new generation of right-wing terrorists has financed its plots by robbing banks and armored cars, counterfeiting, and stealing cars. So what's new? Kidnapping is a new means of raising money for the radical Right; so are car-jacking, drug trafficking, and credit card theft. Some of these extremists have also become more audacious in their showcasing of imagery and style. In April 2004, for instance, neo-Nazi skinhead Sean Gillespie actually videotaped himself as he firebombed an Oklahoma City synagogue for a film he was making to inspire other racists to violent revolution.

Another new development, and potentially more worrisome, is the fact that America's current defender of national security, the Department of Homeland Security (DHS), does not consider the radical Right to be a threat to the nation's safety. In a controversial report released in 2005, the DHS contended that future terrorist threats will come primarily from al-Qaeda and other foreign jihad groups, as well as domestic radical Islamic groups. The report also lists left-wing domestic groups, such as the Earth Liberation Front (ELF), as terrorist threats, but it does not mention anti-government groups or white supremacist or anti-abortion organizations.[107] Among the sixty plots waged by the radical Right over the past ten years, however, several cases demonstrate that the movement is still worthy of the government's attention. One case in particular, and the final case explored here, is not only an outstanding example of that threat, but is also an outstanding illustration of what it means to police terrorism in the new millennium.

Chemical Warfare

The story begins in April 2004 when an informant in rural McKenzie, Tennessee (population 2,489), provided an officer of the state's drug task force with information about a methamphetamine dealer who had asked the informant questions about acquiring nuclear waste.[108] The Tennessee Bureau of Investigation passed the tip onto the FBI office in Jackson, and an agent began an investigation of the suspect, a thirty-nine-year-old farmhand from McKenzie named Demetrius "Van" Crocker, who was known to local authorities as a member of a white supremacist group during the 1980s. The informant told the FBI that Crocker "had absolute hatred for the United States government and had made comments . . . to the effect that the country needs to be taken back by the people."

On September 16, the informant introduced Crocker to an undercover FBI agent. In the course of that meeting, Crocker told the agent that he hated the government, adding that "it would be a good idea if somebody could detonate some sort of weapon of mass destruction in Washington, D.C., while both the U.S. Congress and Senate were in session." Crocker said that he admired Adolf Hitler and the Nazi ideology, that he hated Jews, and that he believed that setting up a concentration camp for Jewish insurance executives "would be a desirable endeavor."

The agent met with Crocker again on September 29. This time Crocker candidly talked about his previous experience working at an electroplating factory where he had had access to various chemicals. Once, Crocker said, he had produced a batch of nitroglycerin and went on to describe how to use it in a booby trap. On another occasion, Crocker said he had produced mustard gas.

Saying that he owned an AK 47 and would willingly kill any cop who tried to take it away from him, Crocker also boasted of his ability to "kill government people" and blacks with his assault rifle. He then inquired about the agent's ability to get automatic weapons and chemical weapons, including nerve agents. Crocker said that he had targeted a federal courthouse and that he "enjoyed hearing the news" of the sarin nerve-gas attack on a Japanese subway system years earlier. Crocker asked if the agent had access to VX, a nerve agent. The agent did not have access to VX, but said he could get Difluoro, a precursor and key component for sarin nerve gas, stolen from Pine Bluff Arsenal, the state's weapons depot.

On October 7, Crocker met with the agent again and gave him $500 cash to steal the Difluoro from Pine Bluff. The agent told Crocker he could also deliver some stolen C-4 plastic explosives to him, to which Crocker enthusiastically agreed.

The two met for the final time in Jackson on October 25, where the agent gave Crocker a container marked "Difluoro" and a block of C-4. Both the precursor and the explosives were made of inert substances, however, and at this point Crocker was surrounded by FBI agents and arrested on charges of attempting to acquire weapons of mass destruction intended to "blow up" government buildings. The seven-month federal investigation was, in effect, a sting.

The Crocker case is significant on a number of levels. To begin with, it signals a trend: In recent years domestic terrorists have been arrested with a number of poisons, including ricin (a deadly white powder distilled from castor beans), *Yersinia pestis* (which causes bubonic plague), and bacteria that cause cholera.[109] Yet sarin nerve gas, developed by Nazi doctors during World War II, is one of the deadliest weapons in the terrorist's arsenal, 500 times more toxic than the cyanide discovered at the CSA compound in 1984, in what was then the biggest terrorism investigation ever conducted by the FBI. When the Japanese religious cult Aum Shinrikyo released sarin into the Tokyo subways in 1995, it killed twelve people and sent more than 5,000 to hospitals. Witnesses said that the subway entrances resembled battlefields as injured commuters lay gasping on the ground with blood gushing from their noses and mouths. The attack demonstrated how easy it is for a small group to engage in chemical warfare. Sarin is made into a weapon by synthesizing the gas with other readily available chemicals; and today, the instructions for doing that can be found on the Internet, in books like *Silent*

Death available on Amazon, or in self-published books like *BioToxic Weapons* sold at gun shows. Experts claim that a college chemistry student could follow these instructions.[110]

The greatest mistake made by authorities over the years has been to underestimate terrorists. That was the lesson of Munich, of 9/11, of Oklahoma City, of Madrid, and of London, to mention but a few instances of massive intelligence failures. The Crocker case, then, should be of profound concern to Homeland Security. Given the radical Right's hoary history of murder and mayhem, Crocker's mere *intention* to use sarin nerve gas is a far greater threat to national security than anything done by ELF. They have killed no one.

And if this were not enough, it is entirely possible that the radical Right's intention to use chemical weaponry against the U.S. government could be of interest to the jihad movement. Shortly before he was killed in a roadside attack near Kabul, Afghanistan, in November 2001, Spanish journalist Julio Fuentes found 300 bottles of Russian-made sarin nerve gas at an abandoned Qaeda base known as Farm Hada, some 25 miles south of Jalalabad.[111] In May 2004, an IED containing sarin nerve agent exploded near a military convoy en route to Baghdad International Airport, causing two soldiers to be hospitalized with low-level chemical exposure. Experts claimed that the sarin gas had been smuggled into Iraq by terrorists from Syria.[112] It was with radicals from Syria, it must be remembered, that Robert Mathews and the Order attempted to forge an Aryan-Islamic alliance capable of mounting a campaign of urban terrorism in the United States. Such intentions have persisted into the post–9/11 era. A collection of internet postings by hate groups examined by the *New York Times* after the September 11 attacks include a message written by Billy Roper, a ranking officer of (*Turner Diaries* author) William Pierce's National Alliance. "The enemy of our enemy is, for now at least, our friend," Roper wrote. "We may not want them marrying our daughters, but anyone who is willing to drive a plane into a building to kill Jews is alright by me."[113]

Finally, the story of Demetrius Crocker confirms the importance of policing as an effective counter-terrorism strategy. Once more, the case was made not by an elite federal counter-terrorism unit operating under the wide sweeping legislative powers of the Patriot Act, but by FBI agents' developing a single informant, patiently working a suspect, and then allowing that suspect to expose his own criminal vulnerabilities.

CONCLUSION

The main finding of this study is that the most successful method of both detecting and prosecuting cases of terrorism is through the pursuit of conventional criminal investigations. By focusing on the broad spectrum of crimes committed by terrorist groups and by acting on solid intelligence, the FBI and other policing agencies may forestall larger conspiracies designed to kill hundreds if not thousands of civilians. This comes as no surprise to investigators who have spent their careers in the trenches, nor has it escaped the attention of experienced counter-terrorism officials in Washington.

As David Kaplan points out in his exhaustive exposé on the growing criminality of terrorist groups around the world, the National Security Council has recently adopted a new policy on transnational crime that makes the crime-terrorism connection a top priority. The CIA's Crime and Narcotics Center has also implemented new policies to deal with international crime, focusing on the linkages between drug smuggling, organized crime, and terrorism. On the domestic side, the federal Joint Terrorism Task Force has begun to take a harder look at the criminal inroads made by terrorist groups. A similar program is underway in Britain, where London's Metropolitan Police now routinely monitor low-level criminal activity for suspected links to unfolding terrorism conspiracies.[114]

Getting a grip on the pervasive criminality of terrorist groups will not be easy, though. Despite recent law enforcement advances, the U.S. approach to the crime-terrorism problem is for the most part embedded in military measures, both practically and metaphorically. The U.S. response to terrorism is primarily a military venture fought by the U.S. Army, Navy, Air Force, and Marines. Dismantling and degrading the international jihad network will require unprecedented international intelligence and law-enforcement cooperation, not expensive new airplanes, helicopters, and armed personnel carriers. The vision of heroic U.S. soldiers hunting down Osama bin Laden may play well to American television audiences, but it is not the model to deal with passport fraud, credit card theft, cell phone cloning, motor vehicle violations, low-level drug dealing, or arms smuggling. These crimes are rooted in local communities, and they cannot be solved by military incursions or specially designed judicial proceedings at offshore detention facilities conducted under the auspices of a war on terrorism. Terrorism is a tactic, and it is impossible to wage "war" against a tactic.

In the long term—and the Bush administration has repeatedly argued that the global war on terrorism could last ten, twenty, or even thirty years—effectively countering terrorist-oriented criminality requires taking such unglamorous steps as strengthening law enforcement management capabilities in the developing countries of Central Asia and North Africa. Black market economies, heroin smuggling, graft, and fraud thrive in that part of the world. It is no accident that these regions produce some of the world's most violent jihadists.

Effectively countering terrorism also requires assisting some nations in developing strong school systems to counteract the appeal of the madrassas that have become terrorist breeding grounds. It also requires what Francis Fukuyama calls *"realistic Wilsonianism . . . a dramatic demilitarization of American foreign policy and re-emphasis on other types of policy instruments."*[115] These include, on the one hand, abandoning incendiary rhetoric about a global war on terrorism and, on the other promoting political and economic development abroad through "soft power" (job training, advisement, and financial incentives to weaken cultures of terrorism).

But perhaps most importantly, the United States must repair its appalling public diplomacy record in the Muslim world. It is well known that the photographs of abuses by American soldiers at Baghdad's Abu Ghraib prison—of a man standing hooded on a box with electric wires attached to his hands; of guards leering as a pile of naked men simulated sexual acts; of a man led around on a dog leash by female guard Lynndie England (three of the guards involved in the abuses were women); of Lynndie England posing in front of a line of naked men, cigarette dangling from her mouth, her finger pointed towards the genitals of naked victims; of a man handcuffed and gagged, lying in his own feces with a banana protruding from his rectum; of a plastic-wrapped corpse of a man beaten to death—infuriated Muslims around the world. Copies of these photos are now sold in marketplaces from Karachi to Bangkok, vividly demonstrating the worst suspicions of Muslims everywhere: that Americans are corrupt, heartless, and hell-bent on humiliating Muslims and mocking their values. "If Osama bin Laden had hired a Madison Avenue public relations firm to rally Arabs' hearts and minds to his cause," observes military analyst Phillip Carter, "it's hard to imagine that it could have devised a better propaganda campaign."[116]

The damage done to the credibility of the United States by military guards at Abu Ghraib will never be fully rectified. However, a meaningful step *was* in fact taken by the person ultimately responsible for what an internal U.S. Army report on Abu Ghraib described as "numerous incidents of sadistic, blatant, and wanton criminal abuses": President George W. Bush.[117] After the abuses became public, Bush proposed to demolish the Abu Ghraib facility as a gesture to the local population. Blowing the prison up, bulldozing its remains underground, and allowing al-Jazzera to broadcast these scenes would have sent the Arab world a powerful message about America's repentance for the sins of Abu Ghraib. Ironically, an American military judge ordered that the prison be preserved as a crime scene.[118] A potentially significant political stride in fighting terrorism's global criminal threat—reducing the bitter anger against America that is now spreading across the Muslim world like an unchecked fire in a vast field—was itself usurped by crimes committed by the United States. Consequently, Abu Ghraib remains a symbol of all that has gone wrong with the U.S. occupation of Iraq and a potent recruiting tool for terrorists around the world.

Much the same can be said for that other American military gulag, the naval base at Guantanamo Bay, Cuba. In 2006, the United Nations recommended that Guantanamo be closed down "without further delay" because practices at the camp violated the U.N Convention against Torture. The United States has failed to follow the United Nations' recommendation and continues to incarcerate approximately 505 men who are being held in long-term detention as suspected terrorists, even though the U.S. Supreme Court has ruled that no legal grounds can be found to warrant their continued imprisonment. Since 2002, over three hundred specific cases of serious detainee abuse have surfaced, yet the United States has failed to put an end to "special interrogation techniques" widely considered torture. These practices include subjecting detainees to excessive cold and heat, loud music, sleep deprivation, and "gender coercion" by female guards. Female guards at Guantanamo have doused a detainee with perfume; smeared a prisoner with what was meant to appear to be menstrual blood; stripped off their uniforms and rubbed up against prisoners in a sexually provocative manner; forced a prisoner to wear a bra and put women's underwear on his head; and performed a pseudo lap dance on a prisoner (by straddling the prisoner's lap and massaging his neck).[119] These women, like Private Lynndie England and the other women at Abu Ghraib, were following orders of their co-abusing male superiors. Unlike the FBI agents at the CSA siege in 1985, who appreciated the social role of women in terrorist groups and used that knowledge to mediate violence, officials at U.S. military prisons have created a culture supporting the exploitation and debasement of women soldiers by having them behave like sexual predators. The effect is also to further inflame the Muslim rage that incites terrorism.

In addition, the United States has failed to stop the process of "extraordinary rendition"—the secret transfer of detainees to countries where they might be tortured. A 2005 Amnesty International report reveals that the United States is believed to have rendered over one hundred detainees in the war on terrorism to countries that the U.S. State Department cites for torture or ill-treatment of prisoners; these countries include Jordan, Syria, and Egypt, where prisoners are routinely beaten, deprived of sleep, and left hanging in the air by their wrists.[120] Using torture to solve the problem of terrorism is like eating rat poison to cure a stomach ache. It was the United States' rendition of Ayman al-Zawahiri's brother from Albania to Egypt, where he was likely to be tortured (as was Ayman al-Zawahiri himself in the early 1980s for his suspected role in the Sadat assassination), that contributed to the grievances behind al-Qaeda's bombings of the East African embassies in 1998—the prelude to 9/11. Over and over again, U.S. policy makers have failed to realize that the campaign against international terrorism is as much a battle for the political and moral high ground as it is a struggle to collect meaningful intelligence.

Fighting terrorism requires a full recognition of this hard lesson, along with improved international law enforcement, economic assistance, and humanitarian aid on a scale equivalent to the $100 million that the United States spends each day on the deceitfully perpetrated and abysmally failed war in Iraq. Without drastic steps like these, crime and terrorism will endure as global problems.

Notes

NOTES TO THE INTRODUCTION:

1. See Michael Barkun (2003) "Defending Against the Apocalypse: The Limits of Homeland Security." *Governance and Public Security*, 3: 17–28.

2. See Mark S. Hamm (2003) "Agony and Art: The Songs of 9/11." In Steven Chermak, Frankie Y. Bailey, and Michelle Brown (eds.), *Media Representations of September 11*. Westport, CT: Praeger, pp. 201–20.

3. Marcus Felson (2004) "The Basic Routine Activity Approach to Crime Analysis." In Margaret A. Zahn, Henry H. Brownstein, and Shelly L. Jackson (eds.), *Violence: From Theory to Research*. Cincinnati: LexisNexis, p. 121.

4. Edwin Sutherland (1947) *Criminology*. Philadelphia: Lippincott.

5. Ronald L. Akers and Adam L. Silverman (2004) "Toward a Social Learning Model of Violence and Terrorism. In Zahn et al. (eds.), *Violence*, p. 19.

6. Mark S. Hamm (2002) *In Bad Company: America's Terrorist Underground*. Boston: Northeastern University Press.

7. See Martha Crenshaw (ed.) (1983) *Terrorism, Legitimacy, and Power*. Middletown, CT: Wesleyan University Press.

8. Jonathan White (2002) *Terrorism: An Introduction*. Belmont, CA: Wadsworth.

9. Chris Dishman (2001) "Terrorism, Crime, and Transformation." *Studies in Conflict & Terrorism*, 24: 43–58; C.J.M. Drake (1991) "The Provisional IRA: A Case Study." *Terrorism and Political Violence*, 3: 43–60.

10. James Adams (1986) The *Financing of Terrorism*. New York: Simon & Schuster.

11. G. Davidson Smith (1993) "Sources of Terrorist Weaponry and Major Methods of Obtaining Weapons and Techniques." *Terrorism and Political Violence*, 5: 123–29.

12. Walter Laqueur (1999) *The Age of Terrorism*. Boston: Little, Brown.

13. White, *Terrorism*.

14. Dishman, "Terrorism, Crime, and Transformation."

15. Rensselaer Lee (1999) *Smuggling Armageddon: The Nuclear Black Market in the Former Soviet Union and Europe*. New York: St. Martin's Press.

16. David E. Kaplan (2005) "Paying for Terror." *U.S. News & World Report*, December 5.

17. Lee, *Smuggling Armageddon*.

18. Rachel Ehrenfeld (2002) "Arafat's Legacy: A Case Study of Terror Funding." *National Review Online*, October 31.

19. Lee, *Smuggling Armageddon*.

20. Daniel Benjamin and Steven Simon (2002) *The Sacred Age of Terror*. New York: Random House; Rohan Gunaratna (2002) *Inside Al Qaeda: Global Network of Terror*. New York: Columbia University Press; Robert McMahon (2002) "Afghanistan: UN Official Describes Efforts to Track Al-Qaeda." *Radio Free Europe*, January 28.

21. See Brian Jenkins (1985) *International Terrorism: The Other World War*. Santa Monica: Rand.

22. Claire Sterling (1983) *The Terror Network*. New York: Berkley Books.

23. Smith, "Sources of Terrorist Weaponry and Major Methods of Obtaining Weapons and Techniques."

24. U.S. Department of State (1999) *Patterns of Global Terrorism*. Author.

25. Kaplan, "Paying for Terror."

26. Kevin Flynn and Gary Gerhardt (1989) *The Silent Brotherhood: Inside America's Terrorist Underground*. New York: The Free Press.

27. John Follain (1988) *Jackal: The Complete Story of the Legendary Carlos the Jackal*. New York: Arcade Publishing.

28. Lee, *Smuggling Armageddon*.

29. Gunaratna, *Inside Al Qaeda*.

30. Benjamin and Simon, *The Age of Sacred Terror*; Peter L. Bergen (2002) *Holy War, Inc.: Inside the Secret World of Osama bin Laden*. New York: Simon & Schuster.

31. Ibid.

32. Hans Josef Horchem (1991) "The Decline of the Red Army Faction." *Terrorism and Political Violence*, 2: 61–75.

33. Sterling, *The Terror Network*.

34. Horchem, "The Decline of the Red Army Faction."

35. Mark S. Hamm (1997) *Apocalypse in Oklahoma: Waco and Ruby Ridge Revenged*. Boston: Northeastern University Press.

36. Steven Emerson (2002) *American Jihad: The Terrorists Living Among Us*. New York: The Free Press.

37. Follain, *Jackal*; Harvey W. Kushner (1998) "The New Terrorism." In Harvey W. Kusher (ed.), *The Future of Terrorism: Violence at the New Millennium*. Thousand Oaks, CA: Sage, pp. 3–20.

38. U.S. Department of State, *Patterns of Global Terrorism*.

39. Drake, "The Provisional IRA"; White, *Terrorism*.

40. Flynn and Gerhardt, *The Silent Brotherhood*; Hamm, *In Bad Company*.

41. Benjamin and Simon, *The Age of Sacred Terror*.

42. The following account is based on the works of Benjamin and Simon, Gunaratna, and *The al-Qaeda Documents Vol. 1.* Alexandria, VA: Tempest Publishing, 2002.

43. Ariel Merari (1991) "Academic Research and Government Policy on Terrorism." *Terrorism and Political Violence*, 3: 99.

44. Ibid.: 89.

45. Brent L. Smith and Kelly Damphousse (2003) *The American Terrorism Study.* Oklahoma City: Memorial Institute for the Prevention of Terrorism.

46. The ATS uses the FBI's definition of terrorism, thereby restricting its cases to those that occur as a result of an indictment stemming from a federal "domestic security/terrorism investigation" as specified in the *Attorney General Guidelines on General Crimes, Racketeering Enterprises, and Domestic Security/Terrorism Investigations.* This document defines "the prediction threshold for investigations of crimes . . . in support of terrorist objectives."

47. The Pearson Chi-Square value for these differences was 2956.20, df, 40, p<.000. For a complete review of the statistics, see Mark S. Hamm (2005) *Crimes Committed by Terrorist Groups: Theory, Research, and Prevention.* Washington, DC: National Institute of Justice. Award #2003 DT CX 0002.

48. The majority of mail fraud counts among domestic groups relate to the 1996 Montana Freeman case. Trial transcripts for the case were not available from the federal courts, however, so the case was dropped from the study.

49. Benjamin and Simon, *The Age of Sacred Terror*, pp. xii–xiii.

50. Intelligence Resource Program (2005) "Irish Republican Army." July 21.

51. Andrew Blejwas, Anthony Griggs and Mark Potok (2005) "Terror from the Right." *Intelligence Report* (Southern Poverty Law Center), Summer: 33–46.

52. Center for International Strategic Studies (2004) *Transnational Threats Update*, June: 3; see also Kaplan, "Paying for Terror."

NOTES TO CHAPTER I

1. Special Agent Louis Vizi. *To the Best of My Knowledge.* Penn State University Radio. May 5, 1998.

2. Richard A. Clarke (2004) *Against All Enemies: Inside America's War on Terror.* New York: Free Press, p. 218.

3. John Kerry (2004) "Fighting a Comprehensive War on Terrorism." Remarks by Senator John Kerry at the Ronald W. Burkle Center for International Relations. University of California at Los Angeles. February 7.

4. Unless otherwise noted, information on the 1993 World Trade Center bombing is based on the following court transcripts: *United States of America v.*

Mohammad A. Salameh, Nidal Ayyad, Mahmud Abouhalima, Ahmad Mohammad Ajaj, Ramzi Ahmed Yousef, and *Abdul Rahman Yasin,* S593 Cr. 180 (KTD); *United States of America v. Ramzi Ahmed Yousef, Abdul Hakim, Murad Wali Khan* S1293 Cr. 180 (KTD).

5. Lauri Mylroie (1995/96) "The World Trade Center Bomb: Who Is Ramzi Yousef? And Why It Matters." *The National Interest,* Winter.

6. Robert E. Precht (2003) *Defending Mohammad: Justice on Trial.* Ithaca, NY: Cornell University Press.

7. John Miller and Michael Stone with Chris Mitchell (2002) *The Cell: Inside the 9/11 Plot, and Why the FBI and CIA Failed to Stop It.* New York: Hyperion.

8. Ibid.

9. Emerson, *American Jihad.*

10. Miller et al., *The Cell.*

11. Ibid.

12. Ibid.

13. Precht, *Defending Mohammad.*

14. Jim Dwyer, David Kocieniewski, Deidre Murphy, and Peg Tyre (1994) *Two Seconds Under the World Trade Center: Terror Comes to America—The Conspiracy Behind the World Trade Center Bombing.* New York: Crown.

15. Rex A. Hudson (1999) *Who Becomes a Terrorist and Why: The 1999 Government Report on Profiling Terrorists.* Guilford, CT: Lyons Press.

16. *The 9/11 Commission Report: Final Report of the National Commission on Terrorist Attacks Upon the United States* (n.d.). New York: W. W. Norton; U.S. Senate Select Committee on Intelligence and House Permanent Select Committee on Intelligence (2002) *Joint Inquiry into Intelligence Community Activities Before and After the Terrorist Attacks of September 11, 2001.* Authors.

17. The fact that Yousef was able to purchase such a quantity of dangerous chemicals, no questions asked, highlights the degree to which the United States was institutionally unprepared to combat terrorism prior to 9/11. In 1994, Timothy McVeigh and Terry Nichols would make a similar purchase from a farm cooperative in Kansas, no questions asked.

18. Mylroie, "The World Trade Center Bomb."

19. Mark Juergensmeyer (2000) *Terror in the Mind of God: The Global Rise of Religious Violence.* Berkley: University of California Press.

20. Simon Reeve (2000) *One Day in September: The Full Story of the 1972 Munich Olympics Massacre and the Israeli Revenge Operation "Wrath of God."* New York: Arcade Publishing.

21. Simon Reeve (1999) *The New Jackals: Ramzi Yousef, Osama bin Laden, and the Future of Terrorism.* Boston: Northeastern University Press. P. 177.

22. Dave Williams (1998) "The Bombing of the World Trade Center in New York City." *International Criminal Police Review,* 4: 469–71.

23. There is some confusion as to who actually drove the truck. While the

Palestinian Eyyad Ismail would later be charged with having driven the bomb-laden van, Ismail was not seen at the gas station. Nor was he known to operate a motor vehicle for any of the cell's other operations preceding the attack. Salameh, on the other hand, was unquestionably the cell's driver. He received instructions on driving the truck from Yasin, made surveillance runs to the Twin Towers, and was seen at the Shell station.

24. Dwyer et al., *Two Seconds Under the World Trade Center.*

25. Miller et al., *The Cell.*

26. Dwyer et al., *Two Seconds Under the World Trade Center,* p. 143.

27. *The 9/11 Commission Report,* p. 42.

28. Quoted in Bergen, *Holy War, Inc.,* p. 140.

29. *The 9/11 Commission Report,* p. 53.

30. Reeve, *The New Jackals.*

NOTES TO CHAPTER 2

1. Unless otherwise noted, information on the East African embassy bombing is derived from the 8,000-plus pages of transcripts in the *United States of America v. Usama Bin Laden et al.,* S(7)98 cr. 1023. Background information on al-Qaeda comes from the testimony of Jamal Ahmed al-Fadl, Feb. 7, 2001; and FBI (1998) Osama bin Laden. Executive Summary. (Author). Material on Mohammed al-Owhali is based on the testimony of FBI Special Agent Stephen Gaudin, Jan. 8, 2001.

2. Mary Anne Weaver (1996) "Blowback." *The Atlantic Online.*

3. Material on Mohamed Odeh comes from the testimony of FBI Special Agent John Antivec, Feb. 27, 2001, and the Sealed Complaint for *United States of America v. Mohamed Sadeek Odeh.*

4. Quoted in A. Brownfeld (2001) "Bin Laden's Activities Exposed in New York Trial." *Jane's International Security News,* March 14, p. 1.

5. *The 9/11 Commission Report.*

6. Michael Griffin (2003) *Reaping the Whirlwind: Afghanistan, Al Qa'ida and the Holy War.* London: Pluto Press.

7. Anonymous (2002) *Through Our Enemies' Eyes: Osama bin Laden, Radical Islam, and the Future of America.* Washington, D.C.: Brassey's Inc., p. 178.

8. See Robert A. Pape (2005) *Dying to Win: The Strategic Logic of Suicide Terrorism.* New York: Random House.

9. John Miller (1999) "Greetings America: My Name is Osama bin Laden, Now That I Have Your Attention . . . A Conversation with the Most Dangerous Man in the World." *Esquire,* February (internet version).

10. Yosri Fouda and Nick Fielding (2003) *Masterminds of Terror: The Truth Behind the Most Devastating Terrorist Attack the World Has Ever Seen.* New York: Arcade Press.

11. Bergen, *Holy War, Inc.*

12. As will be pointed out momentarily, Mohamed's honorable discharge from the U.S. military, despite his having violated army policy by fighting alongside the mujahideen in Afghanistan, may be explained by virtue of the fact that he was an informant for the FBI.

13. Mohamed revealed these details of his life in a hearing before the Federal District Court in Manhattan, October 2000. "Excerpts from Guilty Pleas in Terrorist Case," *New York Times*, Oct. 21, A-14.

14. Steve Coll (2004) *Ghost Wars: The Secret History of the CIA, Afghanistan, and bin Laden, from the Soviet Invasion to September 10, 2001.* New York: Penguin.

15. Leaderless resistance was introduced to American law enforcement in the early 1990s by the racist Louis Beam. See his "Leaderless Resistance: An Essay by Louis Beam." *The Seditionist*. Reprinted in B*reakthrough Texts*, crusadernet, 1992.

16. Youssef Bodansky (2001) *Bin Laden: The Man Who Declared War on America*. New York: Random House.

17. Anonymous, *Through Our Enemies' Eyes*, p. 241.

18. This threat is verified by the testimony of Jamal Ahmed al-Fadl, pp. 8,680–81.

19. Yonah Alexander and Michael S. Swetnam (2001) *Usama Bin Laden's al-Qaida: Profile of a Terrorist Network*. New York: Transnational Publishers.

20. Jessica Stern (2003) *Terror in the Name of God: Why Religious Militants Kill*. New York: Ecco.

21. See Benjamin and Simon, *The Age of Sacred Terror*; Bodansky, *Bin Laden*.

22. Africa News (2001) "Al-Qaeda Hiding in Plain Sight." Sept. 1.

23. Douglas Waller (1998) "Inside the Hunt for Osama." *Time*, Dec. 21.

24. Bergen, *Holy War, Inc.*

25. Marc Sageman (2004) *Understanding Terror Networks*. Philadelphia: University of Pennsylvania Press.

26. Judith Miller, Jeff Gerth, and Don Van Natta, Jr. (2001) "Planning for Terror, but Failing to Act." *New York Times*, December 30.

27. Waller, "Inside the Hunt for Osama."

28. Clarke, *Against All Enemies*, p. 183.

29. Miller et al., "Planning for Terror, but Failing to Act."

30. Waller, "Inside the Hunt for Osama."

31. Ibid.

32. Coll, *Ghost Wars*, p. 404.

33. Mohamed testimony, "Excerpts."

34. Benjamin and Simon, *The Age of Sacred Terror*; Lance Williams and Erin McCormick (2001) "Al Qaeda Terrorist Worked with FBI, Ex-Silicon Valley Resident Plotted Embassy Attacks." *San Francisco Chronicle*, Nov. 4.

35. Mohamed testimony, "Excerpts."

36. Williams and McCormick, "Al Qaeda Terrorist Worked with FBI, Ex-Silicon Valley Resident Plotted Embassy Attacks."

37. Anonymous, *Through Our Enemies' Eyes.*

38. Bodansky, *Bin Laden.*

39. Coll, *Ghost Wars.*

40. U.S. Department of State (2000) *Report of the Accountability Review Boards: Bombings of the US Embassies in Nairobi, Kenya, and Dar es Salaam, Tanzania, on August 7, 1998: Nairobi.* (Author).

41. Ibid.

42. U.S. Department of State (2000) *Report of the Accountability Review Boards: Bombings of the US Embassies in Nairobi, Kenya, and Dar es Salaam, Tanzania, on August 7, 1998: Dar es Salaam.* (Author).

43. Ibid.

44. Sageman, *Understanding Terror Networks.*

45. CNN (n.d.) "Ayman al-Zawahiri: Egyptian Doctor Emerges as Terror Mastermind."

46. U.S. Department of State, *Report of the Accountability Review Boards: Nairobi.* See also Jason Burke (2003) *Al-Qaeda: Casting a Shadow of Fear.* London: I. B. Tauris.

47. Salman Masood (2004) "Pakistan Reports Arrest of a Suspect in '98 Embassy Bombings." *New York Times,* July 31.

48. "Hunting bin Laden: The Trail of Evidence: The Suspects and Charges." *Frontline,* May 29, 2001.

49. Quoted in Scott Shane and James Risen (2005) "Internal Report Said to Fault C.I.A. for Pre–9/11 Actions." *New York Times,* August 26.

50. Quoted in Ed Blanche (2001) "Ayman Al-Zawahri: Attention to the Other Prime Suspect." *Jane's International Security News,* October 3, p. 4.

51. Benjamin and Simon, *The Age of Sacred Terror.*

52. *The 9/11 Commission Report,* p. 120.

53. Clarke, *Against All Enemies,* p. 190.

54. *The 9/11 Commission Report,* p. 76.

55. Ibid., p. 149.

NOTES TO CHAPTER 3

1. Unless otherwise noted, material on the CSA is taken from transcripts in the *United States of America v. James D. Ellison* Cr. 85–2095 and Cr. 85–200017–01. Supporting court documents include: *In the Matter of Gun Violation Investigation: Testimony of James Ellison.* Before the Grand Jury of the United States District Court for the Eastern District of Oklahoma, Sept. 26, 1984; *United States of America v. James E. Ellison* [sic], *Gary Richard Stone, Timothy Wayne Russell, Kerry Noble, Rudy Loewen, David Giles* Cr. 85–200017–01–06;

United States of America v. Kerry Noble Cr. 85–200017–04; Report of Interviews, FBI: with Timothy Wayne Russell by Special Agent (SA) Jack Knox, April 21, 1985; with David Kent Giles by SA Herbert J. Davis, April 23, 1985; with Gary Richard Stone by SA Dan Short, April 24, 1985; Bureau of Alcohol, Tobacco, and Firearms Evidence Log by SA William Buford, June 18, 1985; and Affidavit of SA Jack D. Knox, April 16, 1985.

2. "Stewart" is a pseudonym.

3. Author interview with Kerry Noble, December 16, 2004.

4. Quoted in James Coates (1987) *Armed and Dangerous: The Rise of the Survivalist Right.* New York: Hill & Wang, p. 122.

5. Stern, *Terror in the Name of God.*

6. Flynn and Gerhardt, *The Silent Brotherhood.*

7. Kerry Noble (1998) *Tabernacle of Hate: Whey They Bombed Oklahoma City.* Prescott, Ontario, Canada: Voyageur, p. 84.

8. Michael Barkun (1997) *Religion and the Racist Right: The Origins of Christian Identity.* Chapel Hill: University of North Carolina Press.

9. Quoted in Stern, *Terror in the Name of God,* p. 18.

10. Quoted in Victoria Loe Hicks (1998) "Memoir Traces Author's Journey out of a Violent Racist Group." *Dallas Morning News,* June 6.

11. Flynn and Gerhardt, *The Silent Brotherhood.*

12. Noble interview.

13. Flynn and Gerhardt, *The Silent Brotherhood,* p. 161.

14. Jeffrey Kaplan (1997) *Radical Religion in America: Millenarian Movements from the Far Right to the Children of Noah.* Syracuse, NY: Syracuse University Press.

15. Hamm, *Apocalypse in Oklahoma.*

16. Stephen Singular (1987) *Talked to Death: The Murder of Alan Berg and the Rise of the Neo-Nazis.* New York: Berkeley Books.

17. Jeffrey Kaplan (1998) "Tabernacle of Hate." *Nova Religio;* 165.

18. Noble interview.

19. Noble, *Tabernacle of Hate,* p. 103

20. Stern, *Terror in the Name of God,* p. 22.

21. Kathleen Blee (2004) "Women and Organized Racism." In Abbey L. Ferber (ed.), *Home-Grown Hate: Gender and Organized Racism.* New York: Routledge, pp. 57–58.

22. Noble interview.

23. Noble, *Tabernacle of Hate,* p. 147.

24. Noble interview.

25. Quoted in Rodney Bowers (1987) "White Radical Activities That Led to Indictments Recounted from 1983–85." *Arkansas Gazette,* April 27: 1A.

26. Noble, *Tabernacle of Hate,* pp. 131–32.

27. Ibid., p. 132.

28. Author interview with Danny Coulson, December 15, 2004.

29. Noble interview.

30. Quoted in Jo Thomas and Ronald Smothers (1995) "Oklahoma City Building was Target of Plot as Early as '83, Official Says." *New York Times,* May 20.

31. Noble, *Tabernacle of Hate,* p. 135.

32. Jessica Stern (2000) "The Covenant, the Sword, and the Arm of the Lord." In J. Tucker (ed.), *Toxic Terror.* Cambridge, MA: MIT Press (available at author's website).

33. Noble interview.

34. Flynn and Gerhardt, *The Silent Brotherhood,* p. 260.

35. *U.S. v. Ellison,* 793 F.2d 942 (8th Cir. 1986).

36. Noble interview.

37. Noble, *Tabernacle of Hate,* p. 81.

38. The following account is taken from Coates, *Armed and Dangerous* as well as various Associated Press and *Southwest Times* releases on the CSA siege, April 1985 (entered in Ellison's legal proceedings).

39. Noble interview.

40. Ibid.

41. Coulson interview.

42. Danny O. Coulson and Elaine Shannon (2001) *No Heroes: Inside the FBI's Secret Counter-Terror Force.* New York: Pocket Books. Pp. 254 and 269.

43. Coates, *Armed and Dangerous,* pp. 143–44.

44. Coulson interview.

45. Coulson and Shannon, *No Heroes,* p. 293.

46. Coulson interview.

47. Noble, *Tabernacle of Hate.*

NOTES TO CHAPTER 4

1. Edwin Sutherland (1947) *Criminology.* Philadelphia: Lippincott.

2. William Fried (2004) "Charisma: Belief, Will, and the Power of the Gifted." *Round Robin* (Newsletter of Psychologist-Psychoanalyst Practitioners, Division of Psychoanalysis). American Psychological Association, 39: 1–18.

3. Tom Martinez with John Guinther (1999) *Brotherhood of Murder.* New York: toExcel, p. 53

4. The following account is taken from the exhaustive review of Mathews' background provided by Flynn and Gerhardt, *The Silent Brotherhood,* pp. 23–28 and 30–38.

5. Ibid., p. 27.

6. The following account is also taken from Flynn and Gerhardt, *The Silent Brotherhood,* pp. 112–19.

7. Robert Jay Mathews (n.d.) "Last Letter," p. 1. Unpublished.

8. Unless otherwise noted, information on the Order's crime spree is based on transcripts and related documents filed in *United States of America v. Bruce Carroll Pierce et al.* Cr. 85–001; *United States of America v. Randolph Duey et al.* Cr. 85–001M, Superseding Indictment.

9. Flynn and Gerhardt, *The Silent Brotherhood*, p. 7.

10. See James A. Aho (1990) *The Politics of Righteousness: Idaho Christian Patriotism.* Seattle: University of Washington Press; Barkun, *Religion and the Racist Right;* Jeffrey Kaplan (1995) "Right-Wing Violence in North America." *Terrorism and Political Violence,* 7: 44–95.

11. For an excellent discussion, see William James Gibson (1994) *Warrior Dreams: Violence and Manhood in Post-Vietnam America.* New York: Hill and Wang.

12. Flynn and Gerhardt, *The Silent Brotherhood*, p. 265.

13. Author interview with Tom Martinez, January 12, 2005.

14. Quoted in the CBS documentary "The Order." *Turning Point,* July 10, 1997.

15. Aho, *The Politics of Righteousness,* p. 63.

16. Former FBI Special Agent Wayne Manis, quoted in "The Order."

17. Elinor Langer (2003) *A Hundred Little Hitlers: The Death of a Black Man, the Trial of a White Racist, and the Rise of the Neo-Nazi Movement in America.* New York: Metropolitan Books, p. 153.

18. International Anti-Counterfeiting Coalition (2003) "White Paper: International/Global Intellectual Property Theft: Links to Terrorism and Terrorist Organizations." Author.

19. Quoted in "The Order."

20. Ibid.

21. Martinez interview.

22. Quoted in "The Order."

23. Ibid.

24. The following account draws from both the transcripts and Flynn and Gerhardt's description in *The Silent Brotherhood,* pp. 224–39.

25. Flynn and Gerhardt, *The Silent Brotherhood*, p. xiii.

26. Author interview with Danny Coulson, December 15, 2004.

27. Author interview with Wayne Manis, December 11, 2004.

28. Ibid.

29. Ibid.

30. Ibid.

31. Martinez interview.

32. Flynn and Gerhardt, *The Silent Brotherhood*, p. 274.

33. Martinez interview.

34. Ibid.

35. Coulson and Shannon, *No Heroes,* p. 180.

36. Manis interview.

37. Coulson interview.

38. This was most likely the cyanide acquired by the CSA, discussed in the last chapter.

NOTES TO CHAPTER 5

1. Philip Jenkins (2003) *Images of Terror: What We Can and Can't Know about Terrorism.* New York: Aldine de Gruyter. P. 189.

2. The following is a composite sketch of Carlos the Jackal based on the following works: Christopher Dobson and Ronald Payne (1977) *The Carlos Complex: A Pattern of Violence.* London: Book Club Associates; Follain, *Jackal;* "Illich Ramirez Sanchez." *Wikipedia, the free encyclopedia;* Amir Taheri (2003) "The Axis of Terror: Carlos the Jackal Pledges Alliance to Osama bin Laden." *Weekly Standard,* Nov. 24.

3. Quoted in Taheri, "The Axis of Terror," p. 3.

4. Dobson and Payne, *The Carlos Complex.*

5. Martinez, *Brotherhood of Murder,* p. 63.

6. Martinez interview.

7. Quoted in Taheri, "The Axis of Terror," p. 3.

8. Brian Jenkins, *International Terrorism.*

9. Background information on Langan comes from author interviews with Peter Langan, Federal Detention Center, Milan, Michigan, November 28, 1998; with Langan's sister, December 18, 1998, January 5, 1999; and from Richard Leiby (1997), "The Saga of Pretty Boy Pedro: How a Wheaton Kid Became a Neo-Nazi Bank Robber, and One Confused Human Being." *Washington Post,* February 13.

10. The following profile is based on Guthrie's ninety-one-page confession to the FBI (Federal Bureau of Investigation, FD-302 Richard Lee Guthrie, March 22, 1996); Guthrie's unpublished, hand-written autobiography, "The Taunting Bandits"; as well as interviews with his lawyer, W. Kelly Johnson, December 10, 1999 and Peter Langan (see previous note).

11. Unless otherwise noted, information on the ARA's crime spree comes from the Langan interview, Guthrie's FBI 302, Guthrie's "The Taunting Bandits," and the following transcripts: *United States of America v. Peter Kevin Langan,* CR-2–96–015; *United States of America v. Scott Anthony Stedeford,* CR 96–98; and *United States of America v. Mark William Thomas et al.,* Indictment filed January 30, 1997.

12. Author interview with Matt Moning, August 17, 2005; Leslie Blade and Gregory Flannery (2004), "Queen City Terror: Cincinnati's Links to the Oklahoma City Bombing." *Cincinnati City Beat,* September 16.

13. Background on Stedeford, McCarthy, and Brescia comes from Hamm, *In Bad Company*.

14. Neil Mackay (2005) "International Criminal 'Behind IRA Bank Raid.'" *Sunday Herald Online*.

15. See Marley Brant (1998) *Jesse James: The Man and the Myth*. New York: Berkeley Books.

16. Interview with FBI Special Agent Gil Hendrickson, December 10, 1999.

17. Jeff Ferrell (2006) *Empire of Scrounge: Inside the Urban Underground of Dumpster Diving, Trash Picking, and Street Scavenging*. New York: New York University Press, p. 200.

18. Langan to Author, letter dated October 12, 2001.

19. *State of Oklahoma v. Terry Lynn Nichols*, F-2004–68. Terry Lynn Nichols' Motion to Dismiss Based on the State's Failure to Comply with *Brady v. Maryland*.

20. Ibid., p. 3.

21. Hamm, *In Bad Company*.

22. "U.S. Had Data Hinting of Oklahoma Bombing." Associated Press release, February 11, 2003.

23. FBI. SPLC-OKBOMB Memorandum. Oklahoma City Bombing Case File, No. 174A-OC-56120; *Oklahoma v. Nichols*.

24. Jonathan Franklin (1997) "God City." *Vibe*, November: 101–04; Author interview with Morris Dees, September 20, 1999.

25. SPLC-OKBOMB Memorandum.

26. See Stephen Jones and Peter Israel (2001) *Others Unknown: The Oklahoma City Bombing Case and Conspiracy*. New York: PublicAffairs; Hamm, *In Bad Company*.

27. *Oklahoma v. Nichols*, p. 18.

28. Ibid.

29. Ibid.

30. Elizabeth Gleick (1995) "Something Big is Going to Happen." *Time*, May 8.

31. *Oklahoma v. Nichols*.

32. Associated Press (2004) "Secret Service Documents Cite Mystery Video in Oklahoma City Bombing." Press release, April 19.

33. *Oklahoma v. Nichols*.

34. CNN (2004) "FBI Suspected McVeigh Part of Conspiracy." February 25.

35. John Leland (2004) *Hip: The History*. New York: Ecco, p. 290.

36. Jack Katz (1988) *Seductions of Crime: Moral and Sensual Attractions in Doing Evil*. New York: Basic Books.

37. Wayne Morrison (2004) "Reflections with Memories: Everyday Photography Capturing Genocide." *Theoretical Criminology*, 8: 341–58.

38. Blade and Flannery, "Queen City Terror."

39. Author interview with FBI Special Agent Ed Woods, March 6, 2001 (e-mail).

40. Reeve, *One Day in September.*

41. Hendrickson interview.

42. *Oklahoma v. Nichols.*

43. FBI. Mid West Bank Robbery gang, BOMBROB Case File, No. 91A-OM-41859.

44. Hamm, *In Bad Company.*

45. Quoted in "FBI Linked McVeigh to Group After Bombing." Associated Press release, February 12, 2003.

46. Letter from David Paul Hammer to Author, May 14, 2001. Hammer and McVeigh were celled next to each other on death row. I sent numerous letters to McVeigh asking questions about the bombing. Hammer would reply for McVeigh.

47. Jones and Israel, *Others Unknown*, p. xviii.

NOTES TO CHAPTER 6

1. Daniel Benjamin and Steven Simon (2005) *The Next Attack: The Failure of the War on Terror and a Strategy for Getting It Right.* New York: Henry Holt.

2. D. Kaplan, "Paying for Terror."

3. Ibid.

4. Aparisim Ghosh (2006) "Can Bin Laden Be Caught?" *Time*, January 30.

5. Figures maintained by Marc Herold, Department of Economics and Women's Studies, University of New Hampshire (website). The estimates are based on media and press reports.

6. Sami Yousafzai (2006) "'Got to Take That Shot.'" *Newsweek*, January 23.

7. David Rohde and Somini Sengupta (2005) "Qaeda on the Run? Raids Seem to Belie Pakistani's Word." *New York Times*, August 3; David Rohde and Carlotta Gall (2005) "Word of Secret Terror Camps Brings Denials by Pakistanis." *New York Times*, August 26; BBC News (2005) "Timeline: The Search for Bin Laden." March 15.

8. Alan Cowell (2005) "Britain May Lengthen Time for Holding Terror Suspects." *New York Times*, August 8.

9. Rohde and Sengupta, "Qaeda on the Run? Raids Seem to Belie Pakistani's Word."

10. Quoted in Ghosh, "Can Bin Laden Be Caught?"

11. Quoted in Douglas Jehl (2005) "Experts Fear Suicide Bomb Is Spreading into the West." *New York Times*, July 11.

12. *60 Minutes* interview, "Bin Laden Expert Steps Forth." November 14, 2004.

13. Waller, "Inside the Hunt for Osama."

14. Graham Allison (2004) *Nuclear Terrorism: The Ultimate Preventable Catastrophe*. New York: Henry Holt.

15. Quoted in Evan Thomas (2001) "Gunning for Bin Laden." *Newsweek*, November 26.

16. T. J. Badey (2001) "Nuclear Terrorism: Actor-Based Threat Assessment." *Intelligence & National Security*, 16: 39–54.

17. D. Kaplan, "Paying for Terror."

18. Quoted in Mark Landsbaum (2005) "Al-Qaeda's Illegal Immigration Threat." FrontPageMagazine.com, March 7.

19. See Jehl, "Experts Fear Suicide Bomb Is Spreading into the West."

20. Eric Lichtblau (2005) "U.S. Terror Assessments See Threat of Suicide Attacks." *New York Times*, August 4.

21. MIPT Terrorism Knowledge Base. University of Arkansas.

22. Robert A. Pape (2005) "Al Qaeda's Smart Bombs." *New York Times*, July 9.

23. Lichtblau, "U.S. Terror Assessments See Threat of Suicide Attacks."

24. Anonymous, *Through Our Enemies' Eyes*, p. 236.

25. Ibid., p. 237.

26. Waller, "Inside the Hunt for Osama."

27. Christopher Dickey (2005) "Women of Al Qaeda." *Newsweek*, December 12.

28. John Ashcroft (2003) Testimony of Attorney General Ashcroft, U.S. House of Representatives, Committee of the Judiciary, June 5.

29. Quoted in Benjamin and Simon, *The Next Attack*, p. 117.

30. Benjamin and Simon, *The Next Attack*.

31. This is a composite sketch of the conspiracy based on the following works: Associated Press (2005) "Parachas Known To Associate With Bin Laden, Mohammed." November 20 (press release); Phil Hirschkorn (2003) "Lawyer: Detained Pakistani to Face Terrorism Charges." CNN.com, August 6; Phil Hirschkorn (2004) "Alleged Terrorist Operative Seeks Access to Top al Qaeda Captive." CNN.com, January 9; Julia Preston (2005) "Prosecutor Says Suspect Knew of Qaeda Link." *New York Times*, November 22; Brian Ross and Richard Esposito (2005) "CIA's Harsh Interrogation Techniques Described." *ABC News*, published November 19; Evan Thomas and Michael Hirsh (2005) "The Debate Over Torture." *Newsweek*, November 21; *United States of America v. Uzair Paracha*. Indictment, 03 Cr.

32. Benjamin and Simon, *The Next Attack*, p. 31.

33. D. Kaplan, "Paying for Terror."

34. Alison Pargeter (2005) "The Islamist Movement in Morocco." *Terrorism Monitor*, May 21.

35. Benjamin and Simon, *The Next Attack*, p. 28.

36. Erri Daily Intelligence Report (2003) "Morocco Bombing Update." May 20; Wikipedia, the free encyclopedia (2005) "2003 Casablanca Bombings." November 10.

37. Quoted in Benjamin and Simon, *The Next Attack*, p. 28.

38. Wikipedia, "2003 Casablanca Bombings."

39. D. Kaplan, "Paying for Terror."

40. Sebastian Rotella (2004) "Holy Water, Hashish and Jihad." *Los Angeles Times*, February 23.

41. Ibid.; John Larson and Sachar Bar-on (2005) "Lessons from Madrid Bombing." MSNBC.com, June 6.

42. Larson and Sachar Bar-on, "Lessons from Madrid Bombing."

43. *China Daily* (2004) "Zapatero: Iraq Occupation a Fiasco," March 18.

44. *China Daily* (2004) "Six Moroccans Suspected in Madrid Blasts," March 17.

45. Rotella, "Holy Water, Hashish and Jihad."

46. Mar Roman (2004) "Madrid Terror Suspect Says He Wanted to Give Spain a Lesson." Associated Press (press release), July 28.

47. CNN.com (2003) "Aljazeera Airs Purported bin Laden Audiotapes." October 19.

48. Rotella, "Holy Water, Hashish and Jihad."

49. Ibid.

50. BBC News (2004) "Spain Suspects 'Were Informants,'" April 29.

51. Benjamin and Simon, *The Next Attack*.

52. Ibid.

53. Wikipedia, the free encyclopedia (n.d.) "11 March 2004 Madrid Train Bombings."

54. D. Kaplan, "Paying for Terror."

55. *China Daily*, "Zapatero."

56. Benjamin and Simon, *The Next Attack*, p. 5.

57. D. Kaplan, "Paying for Terror."

58. Mark Hosenball (2005) "Bombers Next Door." *Newsweek*, August 8.

59. Lizette Alvarez (2005) "Lives of Three Men Offer Little to Explain Attacks." *New York Times*, July 14.

60. Sarah Lyall (2006) "Briton Tried to Buy A-Bomb, Prosecution in Trial Contends." *New York Times*, March 23.

61. Elaine Sciolino and Don Van Natta, Jr. (2005) "British Raid Sounded Alert on Pakistani Militants." *New York Times*, July 12.

62. Somini Sengupta (2005) "3 Bombers Visited Pakistan, Land of Their Roots, in 2004." *New York Times*, July 12.

63. Hassan M. Fattah (2005) "Anger Burns on the Fringe of Britain's Young Muslims." *New York Times*, July 16.

64. Tara Pepper and Mark Hosenball (2005) "A Deadly Puzzle." *Newsweek,* July 25.

65. Thomas L. Friedman (2005) "Giving the Hatemongers No Place to Hide." *New York Times,* July 10.

66. Alan Cowell and Raymond Bonner (2005) "Changes in Investigation of Bombing Attacks in London Leave Major Questions Unanswered." *New York Times,* August 15.

67. Sarah Lyall (2005) "In Britain, Migrants Took a New Path: To Terrorism." *New York Times,* July 28.

68. Hosenball, "Bombers Next Door."

69. Pepper and Hosenball, "A Deadly Puzzle."

70. Ibid.

71. Don Van Natta, Jr., and Elaine Sciolino (2005) "Timers Used in Blasts, Police Say; Parallels to Madrid Are Found." *New York Times,* July 8.

72. Eamonn O'Neill (2006) "CSI: London, On the Trail of the 7/7 Bombers." *Esquire* (British edition), February.

73. Kim Sengupta and Jason Bennetto (2005) "CCTV Captures Rehearsal for London Bomb Attacks." *The Independent* (online edition), September 21.

74. Don Van Natta, Jr., and Elaine Sciolino (2005) "Two Thursdays: Echoes and Theories, but No Solid Leads." *New York Times,* July 20.

75. *CNN.com* (2005) "Bomb Suspect: 'No al Qaeda Links.'" August 1.

76. Alan Cowell (2005) "Al Jazeera Video Links London Bombings to Al Qaeda." *New York Times,* September 2.

77. See Frank Rich (2005) "Falluja Floods the Superdome." *New York Times,* September 4.

78. Elaine Sciolino (2005) "Europe Finds The New Face of Terrorism." *New York Times,* August 1.

79. Sageman, *Understanding Terror Networks.*

80. James Q. Wilson (2004) "What Makes a Terrorist?" *City Journal,* Winter (available at city-journal.org).

81. See Benjamin and Simon, *The Next Attack.*

82. Donatella Della Porta (1990) *Il Terrorismo Di Sinistra.* Bologna: Il Mulino.

83. For more examples of this phenomenon, see Mark S. Hamm (1993) *American Skinheads: The Criminology and Control of Hate Crime.* Westport, CT: Praeger.

84. Elaine Sciolino and Don Van Natta, Jr. (2005) "Plastic Vessels May Link Two Sets of London Bombings." *New York Times,* July 27.

85. *The 9/11 Commission Report.*

86. Jim Yardley (2001) "Mohamed Atta Squeaked by in Incident at Miami Airport." *New York Times,* October 17.

87. Arif Jamal and Somini Sengupta (2005) "Two Militants Place Suspect at a Camp in Pakistan." *New York Times,* July 26.

88. Kaplan, "Paying for Terror"; Eric Lichtblau (2005) "4 Men in California Accused of Plotting Terrorist Attacks." *New York Times,* August 30.

89. See Dana Milbank and Claudia Deane (2005) "Poll Finds Dimmer View of Iraq War." *Washingtonpost.com,* June 8; Program on International Policy Attitudes (2006) "World Public Says Iraq War Has Increased Global Terrorist Threat." Author. March 8; "Opposition to the Iraq War." *Wikipedia, the free encyclopedia.*

90. *CNN.com* (2005) "Survey: 25,000 Civilians Killed in Iraq War." July 19; Iraq Body Count, "A Dossier of Civilian Casualties in Iraq 2003–2005" (available at IBC website). In late 2005 President Bush would say that 30,000 Iraqi civilians had been killed in the war. Other estimates run as high as 650,000.

91. Francis Fukuyama (2006) *America at the Crossroads: Democracy, Power and the Neoconservative Legacy.* New Haven: Yale University Press.

92. Dana Priest (2005) "Iraq New Terror Breeding Ground: War Created Haven, CIA Advisors Report." *Washington Post,* January 14.

93. Quoted in Mark Danner (2005) "Taking Stock of the Forever War." *New York Times Magazine,* September 11, p. 47.

94. Christopher Dickey (2005) "Saudi Storms." *Newsweek,* October 3.

95. Eric Lipton (2005) "Bin Laden Aide Urged to Attack Outside Iraq." *New York Times,* March 1; Adam Zagorin, Timothy J. Burger, and Brian Bennett (2005) "Zarqawi Planning U.S. Hit? *Time,* March 1. The continued threat to the United States by al-Qaeda in Iraq, even after the U.S. air strike that killed al-Zarqawi in June 2006, was confirmed to the author by two federal agents in June 2006.

96. D. Kaplan, "Paying for Terror."

97. Sciolino, "Europe Finds the New Face of Terrorism."

98. Elaine Sciolino and Helene Fouquet (2005) "Belgium Is Trying to Unravel the Threads of a Terror Web." *New York Times,* October 10.

99. Dickey, "Women of al-Qaeda."

100. Craig S. Smith (2005) "Raised as Catholic in Belgium, She Died as a Muslim Suicide Bomber." *New York Times,* December 4.

101. The possibility that al-Qaeda would cross into the United States from Canada, as Ahmed Ressam did in the millennium bomb plot, is also a serious concern, though it receives less attention than the potential incursions from the southern border.

102. Landsbaum, "Al-Qaeda's Illegal Immigration Threat."

103. Quoted in Faye Bowers (2005) "US–Mexican Border as a Terror Risk." *Christian Science Monitor,* March 22.

104. Ibid.

105. Zagorin et al., "Zarqawi Planning U.S. Hit?"

106. Blejwas et al., "Terror From the Right."

107. DHS (2005) "Integrated Planning Guidance, Fiscal Years 2005–2011." January.

108. The following is based on the federal affidavit for the case, covered in Jamie Page (2004) "McKenzie Man Faces Explosives Charges." *Jackson Sun*, October 26.

109. Jo Thomas (2001) "U.S. Groups Have Some Ties to Germ Warfare." *New York Times*, November 2.

110. Council on Foreign Relations (2005) "Aum Shinrikyo." November.

111. Giles Tremlett (2001) "Nerve Gas Find at Camp." *Guardian*, November 20.

112. Fox News (2004) "Sarin, Mustard Gas Discovered Separately in Iraq," May 17.

113. Thomas, "U.S. Groups Have Some Ties to Germ Warfare."

114. Kaplan, "Paying for Terror."

115. Fukuyama, *America at the Crossroads* (Quoted in Michiko Kakutani [2006] "Supporter's Voice Now Turns on Bush." *New York Times*, March 14.)

116. Phillip Carter (2004) "The Road to Abu Ghraib: The Biggest Scandal of the Bush Administration Began at the Top." *Washington Monthly*, November, p. 2 (Internet version).

117. Quoted in Amnesty International (2005) "United States of America." Human Rights Report Covering Events from January to December 2004. London: Author.

118. Robert F. Worth (2006) "U.S. to Abandon Abu Ghraib and Move Prisoners to a New Center." *New York Times*, March 10.

119. David S. Cloud (2005) "Guantanamo Reprimand Was Sought, an Aide Says." *New York Times*, July 13; Daya Gamage (2006) "United States' Human Rights Record Dismal, Says Global Rights Groups." *Asia Tribune*, March 12.

120. Amnesty International, "United States of America."

Index

About the Author

Mark S. Hamm is Professor of Criminology at Indiana State University. He has published numerous books, including *In Bad Company: America's Terrorist Underground* and *Apocalypse in Oklahoma: Waco and Ruby Ridge Revenged.* He is the recipient of the Frederic Milton Thrasher Award for Outstanding Gang Scholarship and the Critical Criminologist of the Year Award from the American Society of Criminology. He lives in Bloomington, Indiana.